Artificial Incubation of Eggs and Brooding of Chicks
A Guide to the Successful Hatching and Rearing of Chicks

by Homer W. Jackson

with an introduction by Jackson Chambers

This work contains material that was originally published in 1919.

This publication is within the Public Domain.

*This edition is reprinted for educational purposes
and in accordance with all applicable Federal Laws.*

Introduction Copyright 2016 by Jackson Chambers

Introduction

I am pleased to present yet another title on Poultry.

This volume is entitled "Artificial Incubation and Brooding" and was authored by Homer Jackson in 1919.

The work is in the Public Domain and is re-printed here in accordance with Federal Laws.

As with all reprinted books of this age that are intended to perfectly reproduce the original edition, considerable pains and effort had to be undertaken to correct fading and sometimes outright damage to existing proofs of this title. At times, this task is quite monumental, requiring an almost total "rebuilding" of some pages from digital proofs of multiple copies. Despite this, imperfections still sometimes exist in the final proof and may detract from the visual appearance of the text.

I hope you enjoy reading this book as much as I enjoyed making it available to readers again.

Jackson Chambers

SUPPLEMENT TO The Feathered World.

DUCKWING. PILE. BLACK-BREASTED RED. BIRCHEN. BROWN-BREASTED RED.

GAME BANTAMS.
(Specially drawn to illustrate Mr. Proud's articles on Bantams.)

[SUPPLEMENT TO The Feathered World, July 3rd, 1896.]

BLACK ROSECOMB.

JAPANESE.

SILVER AND GOLDEN SEBRIGHTS.

BANTAMS.

BRAHMAS.

WHITE ROSECOMB.

BOOTED.

SUITABLE EQUIPMENT IS AN IMPORTANT FACTOR IN SUCCESS IN ARTIFICAL INCUBATING AND BROODING

1—Turning and cooling eggs—Scene in incubator room, Missouri State Poultry Experiment Station. 2—Newly hatched chicks, ready for the brooder. 3—Growing stock on range—Scene at Purdue University. 4—Colony hover brooder house on United States Government Poultry Experimental Farm. 5—Outdoor lamp-heated brooders—Scene on Government Poultry Farm.

CONTENTS

INTRODUCTION

CHAPTER I
Selection of Breeding Stock 9

CHAPTER II
Management of Breeding Stock 15

CHAPTER III
The Hen's Egg and How It Is Formed 22

CHAPTER IV
The Chick Embryo and Its Development 28

CHAPTER V
Operation of Incubators 34

CHAPTER VI
Mistakes in Artificial Incubating 48

CHAPTER VII
Day-Old Chicks and Custom Hatching 54

CHAPTER VIII
Practical Incubator Houses 59

CHAPTER IX
The Selection of Brooding Equipment 65

CHAPTER X
Care and Management of Brooder Chicks 76

CHAPTER XI
Feeding the Brooder Chicks 85

CHAPTER XII
Brooder Houses and How to Build Them 94

CHAPTER XIII
Ailments and Diseases of Chicks 103

Index 111

INTRODUCTION

ARTIFICIAL hatching and brooding of chicks is a practice almost as old as history, and methods substantially the same as those that were in general use before the dawn of the Christian era still are followed in Egypt and other Oriental lands. The secrets of the trade are regularly handed down from father to son and as jealously guarded, as unchanged apparently, and as unaffected by modern ideas as when they were first developed more than 2,000 years ago.

Crude as these methods and facilities undoubtedly are, they are fairly efficient—at least from an Oriental viewpoint, and in Egypt especially, the community "hatcheries" still are the almost exclusive source from which native villagers and small farmers secure their annual supply of chicks. They are, in fact, essential to the existence of the poultry industry, as the fowls kept in that country are practically all non-sitters.

The method of constructing and operating a typical Egyptian hatchery is described in a U. S. Consular report issued by the Government, from which the following extracts are taken:

"The artificial hatching of eggs has been so long practiced in Egypt that the hens have completely abandoned that part of their work to man. It is a regular industry and the professors form a very close corporation, handing down their secrets from father to son. For three months of the year their time is completely absorbed by constant attention at the incubatories.

"The population of Egypt is very dense, about 700 per square mile. This agglomeration fosters the use of large incubatories, each turning out from 300,000 to 600,000 chicks each season. In some villages there are from three to five of these establishments. They are generally near some important market place, and each one apparently in the center of a district of about 50,000 population. That is, each one is the center of a circle having a radius of five miles. It is this density of the population that has allowed this system of artificial hatching to become so very successful.

"The hatchers do not attempt to rear the young broods. Forty-eight hours after the chicks emerge from the shell they are scattered over the country; overcrowding is thus prevented. This distribution is affected in a very simple manner. As the incubator is near a market place, word is sent there that on such a day there will be so many young chicks. This news is quickly disseminated among the villages, and on the appointed day the women arrive with their cages and purchase the young chicks, which are generally sold by the hundred for about $1.50 per hundred. There are also a number of brokers or dealers who take the young chicks to the more distant villages.

"Once in the village the chicks become the property of the women, who take great care of them during the first week. For two or three days they are kept in cages in lots of twenty or thirty and fed on broken grains slightly moistened. At night the cages are taken into the houses and sometimes covered with a bit of cloth. After these first few days the young birds are strong enough to forage for a living; they then are allowed to roam about freely, and at night are kept in a sort of oven placed in the corner of the courtyard. This oven is made of unburnt clay and in shape is like the letter U laid on one side. The top is slightly perforated. The entrance is closed by a heavy stone to keep off foxes and other vermin.

"It is difficult to get any exact figures as to the number of these incubatories, but judging from those personally known to me, and their distances apart, I should estimate the number at 150, with an average production of 300,000 chicks per season. This estimate must be well within the mark, as the population of Egypt is nearly 7,000,000 and fowls form a very large part of the Egyptian diet, so that the production of 45,000,000 table fowls annually would be a short supply.

"The Egyptian incubatory of today is but a reproduction of the one of thousands of years ago. The ordinary form is an oblong, 100 feet in length by 60 feet in width, the height varying from 12 to 15 feet. The illustration on page 7, though not drawn exactly to scale, shows the general arrangement. The outer chamber A is divided into three rooms, the middle one masking the entrance to the ovens and thus excluding the outer air. The door leading from A into the central hall is very small. B represents the ovens of the upper tier. C is the manhole; the attendant stands in this and manipulates the eggs. D D are spaces in the central hall for the reception of the young chicks. These spaces are marked off by ridges of dried mud about 9 inches in height. Fig. 3 is a door giving access to the interior of the oven. Around the walls and parallel to it runs a raised ridge 6 inches in height; between this and the wall the fires are lighted. In the top of the dome is a small aperture about two inches square for the exit of smoke and for regulating the heat.

"The outer wall, 4 feet thick, is generally built of sun-dried bricks; the mortar is simply mud. The space contained within the walls is divided as shown in Fig. 1. The circular ovens are built up and the spaces between them and the wall filled in with brick and mortar, the same as the outer wall. Each set of ovens, the upper and the lower, is perfectly independent and is covered by a dome having a very small aperture in the crown. Fig. 2 represents the elevation on the line A B of Fig. 1. The height of the lower oven is 4 feet and that of the upper one 9 feet. The interior diameter between the ridges D D is 15 feet. Fig. 3 represents the elevation on the line C D of Fig. 1, and shows the disposition of the central wall and the doors of the ovens. For this particular incubatory the attendants consist of two men and a boy.

"In the month of January, about the 10th, fires are lighted in all the ovens and on the floor of the central hall. The entire building is thoroughly warmed to a temperature of 110 degrees Fahrenheit. The fires are at first composed of gelleh or dried cow dung, but when the eggs are placed in the oven, coarse broken straw; mostly the joints, and sheep or goat dung is used. The fuel is placed in the trough between the hall and the ridge, and is lighted at one or more places, according to the degrees of heat required. This is the only means of regulating the heat. Thermometers are not used. The attendants endeavor to keep the heat a trifle greater than that of their own skin. While the oven is being warmed, notice is sent out to the villages that the establishment will purchase eggs on such a date. The country people arrive with large crates containing from 1,000 to 2,000. These are purchased outright by the establishment at the rate of $4.00 per 1,000.

"The floor of the oven is covered with a coarse mat made of palm leaves; on this a little bran is sprinkled to prevent the eggs from rolling. The attendant changes the position of the eggs twice a day, taking those from near the manhole and placing them on the outer edge of the circle and vice versa. The eggs are tested on the fourth day and again six days later, the infertile and dead germs being removed. After the eggs have been fifteen days in the ovens they are daily examined, and so delicate is the touch of the attendant that he can at once distinguish if the egg is alive by the fact that it should be slightly warmer than his own skin.

"At the expiration of twenty-one days the chicks commence to emerge from the shells, the attendants constantly aiding them. They are placed in the spaces D D, illustration 1, and left to dry for nearly forty-eight hours, but they are not fed. The sale then commences and in a few hours they are spirited away. The temperature in the central hall is maintained at 98 F., and that of the ovens slightly more."

Development of the Modern Incubator

The modern incubator may be said to date from about 1875 when the comparatively crude forerunners of the present type of lamp-heated incubator appeared on the market. To develop the modern incubator, however, with its automatic and exact regulation of heat, its adaptability to a wide variety of conditions, its simplicity and its durability, and to do this without making the cost exorbitant, was by no means a simple or easy matter. These problems however, have been solved—unquestionably so, and the standard lamp-heated incubator of the present day is truly remarkable in efficiency, and low cost, and in ease and accuracy of operation. It will bear comparison with any of the modern, high-grade "tools" that have been perfected for the use of those engaged in other lines of agricultural production.

Lamp-heated incubators now are made in various sizes, from 50 to 400-egg capacity or more, the latter apparently being the practical limit for machines of this type. For larger capacity (500 to 2,500 eggs) there are incubators heated with oil or gas stoves; and for still larger capacity there are mammoth incubators heated with hot water, supplied from a central coal, oil or gas burning boiler or heater, and furnished in any desired capacity up to many thousands of eggs. These huge machines are in especial demand on extensive poultry farms and in hatcheries, where large capacity must be secured along with low operating cost. There also are several makes of small incubators heated by means of electricity, an entirely practical and economical method where current can be secured at reasonable rates.

Development of Modern Brooding Devices

In the development of brooding devices, as great or even greater progress has been made. These artificial mothers are quite simple in construction and operation, are thoroughly practical and efficient, and are moderate in cost. The first lamp-heated brooder that could be said to be really satisfactory was similar to the one illustrated on page 67, the method of heating which is still utilized in many homemade brooders, though the heating capacity is limited and such brooders are far from safe as regards fire. Various types of brooders and methods of providing heat were devised and used to a limited extent until the introduction of hovers of the Universal and Adaptable types which may be said to have solved the problem of thoroughly safe, convenient, and practical lamp-heated brooders. These hovers are installed in regular brooder cases ready-made or homemade, or in small portable houses. They can be operated indoors in mild weather with complete success, without case or other enclosure.

For indoor use, with or without a case, the type of lamp-heated hover known as "portable" is especially convenient, as it can be placed directly on the floor of the house and requires no holes in wall or floor to adapt the building to its use. Portable hovers have a more limited range of usefulness, however, owing to their lower heating power. Small hovers heated by electric current are quite extensively used where conditions are favorable.

Hot water pipe brooding systems have been in use for many years. This method of brooding is rather expensive in first cost, but has no superior where chicks are to be brooded in extremely cold weather. There has been no particular change in this type of brooder for many years, the preference of operators still being divided between the "open-pipe" and the closed pipe systems, the latter with either overhead or underneath installation. For brooding in moderately cold weather, when the great majority of chicks are brought out, there are various types of colony hovers heated with coal, oil or gas. These mammoth hovers brood chicks in flocks of many hundreds and have almost completely displaced lamp-heated hovers where chicks are to be brooded in large numbers.

A Billion Dollar Industry

While artificial brooding and incubating is, as we have seen, an ancient art, it has only been in comparatively recent years that, chiefly through the genius of American inventors, the methods have been modernized and made efficient and practical for poultry growers everywhere. And it is chiefly because poultry keepers now have truly automatic, labor-saving equipment for hatching and raising their fowls that the poultry industry has reached its present great proportions—has become a "billion-dollar industry." Great as the industry now is, the possibilities in the way of still further increasing the profitable production of table fowls and eggs are scarcely realized as yet, and will not be until poultry growers generally learn fully to avail themselves of the help that the modern incubator and brooder can give.

It is freely conceded that chicks can be successfully hatched and reared with hens, and with laborious, painstaking care high averages in eggs hatched and chicks raised can be secured in this way. It is doubtful, however, whether any one has ever realized a dollar a day for the time spent in raising chicks by the natural method. The number that any one person can hatch and tend with hens is simply too small to make it possible to secure anything like adequate returns for the time spent. Those who follow the natural method must give up the idea of volume, because that method makes volume impossible. Two or three or half-a-dozen broody hens can be handled with comparative ease, but beyond that it becomes real labor—and a serious waste of time.

If there were any place where the natural method could be successfully adopted it would be on the farm where there is unlimited room, most favorable natural conditions, and where the hens can take care of themselves with the least possible attention. Most of those who have tried it, however, know that even on the farm it can only be done at the expense of a lot of somebody's time, while the broken eggs, deserted nests, lice-infested fowls, the hens and chicks taken by various enemies, and the many other sources of loss, lay a heavy tax upon the farm flock, which is only endured because the extent of the losses is seldom realized. Without doubt, the general and intelligent adoption of artificial methods of raising chicks would, within a very few years, make it possible to double the annual income now being realized from farm poultry.

There are no grounds for questioning the statement that incubators and brooders offer extraordinary facilities for increasing the earning capacity of those engaged in the work. It is not through a mere notion or through the possession of unlimited funds, that commercial poultry keepers the country over have come to depend almost exclusively on artificial methods. They know that they cannot realize a profit on their work unless they do so. In the saving of time alone the artificial method completely justifies itself. It is common experience that where chicks can be raised by hundreds with hens, they can be raised by thousands with incubators and brooders, and with no more labor. On a smaller scale the saving in time is just as great, proportionately, and just as important from a practical point of view.

Why Incubators and Brooders Are Indispensable

The saving in time is the big thing, of course, but incubators and brooders offer other advantages as well. The person who wishes to raise only a comparatively small number of chicks may not care how much it costs, in point of time, but everyone certainly is interested in raising them the easiest, cleanest, and most pleasant way. To the market-egg producer the ability to bring off his chicks at just the right time to insure a supply of pullets for fall and winter laying, is a most important asset. The great scarcity of eggs at this season (November to February) is due, in large measure, to the limited number of early-hatched pullets, and this condition will continue to exist just as long as hen hatching is generally depended upon to maintain the laying flocks. This is true because hen hatching means late hatching, and late-hatched pullets are late layers and hence late sitters, and that means late hatches again, and so this evil perpetuates itself, year after year. Those who have incubators, however, are able to bring off their chicks at early dates, which practically assures them of a profitable fall and winter egg yield.

There is a double advantage to farmers in being able to have their chicks hatched out early in the season, as this makes it possible for them to attend to the work and to carry the chicks along past the delicate stage of their existence before the regular spring farm work begins to crowd. A little later on, plowing, planting, garden making, and an all but impossible assortment of other jobs come in a heap, taxing the strength and endurance of everyone in the household. But earlier in the season, before it is time to get the crops in, or before the ground is dry enough to work, is just the time for getting the chicks out, and the easiest time, too—if an incubator is used.

Those who wish to raise a definite number of chicks each year in order to have sufficient pullets to keep the laying flock up to its usual size without having to carry over a lot of old hens, find one of the most important advantages in artificial incubation in the fact that they are able thus to shorten the incubation period and get the chicks all off in one or two broods. This brings the work of caring for them within a short period of time, whereas, when hens are used, the hatching must necessarily string along from March to June, as the hens are individually pleased to take over this duty, thus multiplying the trouble of caring for the newly hatched chicks. Most of these, of course, will be too late for winter layers, too late for the cockerels to command the best broiler prices, too late for the most favorable season for raising them— too late for about everything that the wide-awake poultry keeper considers worth while. And moreover, with chicks of various ages and sizes, the later hatches always have a struggle for their lives and often lose whatever chance they originally had for amounting to anything, through

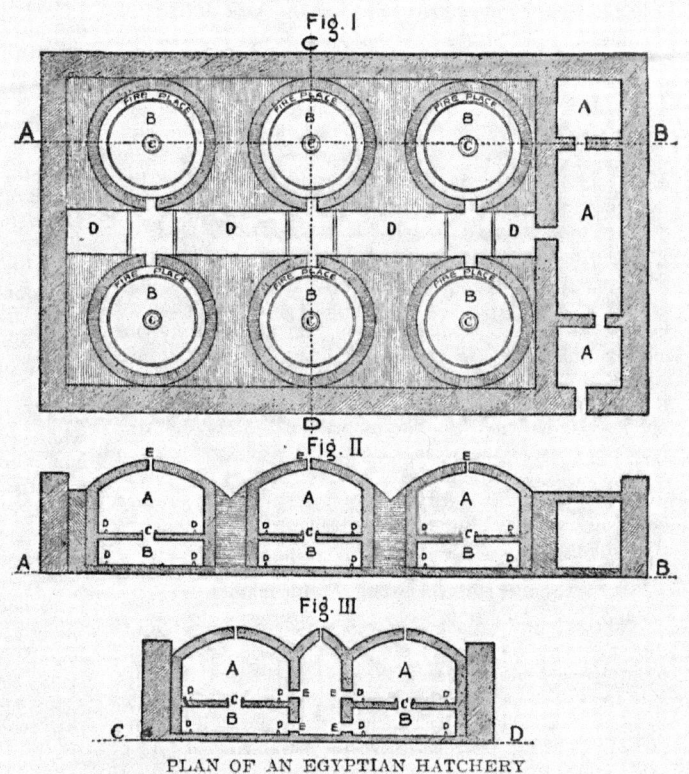

PLAN OF AN EGYPTIAN HATCHERY

Fig. 1—Ground plan: AAA, rooms making entrance to incubatory. BBB, ovens where eggs are hatched. CC, manholes admitting attendants to upper tier. DD, hallway. Fig. II—Sectional view lengthwise. AAA, upper chamber to ovens. BBB, lower chambers. CCC, manholes. DD, fire spaces. Fig. III—Section view lengthwise—same lettering as for Fig. II.

the merciless trampling and crowding that they receive from the half-grown youngsters of the first hatches.

Probably no practical poultry keeper would undertake to prove that incubators will hatch more or better chicks than good sitting hens, if unmolested, but there is no question about the fact that properly operated machines will bring off more chicks during the season than will be secured from an equal number of eggs set under "clucks." This is because, when the latter are set in large numbers, it is impossible to give them the time and attention necessary to secure maximum results and, as a consequence, losses are heavy and there is no practical way of preventing them. Even when special hatching rooms are provided and the hens have the best of care, there always will be some deserted nests, some broken eggs, and some lousy hens, which, in the final summing up, almost invariably give the incubator the lead.

Another point that deserves attention is the general increase in average egg production which results from keeping the hens laying right along, as they will do if promptly broken up as soon as they become broody, instead of allowing them to take two months off for hatching and brooding a flock of chicks just at the season of the year when they should be doing their heaviest and most profitable laying. In spite of the higher prices received during the winter, the average hen pays a larger net profit in the spring and early summer than at any other time of the year, if steadily productive.

It is not claimed that hens can be kept laying all summer long simply by breaking them up as fast as they become broody and putting them back into the laying pen again. Most of them have to take a rest sometime during the season, and it is something of an art to determine the right time to let them do this, with the idea of having them resume laying about the time eggs begin to advance in price in late summer. But whenever the time is when they can be given a vacation to best advantage, it certainly is not in the early spring.

Freedom from lice and mites is another important advantage possessed by artificially hatched chicks. There are few persons who realize the annual destruction caused by the ravages of lice among young chicks. The individual poultry keeper is entitled to little sympathy in his losses from these annoying pests if he refuses to adopt the one method that will give him almost complete immunity from them. But the annual loss to the industry from so unnecessary a cause, certainly is deplorable from an economic viewpoint—a loss that, each year, represents a sum almost sufficient to pay for all the necessary hatching and brooding equipment that would make it a thing of the past.

Brooders As Important As Incubators

The value of brooders is even less appreciated than is the case with incubators, for which reason especial emphasis should be placed on the great help that they are able to render in profitable poultry growing. It is worse than useless to hatch chicks unless proper facilities are provided for raising them after they are hatched. It is little more trouble to raise one hundred chicks in a brooder than ten with a hen; and when they are raised in still larger numbers by the use of colony hovers which brood several hundred in a single flock, the labor cost per chick becomes almost negligible.

Many complaints made by persons who have bought incubators and have not been satisfied with the results secured with them, can be traced to the fact that they did not have sufficient brooding capacity to care for the chicks after they were hatched. This false economy in providing brooders is almost universal, even among experienced poultry keepers who certainly ought to know better. With good brooders, chicks can be raised at any season, the losses will be fewer than with hens, chicks will be practically lice-free, can be protected from enemies, storms, and cold much better than when running with hens, and can be given about every other advantage that is required for their best and most profitable growth and development.

Incubators and Brooders Easy to Operate

Modern incubators and brooders, especially those of the better sort, are now so well developed and so nearly automatic in action that they require a surprisingly small amount of attention, and are so simple that any average man or women, boy or girl, can operate them successfully, and with ease. In a general way, the directions that are supplied by the manufacturers with every incubator or brooder they sell, contain information sufficient for their operation under ordinary conditions. These directions present, in condensed form, not only the general instructions that are applicable to all incubators alike, but also the special detailed information that is essential to the successful operation of their particular type of machine.

No better advice can be given the beginner than to say with all possible emphasis: **Follow the manufacturer's directions; follow them to the letter!** If, after one or two trials, results do not seem to be as good as they should, write direct to the manufacturer, giving him all the information needed to enable him to understand the particular conditions under which the machine is being operated, and depend upon it, he will be glad to give whatever additional instructions are required to insure complete success.

It is not the purpose of this book, therefore, to give directions that will take the place of the instructions of the manufacturer. These must, as far as they go, take precedence over all other advice, written or spoken. The manufacturer's instructions however, are necessarily quite brief and general, and they leave much unsaid that the thoughtful operator wishes to know, and must know if he is to make his poultry work the complete success that it can and should be. It is at this point that this book takes up the subject, supplementing the manufacturer's instructions, but not supplanting them.

In it we have endeavored to give the most reliable, up-to-date information available on artificial methods of raising chicks and on the allied subjects that are directly associated with such work. Recent literature from our various state experiment stations has been freely drawn upon for much of the experimental data presented, and the latest methods of successful, practical poultry growers have received no less attention. It is hoped that this book will prove interesting and helpful to all chick growers, whether they are using but a single incubator or brooder, or are turning out chicks by the tens of thousands.

CHAPTER I

Selection of Breeding Stock

Success in Hatching and Raising Chicks is Determined to a Great Extent by the Breeding Stock—Importance of Constitutional Vigor and How to Breed for It—How to Select Fowls for the Breeding Pen—How to Care for Them During the Breeding Season and Afterward.

SUCCESS in hatching and brooding chicks, either by artificial or natural means, is determined to a great extent before the eggs are placed in the incubator or under hens. No matter how skillful the care, no one can hope to raise chicks successfully or profitably if they lack their normal inheritance of health and vigor when hatched. And conversely, chicks of the right sort will stand a surprising amount of mishandling—will survive many mistakes on the part of the well-meaning but misinformed caretaker, if only they have high constitutional vigor to begin with. This character they can secure through inheritance. In order to begin at the beginning of the subject of "Artificial Incubating and Brooding," therefore, the fowls from which the hatching eggs are to be secured must have first consideration, in order to make certain that these eggs are produced from stock that is suitable for the purpose, and that is being bred under favorable conditions.

Choice of Breed

So far as the problems of artificial incubating are directly concerned, it is immaterial what breed is chosen. The average operator probably gets better hatches from Leghorn eggs than from eggs of the larger breeds, though this is not uniformly the case. Both in hatching and in brooding the percentage of loss is influenced more by the condition of the breeding fowls than by the particular breed or variety to which they belong. It is probable, however, that the greater natural activity of small fowls, such as Leghorns, results generally in their keeping in better breeding condition. This, no doubt, is the explanation for the better results usually secured with Leghorn eggs, and is the basis of the common belief that white-shelled eggs hatch better than those with brown shells.

Persons who expect to make the sale of eggs for hatching, day-old chicks, and breeding stock, a more or less important source of income, will naturally want to consider the preferences of possible customers in regard to breed, also whether the breed selected can reasonably be expected to produce a liberal supply of eggs at the time when they are most wanted for setting. For example, if it is the intention to hatch during extremely cold weather, it will hardly be advisable to depend on Leghorns, as fowls of this breed are apt to lay few eggs under such conditions. It is true that much can be done to correct this by providing comfortable houses for the fowls but, as a rule, more eggs and better fertility will be secured at this time with the so-called general-purpose breeds. Moreover, early-hatched Leghorn chicks are not particularly desirable, as they are not profitable market fowls, and the pullets usually come into laying too early and soon go into the "fall molt," after which they lay few eggs until the approach of spring.

In all cases, regardless of whether chicks are to be hatched on a large or a small scale and regardless of breed selected, fowls of standard quality should be made the basis of the breeding flock. It is simply a waste of time and opportunity to start in any line of poultry keeping with inferior stock. Not only will the sales from standard flocks be better and at higher prices, but the percentages realized in hatching and brooding operations will be distinctly better, owing to greater uniformity in the eggs set and in the chicks after they are hatched. Irregularity in size and shape of eggs, in color and character of shell, in vitality of germs, etc., are all handicaps in the successful operation of incubators and brooders, and without doubt uniformity in these respects can be secured only by the use of standard-bred stock. In addition, such fowls, if from the best strains, will be found to be larger in size, higher in vitality, and more productive than those of inferior breeding.

FIG. 1—STRONG, HEALTHY CHICKS ARE HALF RAISED
Sturdy, vigorous chicks like these do not readily succumb to disease or unfavorable conditions. The first step in securing such chicks is the selection of the right kind of breeding stock.

Constitutional Vigor

In the selection of individual fowls for the breeding pen, constitutional vigor is easily first in importance. As has already been stated, hatching percentages and proportion of chicks raised are largely determined by the health and vigor of the breeding fowls. Constitutional vigor is not a mysterious or accidental quality, but is the result of breeding and careful management. The poultry grower who eliminates from his pens every fowl that shows any evidence of low vitality, as determined by close and constant observation right along from chickhood to the breeding season, and who gives his breeders proper care, will have no difficulty in producing chicks full of vigor and vitality.

There are a number of indications of high constitutional vigor and of the lack of it—some readily distinguished, and some so deeply hidden that only long experience or constant observation throughout the growing period makes it possible to detect them. The poultryman who appreciates the importance of having only strong, vigorous birds in his breeding pens will neglect no practical test. In general, breeding fowls should always be full size for the breed to which they belong, and up to Standard requirements in shape and general breed characters. Of course such familiar and conspicuous evidences of low vitality as poor condition, undersize, flat, narrow breasts, knock knees, long, narrow heads, crow bills, dull eyes, low tails, etc., should eliminate the birds showing them, regardless of any good qualities that they may have, no matter what these may be. Naturally, the reverse of these undesirable qualities will indicate the birds that should be used; such as, broad, well-rounded breasts, broad, full heads (not thick or beefy), strong medium-length beaks, straight legs carried upright under the body and set well apart, an alert carriage, eyes with "snap," and a high degree of activity generally.

FIG. 2—A HIGH-CLASS BREEDING FEMALE
There is every appearance of health and superior breeding value here, but do not depend upon appearances alone; apply the tests for constitutional vigor, as described in text.

There are other indications of physical weakness, aside from outward appearance, that are fully as important, if less obvious. Fowls with cold feet are undesirable. Those individuals that have frosted combs where others similarly exposed escape injury, usually are low in vitality; also males that get out of breath or show dark combs after chasing or treading hens. It should hardly be necessary to say that fowls showing any tendency to diarrhea, having dirty noses (indicating catarrhal trouble) or overgrown toe nails (indicating indolence, if not poor health) must not be bred.

Even after fowls have passed these superficial tests they should be looked upon merely as likely candidates, but not to be introduced into the breeding flock until they have been kept under observation for some time, their appetites and general conduct watched, and the droppings under the perches inspected frequently to see whether there are any signs of weak digestion. Even after the pen is made up, any birds that develop indications of physical unfitness should at once be removed. It requires a high degree of moral courage to discard a fowl that may develop some seemingly minor weaknesses but which in many other respects is a desirable breeder. There is, however, no indication of low vitality that can be ignored with safety. In the case of standard-bred fowls, the tendency to overlook known deficiencies because the birds happen to be especially strong in "fancy" points, cannot be too strongly condemned. No excellence in standard requirements offers any compensation for a lack of constitutional vigor.

At the beginning of the hatching season is not the best time for selecting breeders, as they usually are at the height of their vigor then. Without showing any indications of this fact they may possess weaknesses that will make their use in the breeding pen a source of serious loss. This is the reason why the man who raises his own stock and who closely observes the birds during the growing period, is able to make his selections with much greater certainty of getting only desirable breeders.

Bred-to-Lay Stock

Probably next in practical importance in the selection of the breeding pen is getting hens with good trap-nest records the previous year, if possible, or pullets from such hens. It is believed to be particularly important to secure males from heavy laying hens, and the more generations of such ancestry represented in the strain from which selections are made, the better the results are apt to be. It is true that there are a good many things that yet remain to be learned about breeding for increased egg production. Certainly the development of a strain that can be depended upon to transmit heavy-laying ability to succeeding generations can be accomplished only by long-continued and careful selection and is not to be attained as the result of a single season's work. However, where breeding from heavy layers is persistently and intelligently carried out it undoubtedly will bring results, and it is always wise to purchase breeding fowls and eggs for hatching from breeders who are known to specialize in such stock.

Caution should be used here, however, as there are many who have mistakenly come to attach undue importance to the laying record, making it the all-in-all, and not hesitating to forego standard qualities and even individual health and vigor in favor of phenomenal egg production. Such a policy is unwise, and must sooner or later lead to complete failure. The best possible means of establishing a strain capable of transmitting heavy laying ability is through the use of standard-bred fowls that, along with good to high egg records, will combine established breed characters and the high constitutional vigor which make heavy laying ability transmissible. If choice must be made between fowls with high records, but of non-standard breeding, and others from an established strain, of high constitutional vigor but with only good laying records, it usually will be found that better layers will be produced from the latter. This is true probably because heavy laying is dependent fully as much upon uniform breeding, good health and the ability to digest large quantities of food as it is on an inherited tendency to heavy production.

Breeding Related Fowls

Notwithstanding the general and deep-seated prejudice against inbreeding, the poultry breeder who selects his fowls carefully, rigidly excluding every one that shows any sign of physical weakness, need have little fear of unfavorable results from breeding related birds. There is no other method known to breeders that will so quickly and so certainly improve quality and establish uniformity in the poultry flock—provided, of course, that foundation stock of

FIG. 3—A GOOD MALE FOR THE BREEDING PEN
A sturdy, upstanding male like this one, should head the breeding pen. There is no question regarding the constitutional vigor of fowls of this type. This exhibition-quality breeding male is owned by W. D. Holterman.

superior merit is used to start with. It is true that close inbreeding of fowls having common physical weaknesses will intensify such characters, causing rapid degeneration. On the other hand, strong constitutional vigor is just as certainly intensified in the same way, and if this fact is kept in mind and defective birds regularly discarded, nothing but good results need be expected.

The fact that inbreeding is one of the poultry keeper's greatest helps in establishing his strain should be considered in connection with the common but mistaken practice of securing new males each year in order to avoid the fancied danger of relationship matings. The most successful poultry breeders will under no consideration part with either males or females that have proved conspicuously good breeders, but will deliberately breed them back to their offspring in order to fix their good qualities and the power of transmitting them. There is reason for believing that inbreeding is the most effective known means of securing that greatly-desired quality known as prepotency.

Fertility and "Hatchability"

When fowls are properly mated, practically all eggs produced by them are fertile, regardless of season or other general conditions; but not all fertile eggs will hatch. What usually is meant, however, where the term fertility is used, is "hatchability" (for lack of a better word), which is by no means the same thing. The ability to produce hatchable eggs is not possessed equally by all hens, but varies widely in different individuals. It is moreover, a transmissible character, like shape of comb or color of feathers. That is, hens that produce eggs characterized by high or low hatchability will transmit this tendency to their daughters; and by proper selection it is believed to be possible to develop strains regularly distinguished by this quality. This fact is so clearly established that many careful breeders believe that it pays to utilize trap-nests in their breeding pens if only for the purpose of detecting the individuals that produce eggs of inferior hatching quality. The losses due to spoiled eggs, wasted incubator space and dissatisfied customers more than exceed the labor cost of operating the trap-nests.

Selecting the Male

The male is by all odds the most important individual in the breeding pen, and especial attention must be given to his selection. So far as standard qualities go, there is only one general suggestion that need be given here; get the best male that can be afforded. A high price may be no proof of high quality, but a low price is pretty generally proof of inferiority. The buyer, therefore, while using due care and business judgment in buying, must be willing to pay a good price if he hopes to get a good male. A poor one is dear at any price. In breeding for increased egg production the male becomes of still greater importance, owing to the now generally accepted belief that it is through the sons of heavy-laying dams rather than through their daughters, that heavy egg-laying ability is transmitted.

Individually the male should possess every desirable quality previously mentioned as indicative of high constitutional vigor, adding to these the masculine quality of aggressiveness. The "scrappy" male, and the gallant one that is constantly on the lookout for the members of his flock, are apt to be up to specifications in all physical requirements. A male whose comb or wattles have been injured by fighting or freezing is none the worse for breeding purposes on that account, providing he has fully recovered from the effects of the injury. However, weak birds are more apt to have frosted combs than strong ones, and it is advisable to make sure that such injuries have not resulted from this cause. Scaly leg is not a serious matter unless it has developed to such an extent as to make the bird lame, but it should be treated and thoroughly cured before using the bird in the breeding pen. The male should be fully up to standard size for the breed to which he belongs and good in all breed characters.

Diseases of the male organs, resulting in partial or complete sterility, are more common than is generally realized. There is comparatively little danger of the well-

FIG. 4—RAPID, PROFITABLE GROWTH IMPOSSIBLE WITHOUT VIGOR

These two chicks, like the pair shown in Fig. 9, were hatched and brooded under identical conditions, but the "runt" was of parentage low in constitutional vigor. Courtesy of Missouri State Poul. Exp. Station.

developed, "scrappy" male being impotent, but the test of service is the only certain one. For this reason the pen should be mated up sufficiently in advance of the regular breeding season so as to have an opportunity to make a change in males if necessary. In buying males, or females either for that matter, notice whether there is any discharge, foul smelling or otherwise, from the vent, also whether the feathers below it are badly soiled or matted. Diarrhea, or the tendency to it, is transmissible, and vent gleet apparently is growing rather common. If a single individual in the flock has this disease it will quickly spread to all and may prove a source of serious loss.

Cock or Cockerel

Whether to buy or use cocks or cockerels will depend on circumstances. Cocks can generally be purchased at less cost than cockerels of equal quality and may prove much better value for the money. A good male should be serviceable for four or five years, if properly cared for and not overworked. To discard him at the end of his first season is a wasteful practice and is uncalled for in any rational system of breeding. Hence if one or two-year-old males can be bought at a marked reduction from the price of cockerels they should prove a good investment, especially if it is possible to secure a favorable report on their previous performance, and if they are in good physical condition.

Another advantage in buying cocks is that physical weaknesses that escape notice in the cockerel are more readily detected in older birds. Males are often subjected to brutal neglect and mistreatment out of the breeding season, however, and in buying it is important to be sure that they have received no injuries from this cause. For mating with pullets, cocks are considered especially desirable as they are expected to offset any disadvantage growing out of immaturity in the females. It is generally believed that from a mating of cock and pullets a larger proportion of pullets will be secured than in the case of a cockerel-and-pullet, or cock-and-hen mating.

If cockerels are to be used, select those that are well-matured. Much loss annually results from the use of immature birds in the breeding pen—a frequent cause of poor hatches and weak chicks, especially toward the end of the breeding season when young males are apt to weaken, with a marked falling off in fertility as a direct consequence. Well-developed young birds may go through the season without serious loss of vigor if mated in comparatively small flocks and non-forcing conditions are maintained throughout, but immature ones are almost certain to fail before the end of the season. In selecting cockerels avoid those that have plainly been cowed. It is not a mark of inferiority from a breeding viewpoint for one cockerel to be whipped by another in a fight. That test literally applied would eliminate all but one from any flock. But cockerels that are distinctly cowed and willing to accept "peace at any price," are worthless as breeders.

Selection of Females

The poultry breeder's problems would be comparatively simple if males and females of equal quality could always be mated together, in which case they should transmit their characters uniformly and without change. Unfortunately such matings are not possible in practical breeding, and it is necessary to try to strike an average by matching the respective weaknesses and good qualities of the fowls; selecting females that are strong where the male is weak, or the other way around. For example, if the male is a little undersize for the breed, hens are selected for mating with him that are somewhat oversize. If the male's color is not quite what it should be, females mated with him must be especially strong in that respect. This method of mating, when properly handled, often produces fowls better in quality—that is, more closely corresponding to the Standard description—than either of their parents, but it has distinct limitations and must not be carried to extremes, as in the mating of violent contrasts, which practice never gives satisfactory results.

One and two-year-old hens are almost always better breeders than pullets, and they should be employed for this purpose as far as possible. If there is opportunity to consult trap-nest records made by the hens during the preceding year, all that have made conspicuously poor records will, of course, be discarded; also all that lay misshapen eggs or very small or overlarge ones, and those marked by irregular shape or texture of shell. In the absence of trap-nest records, apply the various recognized tests for laying ability, such as the shank color test, spread of pelvic bones, date of molting, etc. All of these are of practical value in determining the previous performance of hens.

Future egg production may be determined with a fair degree of accuracy by performance in the pullet year. This is not an infallible test, as there will always be some that will make high records in the pullet year that will not "come back" in the second season, while others will prove better layers in their second year than in the first. Speaking generally however, the chances for good egg yields in the second year are always in favor of the hens that have laid well as pullets.

It has been definitely shown that yellow-skinned fowls rapidly lose the bright color of shanks and beaks when laying heavily, so that pale shanks and beaks in late summer usually are characteristics of the best layers. In applying this test it is necessary to discriminate between hens that have faded shanks as a result of heavy laying, and those that are naturally pale in shank color, or that have become so as the result of ill health or through the action of the soil, some kinds of which will bleach out the shanks regardless of whether the hens have laid well or not. With suitable correction for these exceptions, however, and considering beaks as well as

FIG. 5—A STANDARD-BRED LEGHORN COCK
This splendid exhibition cock is a good example of the kind of high-vigor males that should head the breeding pen. It is NOT necessary to sacrifice standard qualities to secure practical values. The cock shown in above illustration is owned by Geo. B. Ferris.

FIG. 6—EXHIBITION QUALITY HEN WITH HIGH EGG RECORD
This S. C. White Leghorn hen made a record of 288 eggs in twelve months and is of a famous show strain in which high egg production also is demanded. Hens of inferior quality may be good layers, but they have no place in the breeding pen.

shanks, this test will prove to be fairly reliable, especially if applied about the time the fowls have stopped for the fall molt. The color comes back into the shanks gradually after laying ceases, so that after some time has elapsed the test cannot be applied with any degree of accuracy. Fowls that are good layers also have quite pliable pelvic bones, set wide apart, the position being readily determined by a slight pressure of the fingers on the fowl's body, just below the vent. This test should be applied in connection with the shank-color test.

It has been found that late molting hens are almost invariably the best layers of the preceding year, while the hens that molt early and have their new coat of feathers well in advance of cold weather generally are the poorest layers of the flock. Late molters may be handicapped by the necessity for making the change in cold weather, and often need special protection to keep them from suffering. They make short work of the molt when they get at it, however, and almost invariably will lay more winter eggs, in spite of this, than the hens that have molted weeks or months before.

Care of Breeding Fowls Out of Season

If in position to do so, it often is desirable to purchase breeding fowls for the next season's use, in the summer. They usually can be bought at moderate prices then, and this is the most favorable time for selection, as they are more likely to show their defects at the end of the breeding season, and it is, of course, just the right time to select the best layers. Moreover, the value of old birds as breeders the next season will depend a good deal on the way they are handled during the fall and winter.

FIG. 7—A POOR LAYER AND BREEDER
This hen molted in late summer and only laid 36 eggs in her pullet year. Avoid early molters for the breeding pen. Photo from Cornell University.

The common recommendation to separate males from females out of the breeding season, is of questionable value under average conditions. Whether it is true, as some believe, that this violent change in habits is liable to result in injury to the sexual organs of the males does not appear to have been definitely proved by experiments, but there are some good practical reasons for believing that the average person will get better results by letting the males run with the flock or, better still, confining them in comfortable, roomy quarters with a small number of females, unless especially favorable conditions can be provided for them elsewhere. It is not necessarily so but, as a rule, males that are penned together or singly are almost certain to suffer from neglect, and anything that results in their getting out of condition will prove a distinct disadvantage in the long run.

The practice of penning single males in small coops, such as exhibition coops, with barely room to turn around and without any outdoor runs is probably the worst plan of all, if such imprisonment is continued for long periods. It often is necessary to do this where the fowls are of exhibition quality or are kept for sale later on in the season, in which case it is not wise to risk the injuries that may result from fighting. It is highly important, however, that during the off season, the male shall have every facility for regaining his strength and vigor, and he can not do this if cooped up in close quarters, under questionable sanitary conditions or where he is liable to be neglected and poorly fed. Where there are several strange males running together either in stag flocks or with hens, there is apt to be some fighting, but if there is plenty of range or large yards, and the precaution is taken to trim the toe-nails and the beaks so as to make them blunt and a little sensitive, the birds will establish their "spheres of influence" without serious injury to each other.

FIG. 8—ROOSTING CLOSET FOR BREEDERS
In cold climates fowls with large combs need special protection to prevent frost bites, which may destroy their breeding value for many weeks.

The rations of the breeders, males and females alike, should be non-stimulating during the off season, and may consist mainly of hard grains scattered broadcast or buried in the litter to promote exercise. There should be little meat in the ration and what mash is fed should be given dry in hoppers. Supply all the green feed the birds will eat.

Cloth-front houses are ideal for breeders, and close, warm houses should never be used. Except in extremely cold weather the birds should have access to the yards or range all day long. The more time they spend outdoors the better it will be for their general health. Warm houses are debilitating, and experiments have shown that breeding stock confined to them invariably lose in vitality and in ability to produce good hatching eggs. There is a wide difference between cuddling and unlimited exposure, however, and the breeder will do well to avoid either. Be careful to prevent frosted combs, especially at the opening of winter, but not over-careful. If cold weather comes on gradually the fowls will become accustomed to it and will stand much lower temperatures

FIG. 9—EFFECT OF CONSTITUTIONAL WEAKNESS
These chicks were hatched in the same incubator and brooded together under identical conditions. The difference in growth is directly due to difference in constitutional vigor. It pays to cull out every breeding fowl that is low in vitality. Also see Fig. 4.

without injury than is possible when the cold sets in early in the winter.

Males are more liable to injury from frost bites than hens, owing to the larger size of their combs and wattles. It often pays to provide a small cloth-covered roosting coop where they can be confined on extremely cold nights. The small coop often provided for brooding hens at one end of the perches, will answer nicely for this purpose if the sides are curtained. The male will be safe from injury here while the rest of the flock will have all the advantage of the hardening that comes from continued exposure to low temperatures. Remember, however, that extreme exposure is of no practical advantage; fowls are hardened by cold, even severe cold, but they are injured and in no way benefitted by exposure to conditions so severe as to cause actual suffering.

After winter sets in the breeders should have separate quarters with as much room as possible. It is not at all desirable to have them do any laying until about the opening of the breeding season, and they should be fed accordingly. Do not neglect them at this time, however, simply because they are not producing eggs. While the average one and two-year-old hens are at their best as breeders, if in good physical condition, lack of exercise, unsanitary quarters, and feeding for egg production previous to the breeding season, will seriously impair their value. At this time they should be kept in good flesh, but not fat. Overfed fowls and those that are half starved are alike undesirable.

A good ration for idle breeders is a mixture of equal parts of cracked corn and whole oats, with an equal portion of wheat or barley if obtainable. Feed this in plenty of litter so that the fowls will have an abundance of exercise in digging it out. The mash may consist of equal parts, by weight, of bran and middlings, with ten per cent of meat scrap added, feeding it dry in hoppers. With a dry mash formula like this there is little danger of their eating too much, but it should always be kept before them. Plenty of green food should be supplied, of course, sprouted oats being by far the most desirable if they can be provided.

Care of Young Breeding Stock

During the growing season chicks that are intended for the breeding pen should have all possible range, and plenty of nourishing but non-forcing food. All through the growing season they should be under observation, culling out the ones that develop defects or show any indication of low vigor. It is a good plan to mark all the chicks that, at any time during their growth, show undesirable qualities, doing so by clipping the point of the toe, punching the web of the foot or otherwise marking them in some unmistakable manner so that there will be no chance of their being overlooked and getting into the breeding pen later on. It often happens that birds that at some stage of their growth develop unmistakable signs of weakness, afterward recover and at the breeding season appear to be as good as any of the rest, but are inferior in vigor in spite of their appearance.

One point that is of great importance in the handling of young stock is to see to it that none that are intended for the breeding pen are allowed to crowd in brooders or coops during the growing period. It never pays to permit crowding, but in the case of next year's breeders it is doubly objectionable. Feed a good growing ration, with plenty of oats and succulent green stuff, and a reasonable allowance of meat scraps or other animal food, and give all the liberty possible.

If pullets and cockerels are to be used they should be selected from those hatched neither too early nor too late. Pullets hatched quite early, so that they begin laying in the fall, are apt to be undesirable as breeders, as they will be more or less exhausted by heavy laying. They can often be used to good advantage in the early part of the season, but should not be depended upon after the season is well advanced.

It is not wise to attempt to hold back early pullets, however, and prevent their laying, with the idea that in this way their strength and vigor will be conserved for the breeding season. It is much better to let them lay, if they do so naturally, using them early in the season, if necessary, but depending upon hens or later-hatched pullets for the major part of the supply of hatching eggs. Pullets that are not fully grown or are just beginning to lay must not be used, as chicks hatched from their eggs will be undersized and weakly, difficult to raise, and not desirable even when grown. If pullets must be placed in the breeding pen, therefore, select those that have come naturally to maturity without any forcing, and that have laid for a short time only before the season opens.

FIG. 10.—A FINE BREEDING PEN OF WHITE WYANDOTTES
Bred by J. C. Fishel & Sons

CHAPTER II

Management of Breeding Stock

When to Mate the Breeding Pens—Number of Females to the Male—General Directions for Housing, Feeding, and Caring for Breeding Fowls so as to Insure High Fertility and Strong Chicks—Some Common Mistakes That Result in Poor Hatches, and How to Avoid Them.

SO FAR as the subject of "Artificial Hatching and Brooding" is concerned, interest in the breeding pen centers in the production of fertile eggs that will hatch strong, vigorous chicks, and the management of the flock is considered here solely from that viewpoint. In general, the breeding pen should have about the same housing conditions as are found most desirable for the laying flock, differing only in the respect that the breeders must have more room, both in and outdoors, and in extreme climates the house must be warm enough to afford reasonable protection. The breeding flock must under no conditions be coddled, but hardened to the greatest extent possible without exposing them to conditions that will cause actual suffering or injury, which might destroy their breeding value for weeks to come. However, there is no wisdom or practical advantage in exposing fowls to such an extent that their combs will be frozen, and it should be possible to make the house warm enough to prevent such injuries.

It should be remembered in this connection, that since breeding fowls have, or should have, more floor space per hen than usually is the case in laying pens, and are kept in much smaller flocks, they will be less able to keep each other warm on the perches at night, and for this reason need warmer houses than the layers. As a rule, if the house is well built with the open front provided with muslin-covered frames or curtains that can be closed tight in extreme weather, nothing more will be required, except in the coldest sections, where roosting closets such as the one shown in Fig. 8 will prove desirable.

The size of the house or pen will be determined by various factors, but it is desirable in all cases to give the breeders plenty of floor space. Not less than six square feet per hen should be provided in all cases, and eight square feet is better for small flocks. For example, if the breeding pen is to consist of about twelve hens, the pen or house should be 8x10, 8x12, or even 10x10 feet. Many poultry plants are equipped with a number of portable houses of about this size and when such are available they should by all means be utilized.

Extra small breeding pens can be provided for quite cheaply by using portable buildings like the one shown in Fig. 13. There are various inconveniences connected with caring for fowls in extremely small structures, but where the breeding pen is small and is to be kept mated for only a short time, it hardly is practical to provide expensive permanent houses and yards. The coop and yard here illustrated can readily be shifted to new ground at frequent intervals, little cleaning will be required and, during the growing season, the supply of green food will be taken care of without trouble. A convenient house, suitable for a single breeding pen, is shown in Fig. 12. It is portable and comparatively low in cost and may be

FIG. 11—A PERMANENT BREEDING HOUSE
Where the poultry plant is permanently established and the breeding of fowls is to be carried on extensively, a permanent breeding house suitably planned, with yards of ample size, will prove a profitable investment. The house here shown is excellent for mild climates, but for use in the north it should have smaller openings in the front, protected by tight-fitting muslin-covered shutters.

utilized as a colony house for brooder chicks or growing stock when no longer required for the use of breeding fowls.

A permanent compartment breeding house is shown in Fig. 11. Houses of this type are desirable where special attention is given to systematic breeding, in which case the fowls must necessarily be kept yarded in separate flocks. If regular laying houses are to be used for breeding fowls, flock matings usually will be resorted to. A pen 20x20 feet or 16x25 feet will readily accommodate 50 to 70 females for which number three to five males must be provided. As a rule it is more practical to follow this plan than to attempt to divide the space into the necessary small compartments for single flock matings.

Whether small or large flocks are kept, the yards should be as large as it is practical to make them. The birds will do better, fertility will be higher, and the chicks will be better and stronger if the fowls can have plenty of room. Open range for the breeders is the ideal con-

FIG. 12—SMALL COLONY HOUSE FOR BREEDING PEN
Colony houses of the above type provide ample room for a medium-sized breeding flock and can be located wherever convenient for the care of the fowls. When not needed for the breeding pen they afford excellent quarters for growing stock. Photo from U. S. Department of Agriculture.

dition, of course, but this can seldom be provided, and large yards then become the only practical alternative. A grass sod should be maintained on the yards, if possible, so that the birds can secure their green food in the natural way, and the yards should be located where there is plenty of natural shade, if choice in the matter is possible. There is no question that fowls confined in yards such as are illustrated in Fig. 14 will do better and their chicks will do better, other things being equal, than would be the case with fowls confined in small bare yards like the unfortunates shown in Fig. 16.

Mating the Breeding Pens

The exact date at which the breeding pens should be mated will depend to a great extent on the plans of the breeder, also on available houseroom. There are so many advantages in favor of early mating and so little practical objection to it that, if regular breeding houses or laying pens are to be used and are available at this time, it is advisable to place the fowls in their permanent quarters when they are housed for the winter. This will make it possible to give them the special feeding and care that they should receive from this time on, and to do this in the most convenient manner. It is not meant by this that the fowls are to be mated up for the breeding season at that time; the final adjustments will be made later. But it is just as well to sort and pen the birds carefully so as to have as few changes as possible to make later on.

Keep the birds under close observation and make notes regarding final combinations but do not keep shifting them from pen to pen, as one or two strange birds in a flock are apt to be set upon and abused by the rest. For this reason the shifting should all be done at one time if possible. If cockerels are to be used they may be left running together until the pens are finally mated up and there will be little quarreling among them if they are separated from the rest of the flock. Adult males may be left running with small pens of hens or confined separately if desirable, provided they are well cared for (see Chapter 1).

Whatever the date at which hatching operations are to begin, the pens should always be mated up well in advance of that time. About five weeks may be allowed from the date when the first eggs are saved until the hatch comes off, and then it is wise to allow at least two weeks more to give the birds time to get acquainted, to detect sterility in the male, if it exists, and to make any final adjustments among the females, due to partiality on the part of the male or to other causes. After the hatching season begins delays are always unfortunate and readjustments in the breeding pen then may cause serious loss.

Even in the northern states it is practical to bring chicks off as early as the latter part of February, provided there are proper facilities for caring for them, and this means that collecting eggs for hatching must begin about the middle of January. In that case the first of the year is none too soon for mating the pens. Pullets of the Asiatic breeds, or Brahmas, Cochins and Langshans, if hatched by March 1st, should begin laying in October, while the cockerels will be salable as squab broilers the latter part of April, or as regular broilers two weeks to a month later, when they should command the highest prices of the season.

With some strains and under some conditions as to care and feeding, there is danger that pullets hatched before March will begin laying too early in the fall, resulting in the objectionable "fall molt" later on, but this does not often happen with the breeds mentioned. If Wyandottes or R. I. Reds are to be hatched it will be better to delay the hatching date until after the middle of March, unless there is sale for the chicks. With the same exception it will be found better, as a rule, to delay hatching Leghorns and similar breeds until the first of April or later.

Size of Breeding Flock

The size of the breeding flock or the number of fe-

FIG. 13—PORTABLE COOP AND RUN FOR SMALL BREEDING PEN
Close confinement for breeding fowls, while not desirable, is often necessary. For a small flock, or a few specially mated fowls, this combination portable outfit can be used to good advantage. The fowls will keep in good condition if carefully fed and the coop and run frequently moved to new locations.

males that may be mated with one male can not be arbitrarily fixed, as there are a number of things to be considered. The age and individuality of the male has much to do with determining the number of females with which he should be mated. There are instances on record of flocks of 40, 60, and even 80 females mated to one male, with excellent fertility resulting, but such matings are too extreme to be considered in practical breeding. Especially with fowls in confinement, poultry breeders have found that the breeding pen must be comparatively small if good results are to be secured throughout the season. It is possible successfully to mate large numbers of fowls with a single male for a limited time, especially if the latter is young, but if long continued the practice will result in the cockerel's exhaustion.

If the breeder cares to go to the trouble of stud mating (that is, keeping the male confined separately and placing individual hens with him only for service) the number served by one male can be largely increased, especially since it is by no means necessary that the hens be served daily. Many poultry breeders having valuable males that they are desirous of using in the most efficient way, are following this plan with good results. Comparatively few breeders will be interested in this method but will want to allow the usual free mating, and where this is done the number of hens will be found to be limited by the season of the year, the amount of liberty the birds have, the age and vigor of the male, the breed to which the fowls belong, and the length of time that the pen is to be mated.

In cold weather the fowls are not as active and do not mate as readily as in warmer weather, neither will yarded fowls or those confined to house pens mate as readily as on open range or in large yards. It is hardly necessary to call attention to the fact that there is a wide difference in the mating ability of individual males, and it is common knowledge that the larger and heavier fowls do not mate as readily or as freely as the more active breeds, such as Leghorns. Finally, if it is the intention to use eggs from the pen for a long period it will be necessary to conserve the powers of the male to some extent, by keeping the number of females well below the extreme limit.

With all these factors in mind, the breeder who is anxious to secure the best practical results from his fowls will mate about as follows: With the larger breeds such as Plymouth Rocks, Orpingtons, Brahmas, Wyandottes, etc., and in the winter season, the number of females will be limited to not more than six or eight if a cock is used, or two or three more if mated with a vigorous cockerel. Later in the season, when the fowls have outside runs, the number may be increased 25 per cent or more. In the case of Leghorns the minimum number need not be below ten and may be increased to as many as 20 to 25, with vigorous young cockerels, and during mild weather. With fowls on open range, in the height of the breeding season, the number may be still further increased. However, since the pens usually are mated up well in advance of the natural breeding season and are kept in more or less close confinement, it seldom is practical to make successive additions to the flock as here described, and it is advisable to keep within the general limits of 10 to 20 females to one male, reducing the minimum number if results demand it, and increasing the maximum only under most favorable conditions.

What are known as flock matings, in which large numbers are kept in one flock with males provided in the proportion of 4 to 6 for each hundred females, are quite common and are entirely practical where eggs are to be produced for incubation without regard for individual breeding. This practice is especially common with Leghorns, and on farms generally. Where flock mating is practiced it is desirable to provide plenty of males in order that if any prove to be undesirable or defective they can be removed without the necessity of putting in additional ones. When males are raised together, or are penned together for a time so that they can get acquainted before being put with the hens, there should be little fighting, but if strange males are used or new ones are introduced into the flock after the season opens, fighting is about certain to ensue and may cause serious trouble.

It is well known that males often develop preferences among the hens in their flock, paying especial attention to some while others are almost entirely neglected. This is a common cause of low fertility. The only practical way to correct this in pen matings is to detect the neglected hens, which may readily be done by the use of trap nests, and they may then be removed and placed in other pens, when the fertility of their eggs usually will improve at once. This is one of the chief reasons why flock matings often produce better fertility than is secured in single pens.

FIG. 14—A WELL-SHADED YARD IS DESIRABLE FOR THE BREEDING PEN

In flock matings there is always considerable interference among males, especially when the fowls are more or less closely confined, and it is worth while to provide a degree of privacy for the mating birds. Short partitions extending out about midway into the pen, are a help, also large yards. Some breeders find it worth while to provide breeding boards such as the one illustrated in Fig. 15.

Rations for Breeding Fowls

The method of feeding the breeding flock out of season is described in the preceding chapter. As the hatching season approaches and the fowls are to be put into good laying condition, the ration should be changed so that they will get a better laying ration, though forcing must be avoided, especially if the breeding season is to be a long one. Poultry rations generally are subject to such modifications as are indicated by market prices

FIG. 15—A BREEDING BOARD
In flock-mated pens it often is desirable to afford some privacy for mating fowls, to prevent interference from other males. A few inexpensive screens like the one shown above, properly placed, will accomplish this purpose. Photo from McDonald (Que.) College.

and availability, and it is not always practicable to provide just what is wanted or would be considered essential under more favorable conditions. It is only practical to suggest here what may be called a good all-round ration, leaving it to each feeder to modify this to meet the conditions existing in his own feed market.

It is desirable at all times to provide reasonable variety in the ration of the breeding flock, though it also is possible to get along with comparatively limited range of choice in foods if the feeding is carefully done. For the grain part of the ration, equal parts by measure of cracked corn, feeding wheat, heavy oats, and barley will make an excellent mixture. Wheat and barley may be omitted if necessary, making the mixture then about two parts of cracked corn to one of oats, by measure, if oats are used also in the mash and as a source of green food, otherwise use equal parts of corn and oats, provided the oats are plump and heavy. Any other grains that are available may be used in reasonable proportion.

For the mash mixture an ideal formula is: Bran, middlings, corn meal and rolled or crushed oats, in equal parts by measure; one-half part each of gluten feed and meat scrap; five to eight per cent of oil meal. This makes a fairly rich mixture, and does not differ materially from the formula that probably will be fed to the regular laying flock. The portion consumed, however, should be below that recommended for layers. If the mash is fed dry in hoppers it is not likely that consumption will exceed the desired proportion and may fall below it. In this case it will be necessary to give the fowls a feed of moist mash daily, as they will lay better and their eggs will hatch better if they get a reasonable amount of this. If the consumption of dry mash is too low and there are objections to feeding it daily in moist condition, the formula may be changed to make it more palatable, usually by adding more meat scrap and coarse corn meal. If the fowls eat too much of the dry mash, however, the proportion of bran should be increased.

The use of dry mash, giving the fowls access to it at all times during the day, is an important aid to keeping them in good condition and properly nourished, and should not be omitted unless there is some extremely good reason for doing so. If it is not possible to secure the mash ingredients here recommended, the feeder will have to do the best he can to replace them with locally available substitutes or to get along with less variety. Even if it is necessary to limit the mash to bran, white middlings, and meat scrap, it still is possible to get good results, though the fowls may refuse to eat a sufficient amount of it unless fed as a moist mash. Whatever else is used or omitted from the mash, meat scrap, fish meal, fresh butcher's scraps or green cut bone must be liberally supplied—not less than 15 to 20 per cent of the total weight of the mixture. Experiments have shown that rations deficient in animal food will certainly cause poor hatches. Reasonably heavy feeding also is essential to strong fertility and hatches are almost always unsatisfactory where the fowls are kept on scant rations.

Abundant exercise is of the greatest importance in the wellbeing of the breeding flock and to a high hatching percentage in the eggs produced, especially when the fowls are in confinement. For this reason whole corn should not be fed, unless on cold nights, and abundant floor litter must be provided. A variation of 100 per cent in fertility has been observed in experimental pens where the only difference in treatment was the method of feeding, one pen getting its grain in two feeds on a practically bare floor, while the grain ration of the other was fed four or five times a day, and buried in deep litter so that the birds had to dig for it and had to spend practically the entire day hunting for this part of the ration. This extreme method of feeding may not be practical for the average poultry breeder, but he can at least divide the day's grain ration into three separate feeds, giving them morning, noon and evening and always burying the grain in litter, which should be deep enough to hide it thoroughly.

Where this is done, the evening meal must be given early enough so that the fowls will be able to secure a full feed before dark. No harm will be done if some is left in the litter after the fowls are through feeding for the night, as this will be an incentive to get down from the perches next morning as soon as they can see, and get to work again. Remember that breeding fowls need reasonable variety in the ration and it is not desirable to feed too heavily on any one grain, no matter how convenient it may be to do so, or how cheap in comparison with other grains. True economy in the feeding of fowls consists in supplying the ration that they most need and on which they will give the best returns, even though it may cost a little more per pound than something else less desirable or effective.

Much has been said in regard to the necessity for providing a ration for the breeding stock which shall contain everything required, and in just the right propor-

FIG. 16—ONE CAUSE OF POOR HATCHES
Constant confinement in small, bare yards will break down the vitality of the best of fowls.

MANAGEMENT OF BREEDING STOCK

FIG. 17—PARTS OF HOME-MADE TRAP NEST
Galvanized iron door, 9x9 inches square. Edges turned to stiffen. Upper edge has No. 9 fence wire inserted in fold, this wire extending about ¾ of an inch at each end beyond sides of the door. B—Wooden trigger, ⅞x⅞ of an inch in width and thickness, and 2½ inches in length. Has notch cut in lower end. Upper end has common wire staples driven in part way, with an extra staple looped through this one. Is fastened to cross top rail (see Fig. 19) so that galvanized iron door will just clear it nicely when raised. C—Top rail ⅞ of an inch x 2 x 12 inches. Trigger (B) is to be attached to this rail. D and E—Front and back of nest—duplicates; 12½ inches wide x 10¾ inches high. Bottom rail, ⅞ of an inch x 3 x 12½ inches. Top rail, ⅞ of an inch x 1¼ x 12½ inches. Side rail, ⅞ of an inch x 2 x 6½ inches. Strips are ⅞ x ⅞ of an inch x 10¾ inches. Back of nest can be made solid if desired. F and I—Sides of nest each ⅜ of an inch x 10½ x 20½ inches. G—Bottom of nest or floor, ⅜ of an inch x 12⅞ x 20½ inches. H—Strip ⅞ of an inch x 2¾ x 12 inches. Used mid-way between front and back of nest to hold nest material in place. See Figs. 18 and 19, for nest in operation.

tions, for egg formation and the development of the chick. There is no reason for thinking that the practical breeder need concern himself about this matter, beyond observing a few general requirements. While the egg contains a bewildering variety of constituents, it is not probable that any of these are deficient in any ration affording reasonable variety, especially if it carries a fair proportion of oats, bran, and meat scrap. The desirability of increasing the proportion of phosphorus has been widely discussed, but never clearly proved. However, since there is some question on this point and since fowls undoubtedly can and do assimilate both the phosphorus and lime in bones, it is recommended that some cracked bone or bone meal be added to the ration, unless the meat scrap carries a liberal proportion of bone.

Oyster shell and grit will of course, be supplied in hoppers and kept before the fowls all the time. Keep the hoppers clean and free from dirt or litter, as fowls will not eat as much of this material as they really need when laying heavily, if it is mixed with trash from the floor, or if the hopper is clogged with fine particles and dust. Fowls prefer the larger pieces and they want them fresh. Many do not realize that shell and grit will get stale if left standing exposed indefinitely, and in that condition are not relished by the hens. Oyster shell is especially important in the breeding ration as it has been shown that a deficiency in shell-forming material will result in production of much smaller eggs, as well as eggs with thin shells.

As regards grit it must be admitted that little is known concerning its importance in the ration, or the extent to which the fowls are able to assimilate the inorganic substances which it contains. We do know, however, that fowls normally crave grit, and in liberal quantity, also that they are able to assimilate inorganic lime. Hence it would appear wise to use some of the various brands of limestone grit that are on the market, rather than flinty materials that, so far as is known, have no value aside from their "grinding" properties—a function which probably is just as well served by the softer limestone.

Use whatever is available at least expense for litter, so long as it answers the purpose. Most persons will find a mixture of planer shavings and oat or wheat straw best and cheapest. Spread a 4-inch layer of shavings on the floor and then cover with 4 to 6 inches of straw. It costs no more to use plenty of litter, which only need be changed occasionally, than to use it sparingly and be compelled to renew it every little while, and it is impossible to provide sufficient exercise for fowls in confinement without its liberal use.

Green food is one of the most important parts of the ration of the breeding flock. Almost anything green may be given to advantage, but there is nothing better than sprouted oats if they are properly sprouted and free from mold. This can readily be accomplished by sprouting them in a warm room or in one of the special oat-sprouting cabinets that are on the market. With sufficient warmth oats will grow quickly and be ready to feed before mold has a chance to form. It helps also to wash and disinfect all sprouting trays, etc., at frequent intervals, for which purpose formaldehyde is especially good, also any good coal-tar disinfecting solution.

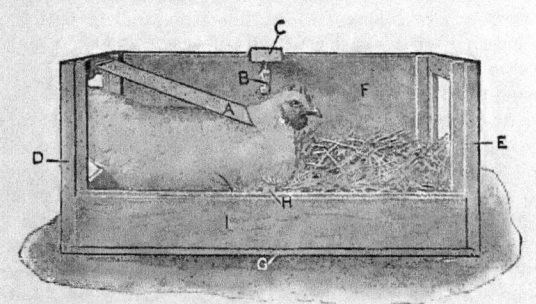

FIG. 18—HEN ENTERING TRAP NEST
For key to lettering see footnote under Fig. 17.

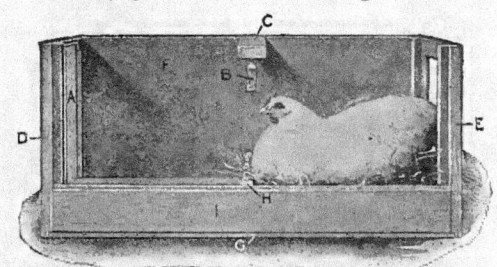

FIG. 19—TRAP NEST WITH DOOR CLOSED
For key to lettering see footnote under Fig. 17.

Pen Hatching Records and Trap Nesting

Whether the breeder attempts systematic or pedigree breeding or not, he certainly will want to keep a record of the results of his matings, and if possible should use trap nests and thus be able to trace the performance of individual fowls, not only through the hatch, but through the growth and development of the chicks. The advantages of being able to do this are too great to be overlooked where it is practicable to attend to the details of the work.

The most elementary form in which it is worth while to keep hatching records is the pen record, where the egg production, hatch, and percentage of chicks raised are followed from day to day. This much, at least, every one who produces eggs for hatching should do. The record should be kept on a specially prepared sheet mounted on stiff backing (pasteboard will answer as well as anything) so that it can be carried at will from pen to incubator room or elsewhere. Blank columns should be provided under suitable heads, following the general outlines of the sample hatching sheet shown on page 46, or the more elaborate one on page 47.

In case the record is to be extended to the individual hen, trap nests and pedigree trays or their equivalent will be needed. For a practical trap nest that will give generally good results with hens of any size and that can be made quite cheaply, the one illustrated in Fig. 17, and shown in operation in Figs. 18 and 19, is recommended. The illustrations and the footnotes that accompany them will be sufficient to enable any one to make the nest successfully. Another type of nest in use at the poultry experiment farm of the U. S. Dept. of Agriculture, near Washington, is shown in Figs. 20 and 21. Pedigree egg trays such as are in use at the Maine Experiment Station are shown on page 44, and more inexpensive appliances for pedigree hatching is shown on page 45. Where pedigree breeding is practiced, record keeping becomes a rather elaborate matter, and it is useless to attempt this method at all unless it is done right. Almost any State Experiment Station will cheerfully furnish specimen record sheets for use in pedigree breeding, and explain their use.

Some Reasons for Low Fertility

With the breeding stock selected, fed, and cared for in the manner just described, there should be no question of low fertility or hatchability. There are, however, a number of ways in which the inexperienced breeder may err in the practical management of his flock, and which will produce unfavorable conditions in the hatch. It may prove helpful to call special attention to some of the more common mistakes of this nature.

Overfat Hens. Hens that are heavily fed and whose exercise has been neglected, are apt to come to the breeding season too fat and more or less out of condition, so that they are not able to produce strongly fertile eggs. It is scarcely possible to place too much emphasis on the importance of taking the best of care of the breeding fowls prior to the breeding season, as well as after hatching operations begin. They should be well-fed but not overfed, and when confined indoors or in yards, special provisions must be made for their exercise. The importance of this may not be so great in the case of Leghorns and other small fowls, as these are naturally active, but fowls of the larger breeds are disposed to take life quite leisurely if supplied with an abundance of easily secured food. The injurious effect of this is found not so much in their getting overfat, as in their being underexercised and thus not in good physical condition for breeding. The reader is advised to turn back and read again what is said in this chapter in regard to providing exercise, no detail of which can safely be neglected in the care of large hens, either during the breeding season or in the months leading up to it.

Exhausted Hens and Pullets. Early-hatched pullets that have been heavily fed for eggs through the winter, and in some cases one-year-old hens also, will not be in condition for the breeding pen in the spring. Eggs for hatching may be secured from winter layers with fairly satisfactory results early in the season, but only then. It is never advisable to depend on pullets or hens that have laid heavily through the winter, for a supply of hatching eggs throughout the season. As far as hens are concerned, it is better to pen them separately and feed them a good nourishing but non-forcing ration and make no effort whatever to get eggs from them until the breeding season has arrived.

Immature Pullets. The use of young pullets is believed to be a general cause of poor hatches and weak chicks. It is not probable that there is any disadvantage in the use of well-matured pullets that have been laying for a short time so that the eggs are good-sized and normal in development. But immature pullets that are laying their first eggs, especially if they have been more or less forced in their development in order to bring them into laying, are extremely undesirable.

Males Not in Good Condition. What has been said in regard to the management of hens, in and out of the breeding season, also applies to males, although these are not apt to become overfat at any time. They undoubtedly will be benefitted by compulsory exercise, however. If very gallant they are more apt to be underfed than overfed and should be watched to avoid any danger of this happening. If necessary, they may have a special supply of grain, provided in a cup or small hopper hung high enough to be out of the reach of the hens.

FIG. 20—U. S. GOVERNMENT TRAP NEST READY FOR USE
For convenience in handling, trap nests may be made in batteries of three or more, as here shown, using light-weight lumber. Dimensions and method of construction are shown in Fig. 21.

Immature Cockerels. The chief objection to the use of cockerels, assuming that they are well developed, is that they are not able to stand service in the breeding pen for long periods, especially when mated to too many females as is almost habitually done. If they must be used singly in large flocks it is a good plan to provide some extra ones so that they can be placed in service alternately, with rest periods between. A better and more practical plan, where it is possible to practice it, is simply to keep the number of females down to a point where the males will not be in danger of being overworked and thus can be continued in regular service throughout the season. Alternating males is a makeshift practice at best. It is much better that the pen, when once mated, be continued unchanged to the close of the season, unless it is found desirable to make a permanent change.

Unsuitable Rations. The rations that the breeders should have are fully outlined in this chapter, and there is no poorer economy than to neglect the provision of what is needed in order to save a few cents on the cost of the ration, if this done at the expense of the nourishment of the breeding stock and the embryo. There is no necessity for making the feeding a complicated mathematical or chemical problem, but wholesome food in reasonable variety and properly supplied, neither too much nor too little, is imperative.

Too Long Breeding Season. It frequently happens that a breeding pen that has given good results early in the year fails to hold up throughout the breeding season, and fertility and vitality in the chicks drop to a low point. There is no practical way of keeping up the vigor of fowls that are laying heavily for long periods, and this must be taken into account in all plans. Winter-laying pullets may be used in the breeding pen early in the season, but for long periods one and two-year-old hens are better. They should be fed so as to keep the egg yield at a reasonable percentage, but avoid all tendency to forcing methods. Egg production may be controlled to some extent by making changes in the rations as suggested in this chapter, such as by increasing or decreasing the percentage of meat scrap, or by regulating the amount of mash. If the fowls are disposed to lay too heavily they may be checked by reducing the proportion of dry mash consumed, doing so by increasing the proportion of bran in the mixture. If the yield falls off too greatly it can be brought back by reducing the bran and increasing the meat scrap and, if necessary, by feeding a moist mash daily.

Too Little Animal Food. Experiments have shown that a lack of animal food will seriously affect the hatchability of eggs, and this part of the ration should always receive attention. Commercial meat scrap is available almost everywhere and should invariably be supplied to breeding fowls in confinement, unless fresh meat, butcher's scraps or green cut bone is used instead. Meat is apt to stimulate the egg organs to too heavy production, however, and must not be fed too freely. The proportion cannot be exactly stated, as much depends on the mash fed, and on other conditions, and must be governed to some extent by the performance of the hens. So long as they are not laying too heavily it is safe to assume that the amount is not excessive, if it conforms in a general way to the percentages suggested in this chapter.

Too Much Green Food. Where sprouted oats are fed liberally, also where efforts are made to reduce the cost of the ration by feeding an abundance of green food, there is danger that the eggs will be watery and far from normal in composition. Such eggs cannot be expected to give good results in the incubator. Green food is important as a means of keeping the fowls in good physical condition, but there is danger in feeding it too heavily.

Poor Sanitary Conditions. It is assumed that good sanitary conditions will be maintained in the breeding pens at all times. Cleanliness, from a poultry-keeping viewpoint, does not mean the same thing that it suggests to the tidy housekeeper, but it certainly should mean freedom from dampness, foul odors, and filthy litter. The condition of the litter is especially important because of the feeding method recommended, which requires the fowls to keep digging in it pretty much all day long to secure their grain feed. It should take no argument to show the importance of having reasonably clean litter, for this purpose—litter that is dry and free from droppings and mustiness. With a dry floor and a well-ventilated house, a thick coat of litter will last for some time, especially where the fowls are no more crowded than is generally recommended for breeding pens. If the house is kept dry by adequate ventilation, the litter renewed frequently enough to keep it bright and fresh, and the droppings boards cleaned often enough to keep the house free from offensive odor, the house can be considered clean and sanitary. Less than this should not be tolerated. A filthy house will certainly react on the health and productivity of the fowls.

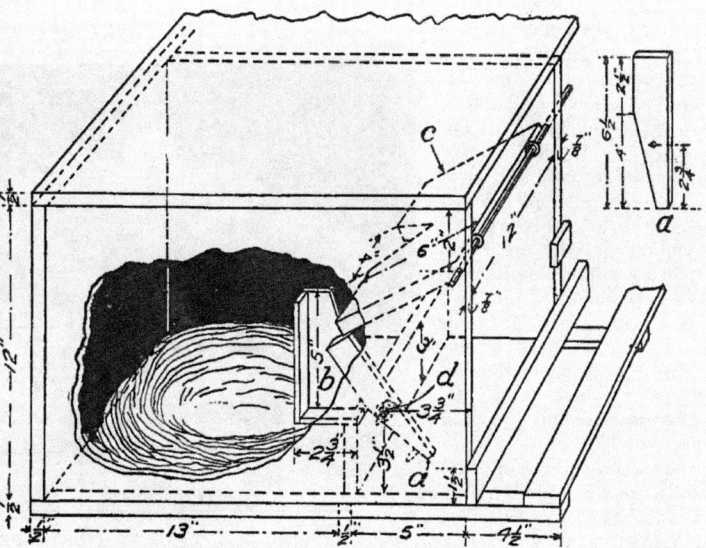

FIG. 21—OUTLINE DRAWING OF U. S. GOVERNMENT TRAP NEST
This drawing shows method of construction and dimensions of trap nest in use at the Governmental Poultry Experimental Farm near Washington, D. C. For complete nest see Fig. 20.

Eggs Chilled or Overheated. Eggs must be protected from extreme temperatures while being held for hatching. Low temperatures that will chill them, or high temperatures that will start germ development are alike injurious. Under ordinary conditions a reasonably dry cellar is a good place for the eggs, and if there is no dampness they may safely be laid in baskets or trays, piled one on top of the other, and covered with a cloth to prevent evaporation. If the cellar is damp or the temperature is liable to fall much below 50 degrees it will be better to keep the eggs elsewhere. A closet in the kitchen or living room frequently offers an excellent place for them, but in this case it is necessary to guard against high temperatures during the day and low temperatures at night. Usually the most practical and convenient way to store eggs for hatching is to place them in one dozen cartons, or in regular shipping cases when large numbers are to be accumulated. These packages provide ideal conditions, as the eggs are protected from sudden changes in temperature, and from evaporation, also from excess moisture, and are easily turned if this is considered necessary.

CHAPTER III

The Hen's Egg and How It Is Formed

Description of the Egg Organs of the Hen—How Eggs Are Developed—Composition of the Egg and How This May Be Affected by Feeding—How Size and Shape of Eggs Are Determined—Securing Large, Uniformly Shaped Eggs for Hatching—Defective Eggs and How Prevented.

A GOOD degree of success in artificial incubation may be achieved with only the most limited knowledge regarding the formation of the egg, its composition, and the growth and development of the chick embryo—that much is readily conceded. The earnest and ambitious poultry keeper, however, who wishes to be well informed generally on matters that directly relate to his work, will want to know at least the details of this complicated but highly interesting subject. There is no question about the fact that he will find all such information helpful to him in practical everyday work with breeding stock and in hatching operations. This information we have attempted to give in this and the following chapters, though it evidently is impossible to do little more in the space available, than to outline the subject and to furnish such details as will enable those who are interested, to follow intelligently the development of the chick embryo. It also is impossible to present such a subject in words made familiar by everyday use, though so far as possible this has been done.

Considering the egg simply as the reproductive body of fowls, it may be described as consisting of a germ, a relatively large amount of food stored up for the nourishment of the developing embryo, and protective coverings. The egg has its microscopic beginning in the ovary of the female fowl, which organ, bearing a slight general resemblance to a bunch of grapes (see Fig. 24) is located close to the backbone and in front of the kidneys. The female normally develops only one ovary—the left one—the right ovary becoming atrophied at an early stage in the development of the embryonic chick.

In mature laying pullets the ovary contains ova in all stages of development, from full-grown yolks down to minute bodies (oocytes) so small that they cannot be detected without the use of a microscope. The number of these is quite large, as many as 3,600 having been counted in a single ovary, only those being considered that were visible to the naked eye (see Fig. 23). How many more might be revealed by the use of the microscope we do not know. Since few hens ever reach a total production of 1,000 eggs, it is clear that the number that any individual may produce is determined by physical limitations, the exhaustion of the supply of ova being a practical impossibility.

The Oviduct

The oviduct (see Figs. 24 and 27) is a whitish tube, located in the abdomen and attached by means of tough membraneous tissue to the upper part of the body wall. In the growing pullet or non-laying hen it is comparatively small, but as the fowl comes into laying condition it increases in size until it reaches a length of fully two feet, with glandular walls of varying thickness and strongly marked with blood vessels. It may be divided into the following parts or sections: The funnel, designed to receive the yolk as it leaves the ruptured yolk sac; the albumen-secreting portion; the isthmus which secretes the shell membrane; the uterus where the hard shell is secreted; the vagina where the coloring matter of the shell and the outer mucilaginous coating are secreted.

Formation of the Egg

The ova or yolks develop in groups, about fourteen days being sufficient for the development of a full-sized yolk from the minute ovum. The yellow part of the yolk consists of round cells filled with fat, which are deposited daily in successive layers, each layer being separated from the rest by an extremely thin layer of white yolk. These layers are so distinct in formation that the yolk of a fresh hard-boiled egg can be peeled off in layers, like an onion, if carefully done. The yolk is enclosed in a membraneous yolk sac, through which it receives from the blood the materials of which it is composed. When the yolk reaches its full development, the sac is ruptured and the yolk, enclosed in an extremely thin envelope known as the vitelline membrane (an essential part of the yolk structure) enters the upper end of the oviduct. The yolk is not a solid mass, but enclosed in it is a central cavity filled with white yolk and connected with the germinal disk on the upper surface of the yolk by a small canal or tube which also is filled with white yolk.

At the time the yolk escapes from the yolk sac, the upper end or mouth of the oviduct opens and more or less envelops it, thus insuring its entrance into the oviduct instead of into the body cavity, which latter frequently happens, however, when the funnel of the oviduct does not function properly. As soon as the yolk enters the oviduct, the glands begin pouring out their secretions of albumen or "white" and as the yolk is gradually pushed along, turning round and round in a spiral manner under the pressure of the muscular walls of the oviduct, it accumulates its share of albumen and, further along, the membranes and the hard shell.

"In the normal egg of the hen there are certainly three and possibly four different albumen layers which can easily be distinguished on the basis of physical consistency. These are: (a) the chalaziferous layer. This

FIG. 22—WELL-FORMED, STANDARD-SIZED EGGS

is a thin layer of dense albuminous material, which lies immediately outside the true yolk membrane. It is continuous at the poles of the yolk with the chalazae, and is undoubtedly formed in connection with those structures. It is so thin a layer that it might well be, and often has been taken for the yolk membrane. (b) The inner layer of fluid (thin) albumen. This layer is extremely thin and there is some doubt as to its existence as a separate layer. (c) The dense albumen. This is the layer which makes up the bulk of the "white" of the egg. It is composed of a mass of dense, closely interlaced albumen fibres with some thin albumen between the meshes of the fibrous network. The dense albumen, as a whole, will not flow readily but holds itself together in a flattened mass if poured out upon a plate. (d) The outer layer of fluid albumen. This is the principal layer of thin albumen, which makes up the fluid part of the "white" observed when an egg is broken.

"Many autopsy records agree in showing that the egg does not receive the outer layer of thin fluid albumen (layer d) during its sojourn in the so-called albumen secreting portion of the oviduct. A detailed and careful study of the weights of the several parts of the egg (yolk, albumen, shell membranes) in eggs taken from different levels of the oviduct, leads to the following results. When the egg leaves the albumen portion of the oviduct it weighs roughly only about half as much as it does when laid. Nearly all of this difference is in the albumen. Thus these weighings fully confirm the conclusion reached from different examinations of the eggs, as already described. The evidence shows that the egg gets all of its thin albumen (layer d), which constitutes nearly 60 per cent by weight of the total albumen, only after it has left the supposedly only albumen-secreting portion of the oviduct, and the shell is in process of formation.

"The weighings show that in general the farther down the oviduct the egg proceeds the more albumen it gets. Very nearly one-half the total weight of albumen of the completed egg is added in the uterus, an organ hitherto supposed to be entirely devoted to shell formation. Clearly much more albumen is added to the egg in the uterus than in the isthmus. This, of course, does not necessarily mean any more rapid rate of secretion in the uterus, because of the time element involved. The egg stays much longer in the uterus than in the isthmus."[*]

The chalazae, to which reference has been made, are attached on opposite sides of the yolk, facing the two ends of the egg, and extend out into the albumen. Their purpose is to hold the yolk in its proper position, allowing it to turn around freely the short way of the egg, but preventing its turning over the long way of the egg. This in connection with the peculiar structure of the yolk, which makes the sides carrying the germinal disk lighter than the other half, keeps the yolk always on the upper side of the egg and near the center, viewing it from end to end, and also keeps the germ side of the yolk uppermost and close up to the source of heat regardless of the position in which the egg is placed.

The covering of the egg consists of two membranes, each a network of fibers, and a hard outer shell. The separation of the inner and outer membranes at the large end forms the air cell with which all incubator operators are familiar. The outer shell is almost pure carbonate of lime and consists of the gelatinous coating, which forms the "bloom" of the egg, an outer porous layer, a middle and denser portion, and an inner

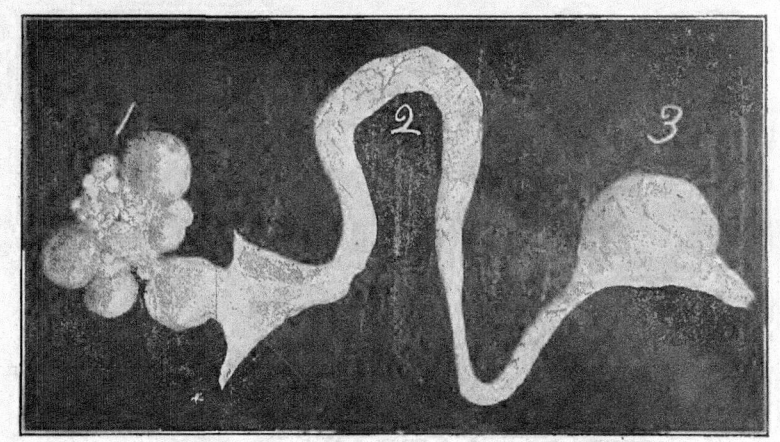

FIG. 24—OVARY AND OVIDUCT OF LAYING HEN
1, ovary with yolks (ova) in different stages of development—one just ready to pass into mouth of oviduct. 2, section of oviduct where the albumen is secreted. 3, the uterus or shell gland, containing full-sized egg. Compare this illustration with Fig. 27. Courtesy of Mo. State Poultry Experiment Station.

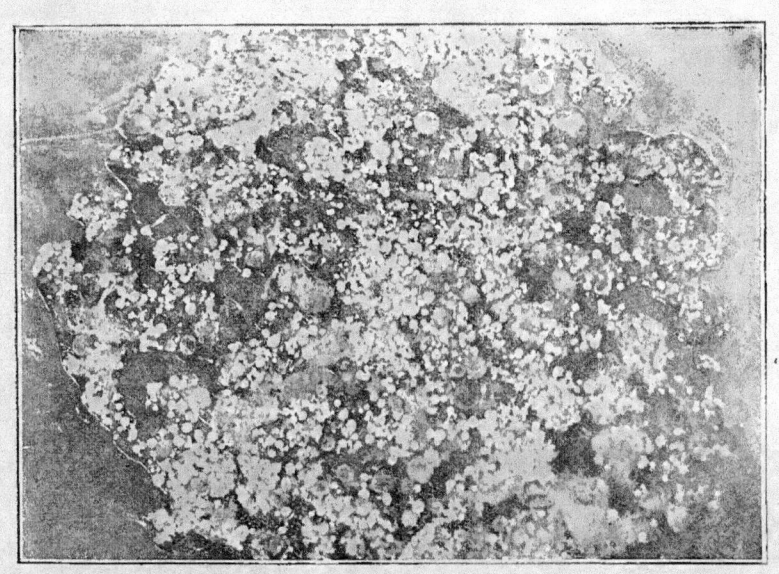

FIG. 23—PORTION OF OVARY OF HEN
This illustration made from a photograph supplied by Missouri State Poultry Experiment Station shows about three-fourths of the ovary of a hen, and gives some idea (though but a faint one) of the great numbers of ova to be found in the ovary of any normal hen, there being many hundreds, possibly thousands more than the hens will ever lay.

[*]Extract from Maine Experiment Station Bulletin No. 216.

or crystalline portion. The shell is quite porous and admits air readily, and bacteria also when kept under unfavorable conditions. The outer gelatinous coating seems to provide some additional protection for the egg, possibly retarding evaporation. If this coating is removed, as when the shells are washed on account of being badly soiled, the eggs seldom hatch as well as when unwashed.

The following statement in regard to the development of the different parts of the egg and the length of

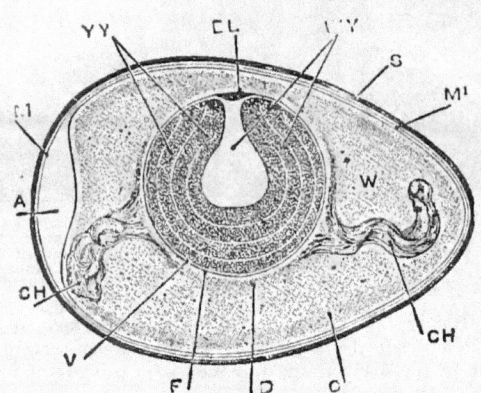

FIG. 25—STRUCTURE OF THE EGG.
S, shell; M, outer shell membrane; M-1, inner shell membrane; A, air cell; C, outer layer of albumen; W, middle layer of albumen; D, inner or chalaziferous layer of albumen; CH, chalazae; V, vitelline membrane; WY, thin layers of white yolk —also central cavity and tube filled with white yolk; YY, layers of yellow yolk; BL, blastoderm or germinal disk.

time occupied in the process, is taken from Bulletin 213 of the Maine Experiment Station:

1. After entering the infundibulum the yolk remains in the so-called albumen portion of the oviduct about three hours and in this time acquires only about 40 to 50 per cent by weight of its total albumen, and not all of it as has hitherto been supposed.

2. During its sojourn in the infundibular and albumen portions of the duct the egg acquires its chalazae and chalaziferous layer, and the "thick" albumen layer.

3. Upon entering the isthmus, in passing through which portion of the duct something under an hour's time is occupied instead of three hours as has been previously maintained, the egg receives its shell membrane by a process of discrete deposition.

4. At the same time, and also during the sojourn of the egg in the uterus, it receives its outer layer of fluid or "thin" albumen, which is by weight 50 to 60 per cent of the total albumen.

5. This "thin" albumen is taken in as a dilute fluid by osmosis through the shell membranes already formed. The fluid albumen added in this way diffuses into the dense albumen already present, dissolve some of the latter and so brings about its dilution in some degree. At the same time the fluid albumen is made more dense in this process of diffusion, and comes to have the consistency of the thin albumen layer of the normal fresh laid egg. The fluid albumen taken into the egg by osmosis is a definite secretion of glands of the isthmus and uterus.

6. The addition of albumen to the egg is completed only after it has been in the uterus from 5 to 7 hours.

7. Before the acquisition of albumen by the egg is completed, a fairly considerable amount of shell substance has been deposited on the shell membrane.

8. For the completion of the shell and the laying of the egg from 12 to 16, or exceptionally even more, hours are required."

Composition of the Hen's Egg

The composition of eggs and the relative proportions of the different substances represented in them vary somewhat in different analyses, but the following averages of a number of tests made at the Kansas Experiment Station probably quite closely approximate the general average:

Weight of egg .... 1.88 oz.
Percentage of white 57.01
Percentage of yolk 32.75
Percentage of shell 9.99
Percentage of protein in white 12.34
Percentage of water in white 87.66
Percentage of protein in yolk 17.58
Percentage of ether extract (fat) 32.23
Percentage of water in yolk 48.63
Percentage of ash in yolk 1.55
Percentage of protein in total egg 12.83

Both yolk and albumen are highly complex compounds. While many of the substances contained in them are present only in the most limited porportions they are not necessarily unimportant to embryonic development on that account. The composition of the yolk of the average egg approximates the following percentages:

Analysis of Yolk.

Water .... 49.32 per cent.
Solids .... 50.66 per cent.
   Fats .... 21.57 per cent.
   Vitellin and other albumens ...... 15.79 per cent.
   Lecithins .... 9.58 per cent.
   Cholesterin .... 1.2 per cent.
   Cerebrin .... .30 per cent.
   Mineral Salts .... 3.33 per cent.
   Coloring matter }
   Glucose   } .... .55 per cent.

The mineral salts in the yolk contain sodium, potassium, calcium, magnesium, iron, phosphoric acid, chlorine and silicic acid. The phosphoric acid and calcium form much the greater proportion of the total.

Analysis of Albumen.

Water .... 83.34 per cent
Solids .... 16.66 per cent
   Albumens .... 11.58 per cent
   Glucose .... .30 per cent
   Extractives .... .58 per cent
   Fats and soap .... Traces
   Mineral salts .... .48 per cent
   Lecithins and cholesterin .... Traces

The mineral salts in the albumen contain sodium, potassium, calcium, magnesium, iron, chlorine, phosphorus

FIG. 26—HOW AGE AFFECTS CONSISTENCY OF YOLK AND ALBUMEN
Eggs rapidly lose consistency or firmness with age. Note the firmness of yolk and albumen in the egg one day old as shown by the way of yolk stands up and the albumen holds together. In the egg one week old both have flattened out noticeably, and in the egg two weeks old the albumen is quite watery and the yolk flat, thin, and easily broken.

acid, carbonic acid, sulphuric acid, silicic acid and fluorine. Of these, sodium, potassium, and chlorine form the greater part of the total.

Variations in Composition of Eggs

Comparatively little information is available, showing the extent to which the composition of the egg may be affected by the rations fed. It is common knowledge that the color is affected by the food supplied, and there are readily observed differences in the consistency of yolk and albumen, which accompany extreme rations such as those composed mainly of soft food, or which contain large proportions of milk, cabbage, or green food in any form, also kitchen scraps. Eggs produced by hens that have a reasonable proportion of animal food in the ration are noticeably different from eggs produced on a meatless ration, and eggs produced by well-fed hens are perceptibly larger than from underfed fowls, while the flavor is noticeably affected by the character of the food provided. The poultry keeper who produces eggs for hatching will therefore aim to supply a nourishing and well-balanced ration, and in liberal proportions, so that the eggs laid will be of full size and normal in their composition.

It is doubtful, however, whether there is any necessity for or advantage in trying to provide a ration that will closely follow the chemical composition of the egg, as is often recommended. If there is any advantage in so doing, certainly the proportions have not been sufficiently investigated to afford any reliable information as to the amounts required. On the whole, there are good practical reasons for thinking that better results will be secured by the feeder who aims simply to supply a normal ration rather than by one who permits himself to get hopelessly tangled up in the complexities of egg and food analyses. As a matter of fact, such investigations as have been made indicate that the great majority of the elements which enter into the composition of the egg are found largely in excess of the fowl's requirements in any good, practical ration such as poultry feeders generally use.

Experiments made at Cornell University, for example, indicate that the relative proportions of fat and protein in the egg vary but little, regardless of the ration fed; that there seems to be no relation between the protein and fat content of the egg and its hatching power or the vitality of the chick; that the phosphorus content of the egg is only slightly modified by the proportions in which this element is present in the ration, and this variation seems to have no bearing on the strength or vitality of the chick; and that the feeding of inorganic phosphorus does not influence the proportion of phosphorus in the egg. If these things are true in regard to phosphorus, which is generally believed to be the element in which the average ration is most likely to be deficient, there can be little reason for anxiety about the other mineral constituents, so long as the ration is well balanced and provides some variety.

The composition of the egg aside from consistency and flavor, appears to vary only in a slight degree as a result of changes in the ration. A conspicuous deficiency in any essential ingredient is much more apt to cause a falling off in egg yield than in the production of eggs showing a noticeable reduction in any of their normal constituents. For example, a marked deficiency of lime in the ration does not necessarily result in soft shells, but usually is followed by reduced productiveness and smaller-sized eggs.

How the Egg Gets Its Oval Shape

As regards the shaping of the egg, the following extract from Bulletin 228 of the Maine Experiment Station gives practically all that is known on this subject:

"The shape of the egg is almost certainly due to the interaction of the two layers of muscle fibers in the oviduct walls. The inner layer of fibers is circular, that is, they pass around the duct. The outer layer is longitudinal and somewhat spiral and extends into both the dorsal and ventral ligaments. Further work on the physiology of these muscles is necessary to determine the exact way in which they act. From their position and from observed activities of the duct it seems that the contrac-

FIG. 27—PHOTOGRAPH OF HEN'S OVIDUCT
Oviduct slit open and flattened out, showing the inside surface. Oviduct was cut in two at "B" in order to get it on the photographic plate. A is the funnel shaped mouth; B, B, B, the albumen-secreting section. The albumen portion stops and the isthmus begins at X. C, the isthmus where the shell membranes are secreted; D, the uterus or shell gland; E, the vagina. Photo from Maine Experiment Station.

tion of the circular fibers contract the duct and move the egg forward. The contraction of the longitudinal fibers, which have a somewhat spiral course, expand the duct, diminishing the resistance to the passage and also gives the egg a spiral motion. If the resistance is slight, i. e., if the contractions are so timed that the duct ahead of the egg is expanded at the time of the contraction of the circular fibers behind, the egg will be long, narrow and pointed. On the other hand, if the resistance is great the egg will be short and broad.

"The individuality of the eggs of a bird in respect

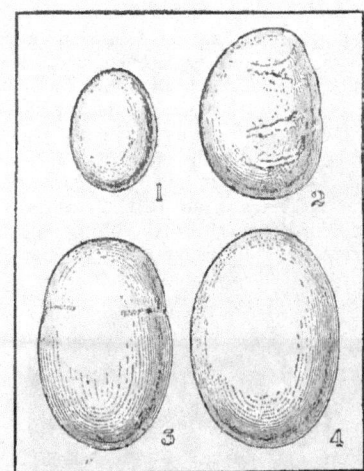

FIG. 28—DEFORMED EGGS
"Wind eggs" (1) usually contain albumen but no yolk. Crooked eggs (2) usually result from an inflamed condition of the oviduct. Ridged or irregularly shaped eggs (3) and double-yolked eggs (4) also are due to inflammation in the oviduct or to weakness in the muscles of that organ, and most commonly are produced by overfat hens.

*Maine Station Bulletin No. 228.

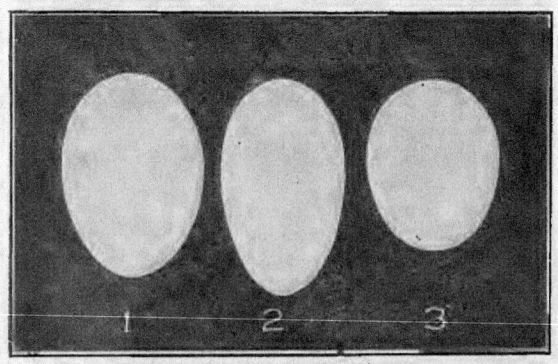

FIG. 29—SELECT NORMAL EGGS FOR THE INCUBATOR
(1) This egg is just about perfect in its proportions. The length is practically 1½ times the diameter, and it weighs two and one-sixth ounces. (2) Extra long eggs are not likely to show a high degree of fertility and are much more apt to have defective shells. (3) Eggs of this type usually are undersized and should be avoided.

to shape must be due to an individuality in the co-ordination of these two sets of muscle fibers and similarly the variation must be due to a variation under different conditions in the degree of coordination."

Size and Shape of Eggs

Since conspicuous variations from ideal egg shape are apt to be due to abnormal conditions in the oviduct, it should be clear that hens that regularly lay such eggs should not be used for the production of hatching eggs. Aside from the fact that such irregularities may be inherited, there is the more immediate disadvantage due to low fertility, which usually is a characteristic of odd-shaped eggs. The shape of the egg bears no relation to the sex of the chick hatched from it.

The eggs of individual hens vary to some extent in size, shape, and color, though conforming more or less closely to certain general breed characteristics. A good degree of uniformity in these respects can be secured in carefully bred strains in any breed. The eggs of any given individual will be found to resemble each other closely in shape and exterior appearance, so that it is possible for the careful observer to identify the hen that laid the egg by its appearance alone, though in a season's production some variation in size, also in color and shape, will be noted. "Egg weight and albumen are about equally variable. They are decidedly less variable than shell weight and yolk weight, and much more variable than either length or breadth."*

The following list arranges the egg characters in the order of their variability; egg weight; yolk weight; albumen weight; shell weight; length; breadth. Eggs during the breeding season have larger yolks and a correspondingly smaller percentage of albumen than eggs at other seasons.

In a general way the size of eggs is greater in the middle of the clutch than at the beginning or the end, and in a period of long-continued laying the eggs tend to average smaller. However, pullets habitually lay smaller eggs in the first clutch than in successive ones and their eggs are not apt to reach maximum size until the second year.

The poultry grower is interested in the variations in size, shape, and composition of eggs for very practical reasons. Regardless of whether eggs are sold by weight or not, size has an important market value. Noticeably small eggs are subject to discount in almost any discriminating market, while large size is almost imperative in securing premium prices. In incubation it is conceded that the largest and best chicks come from large eggs. Color of shell is definitely inherited within the breed. That is, pullets hatched from white-shelled eggs will always lay white-shelled eggs if they are purebred, and hens belonging to breeds that lay eggs with brown shells will never lay white-shelled eggs, though in some breeds the shade of brown in the eggs may vary widely except in strains that have been carefully bred for uniformity in color. Some breeds are much more apt to show uniformity of shell color than others, but a good degree of uniformity can be secured in any breed or variety by persistent selection. That the same rule will apply equally to shape and size is probable, but not so clearly established.

FIG. 30—DEFORMED EGG WITH SOFT SHELL
Eggs with soft shells, in various abnormal shapes, are more or less common, especially in the spring when the fowls are laying heavily and when they often are suffering from long winter confinement. More exercise and a less forcing ration are the remedy.

Defective Eggs and How Caused

There are a number of defects that may occur in eggs, some of them unavoidable, and some the result of poor methods of feeding or care. The appearance of serious defects that are known to be the result of improper conditions should be a sufficient warning immediately to change such conditions, while others that are due to constitutional causes demand the removal of the defective fowls. The following defects may be noticed in almost any flock during the heavy laying season, and while their occurrence now and then is not a serious matter, an appreciable number means improper conditions somewhere along the line, which must be corrected if good hatching eggs are to be produced:

Small Eggs. Extremely small eggs, sometimes called "wind eggs," are generally supposed to be the last of the clutch, or the last eggs laid by a hen before becoming broody. In some cases the wind egg is believed to result from the entrance of the yolk into the oviduct and its later expulsion into the body cavity where it is reabsorbed. The secretion of the albumen having been begun however, the entire process is gone through with, resulting in the formation of a diminutive egg with a regular shell, containing varying amounts of albumen but no yolk. Eggs normal in shell, albumen, and yolk, but quite small in size, may simply be a pullet's first eggs or they may result from rations conspicuously deficient in something essential to egg production.

Overlarge Eggs. Eggs that are conspicuously oversize are generally, but not always, double-yolked eggs, produced by two yolks escaping into the oviduct at the same time, or to a reversal of the muscular action of the oviduct which may result in stopping a yolk at any point in the oviduct, even after it has accumulated most of its albumen, or after a complete shell has been formed, and returning it to the upper part of the oviduct. In the course of this backward movement it meets the following yolk and both then proceed through the oviduct and are enclosed in one shell. Double-yolked eggs indicate irregular functioning of the oviduct and are commonly produced by hens that are overfat, especially if kept in comparative idleness. It is probable that the trouble is not due directly to the hens being overfat, but to a general weakening of the muscles of the oviduct and of the entire abdominal region, as a result of inactivity. At any rate, the remedy lies in providing more exercise for the fowls, and a less forcing ration. As a matter of fact, one of the first and most important steps to be taken in the prevention of defective eggs of almost any kind is to see to it that the hens have plenty of exercise. Normal fowls are highly active, and scratching for their food is the natural way to get both food and exercise. This constant scratching tends to keep the abdominal muscles strong and active, and this firmness of muscle extends to and is an important feature in the health and activity of the oviduct.

Soft Shells. These may be due to a lack of lime or to improper functioning of the egg organs, resulting from lack of exercise. In some instances the presence of soft-shelled eggs is due to forced feeding in which case the shell glands do not appear to be able to secrete material as fast as is required. This may happen even when there is no lack of lime in the ration. In some instances the cause of soft shells will be found in the inability of the hen to take up lime from the material supplied, or simply to failure to eat enough of it.

Watery Eggs. Eggs that are watery when fresh are generally so as the result of defective rations. Fowls that are heavily fed on green stuff, soft food, or kitchen scraps, are apt to lay such eggs, and while they may pass for table use, they are not desirable for hatching. More grain in the ration will remedy this.

Pale Color. The color of the yolk is determined by the presence of a certain coloring matter, which is generally distributed, but is present in especially liberal proportions in yellow corn, clover, alfalfa, grass, etc. There are no tests showing that well-colored yolks will hatch any better than pale-colored ones, but it certainly is wise to try to keep the eggs as nearly normal in all respects as possible. For that reason pale yolks should be corrected by providing some of the above-mentioned foods to supply color.

Rough Shells. Rough shells may be due to lack of a suitable supply of lime, but more commonly to an inflamed condition of the portion of the oviduct where the shell material is secreted. Hens that regularly lay rough-shelled eggs should be removed from the breeding flock. An appreciable number of such indicates something radically wrong with the ration or the condition under which the fowls are kept.

Crooked or Ridged Shells. Various irregularities in the shape of egg shells will be met with from time to time, and all such should be discarded. It is true that crooked or ridged eggs sometimes hatch well, but the

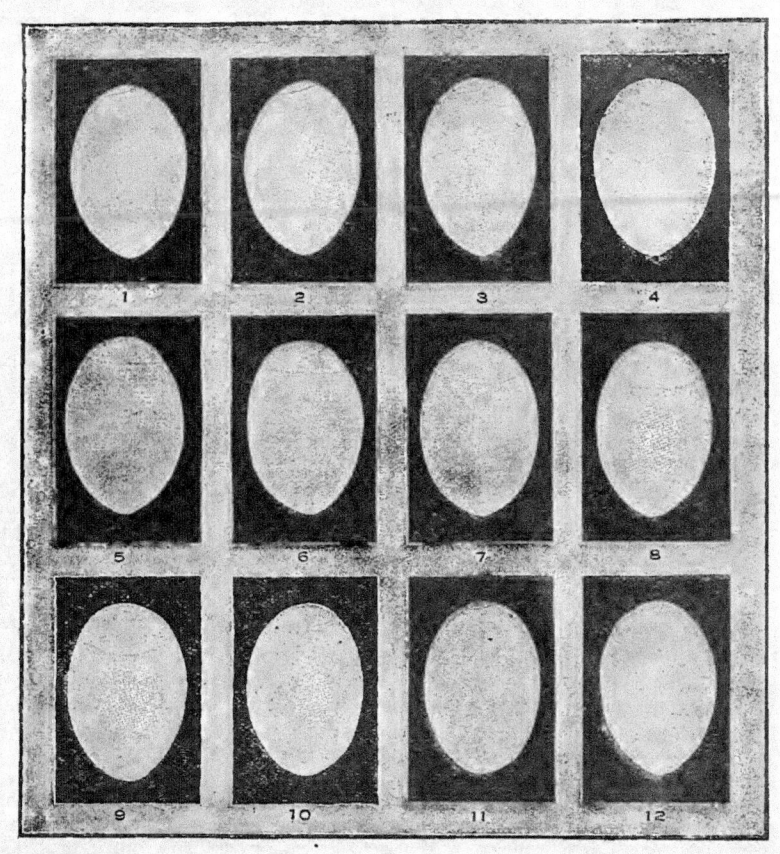

FIG. 31—RATE OF EVAPORATION OF HEN'S EGG
1 to 9. Eggs that have been held for one day, one week, two weeks, three weeks, four weeks, five weeks, six weeks, seven weeks, and eight weeks, respectively. The eggs were kept at a living-room temperature of about 70 degrees Fahrenheit, in an open pasteboard carton. There was no breeze blowing over the eggs, and each egg illustrated is typical of several eggs that were examined at each stage; therefore this series represents the normal results of such holding.
10 to 12. Eggs held for twelve weeks, one week, and one-half week respectively at a temperature of 40 degrees Fahrenheit. Even at twelve weeks of age (10), the egg is less evaporated than at four weeks of age when held at a living-room temperature of 70 degrees Fahrenheit (5). Eggs may be held for two weeks at 40 degrees Fahrenheit without much change. Reproduced from Bulletin 353, Cornell University.

chances are against their doing so, and unless from valuable stock it is hardly worth while to waste incubator space on them. They are usually caused by an inflammatory condition in the oviduct, though some hens lay crooked eggs regularly, apparently as the result of some slight organic malformation that does no harm and does not develop into anything serious.

Transparent Spots in Shells. The exact cause of transparent spots in eggs is not fully understood. It may be characteristic of an individual hen or possibly may occur in hens that generally lay normal eggs. If these eggs can be distinguished either by superficial examination or through the egg tester they should be discarded. Some of them may hatch but the percentage generally will be low.

CHAPTER IV

The Chick Embryo and Its Development

Appearance of Fertile and Infertile Eggs—Stage of Development of Germ When Egg is Laid—How It Is Kept Alive But Dormant Before Incubation Begins—What Happens During Incubation—Position in Which to Keep Eggs and Length of Time They May Be Held.

TO GET a clear idea of the normal position of the yolk and the germinal disk which forms the starting point of the chick embryo, the shell of a fresh egg may be carefully broken away as shown in Fig. 32, when the yolk will be seen floating well up in the albumen, with a thin layer of that substance between the yolk and inner surface of the shell membrane. When this insulating layer disappears through the thinning of the albumen as a result of age, or because the egg has stood too long in one position, the yolk will come in contact with the inner surface of the shell membrane and will adhere to it. The chalazae will be seen opposite each end of the egg, suspended well below the center, sometimes so low as to be almost under the yolk. While the chalazae normally are attached firmly to opposite sides of the yolk, they are subject to rather wide variations in their development, and one or both will sometimes be found apparently floating in the albumen and with no visible attachment to the yolk. Such eggs are not likely to hatch well. On the upper side of the yolk will be seen the germinal disk—a small, round, light-colored spot not much over an eighth of an inch in diameter. This disk is always uppermost, due to a slight difference in the weight of the two sides of the yolk caused by the central cavity and the connecting canal, the outer opening of which is always immediately under the germinal disk (see Fig. 25). The disk, properly called the blastoderm, is close up under the outer envelope of the yolk, known as the vitelline membrane.

When the yolk leaves the ovary, after developing to full size, the germinal disk consists of a small circular spot enclosed in a whitish ring and with the interior presenting a whitish or frothy appearance. The union between the female and male germ (the spermatazoon) takes place in the upper end of the oviduct, immediately after the yolk enters it from the ovary. The spermatazoa traverse the entire length of the oviduct after copulation, and at the upper end or mouth of the oviduct they remain active for some days, suspended in fluid, and awaiting an opportunity to effect a union with a female germ. There is no possibility of such a union until the yolk has entered the upper end of the oviduct, but as the spermatazoa may retain their activity for as long as three weeks in this environment, a single service may result in fertilizing a number of germs, as the successive yolks develop and escape into the oviduct. Experimental tests have shown that hens may continue to lay fertile eggs for weeks after the male has been removed from the flock, though as a rule, fertility is low after six to eight days, and is rare after the fifteenth day.

Appearance of Fertile and Infertile Eggs

It usually is an easy matter to distinguish fertile from infertile eggs when the shells are broken. In the latter the germinal disk will be more or less uniformly opaque, or if closely examined will have a sort of frothy appearance. In the fertile egg the center is also opaque but much smaller than in the infertile egg and this center is surrounded by a transparent ring and this in turn is enclosed by a whitish one, giving a concentric ringing that is an unmistakable indication of a fertilized germ. This concentric ringing is more clearly defined in some eggs than in others, but is nearly always sufficiently developed to make it possible to distinguish fertility if it exists. It is not possible to distinguish between fertile and infertile eggs by candling, until the egg has been exposed to incubating temperature for at least twenty-four hours, and generally forty-eight hours are required, even with white-shelled eggs.

From the time the yolk enters the upper end of the oviduct and is fertilized until the egg is completely formed and laid, fully 24 hours must elapse, and under some conditions the egg may then be carried for a number of hours or even for a day or more before it is dropped. Since the bodily temperature of the hen is around 106 degrees it is clear that the fertilized germ will be subjected to an incubating temperature for that time. During this period cell division or growth actually begins and the germ, therefore, has already reached a certain stage of development when the egg is laid. The exact degree of development attained will depend upon the length of time the egg is retained in the fowl's body after fertilization has taken place, which explains the variation in distinctness of ringing in the germinal disk, as previously noted. The development is slight under any condition, however, and stops instantly after the egg becomes cold, and the germ then remains dormant until again exposed to incubating temperatures.

In natural incubation the germ receives its heat from the body of the sitting hen, the actual degree of heat varying with the fowl's bodily temperature, the character of the nest, and the egg's position in it. The normal temperature of the adult fowl varies with the individual, also with the manner in which it is taken. With a thermometer thrust into the fowl's rectum, temperatures as high as 110 degrees have been noted, though it is probable that 106 represents a fair average. The common belief that the sitting hen has a "fever" and that her temperature is higher than under normal conditions probably is an error growing out of the fact that it is only when broody or sitting that the hen is subject to much handling and therefore the only time when her naturally high temperature is apt to be noticed. If the hen's temperature is taken with a thermometer in contact with the outside of the body the temperature will be lower than given above, running from 103 to 105 on the average.

There is no practical means of recording the actual temperature of the embryo, but careful observations have shown that it is around 99 to 100 degrees during early stages of incubation, gradually increasing until it is in the neighborhood of 103 or 104 at time of exclusion.

While fairly exact and uniform heat is essential to successful incubation, the germ will develop to a greater or less extent under a rather wide range of temperature. At low temperatures the germ will remain completely inactive, but cell division will begin at a little above 70 degrees. At this temperature development will be slow and will continue for only a limited time when, unless

THE CHICK EMBRYO AND ITS DEVELOPMENT

the heat is decidedly increased, the germ will die. At higher temperatures cell division or growth proceeds with increasing rapidity, reaching the normal rate of development at a germ temperature around 99 to 100 degrees.

If the temperature is raised above this point, cell growth will continue with increasing rapidity for a time. At high temperatures, however, the strain on the delicate walls of the embryonic heart and blood vessels becomes severe and it is only a matter of time until the latter will burst, causing hemorrhages and the death of the embryo. At just what temperature this point will be reached depends to some extent upon the development of the embryo, which is much less able to stand high temperatures in early stages of growth than when well on the way to complete development. Also, an embryo may stand exposure to 110 degrees for a very short time, but will break down at even 105 if held at that temperature for some hours.

When the egg is exposed to a suitable temperature, cell division begins at the point when it stopped when the egg was laid. The germ will stand comparatively low temperatures while in dormant condition, the exact degree of endurance being determined by the strength of the individual germ just as, later on, the endurance of the chick will be determined by its individual strength or constitutional vigor. A temperature of around 50 to 55 degrees is generally regarded as most favorable to the dormant germ.

Development of the Chick Embryo

It is impossible, within the limits of this chapter, to give a complete description of the complex operations involved in the development of the chick embryo. There are some general facts, however—some important steps in the process, with which the chick grower should be familiar in order to have a clear understanding of what is going on under the sitting hen or in the incubator. Many of the mistakes which prove common sources of loss to the beginner would be prevented if he clearly understood just how the embryo is produced, and the period of incubation at which certain phases of its development take place. Such details regarding embryonic growth as are here given are intended to supply that information. It is earnestly advised, however, that the beginner in artificial incubation make a practice of breaking a few eggs at various stages of the hatch in order to compare them with the descriptions and illustrations here given, so that he may become thoroughly familiar with the normal rate of development. Before attempting to describe briefly the various stages in the development of the embryo a few special details or definition are necessary, these being mainly condensed from an elaborate treatment of the subject in Lillie's "Development of the Chick."

The Blastoderm. The position of the blastoderm has already been described. The embryo arises within the opaque portion in the center, which becomes pear-shaped as the embryo forms. The embryonic membranes, amnion, chorion, and yolk sac, are parts of the blastoderm but originate outside of the opaque center. The allantois arises directly from the hindpart of the embryo itself. During the first four days the blastoderm spreads rapidly so that the greater part of the yolk is covered by the fourth day.

Position of Embryo. The embryo is always in a definite position with reference to the axis of the egg. If this is placed with the large end toward the left of the observer the head of the embryo will always be directed away from him. There are but few exceptions to this rule. At a later stage in its development the embryo turns lengthwise of the egg, so that the head is in the larger end, unless the air cell happens to be in the small end in which case the normal position of the head will be reversed and, as a rule the chick then will not hatch.

The Amnion. This membrane forms a thin sac completely enclosing the embryo and containing a fluid which appears to act as a cushion, taking up all shocks and jars and thus forming an important protection for the embryo. It also protects the embryo from forming adhesions with the surrounding membranes or with the shell. It has various other functions which need not be

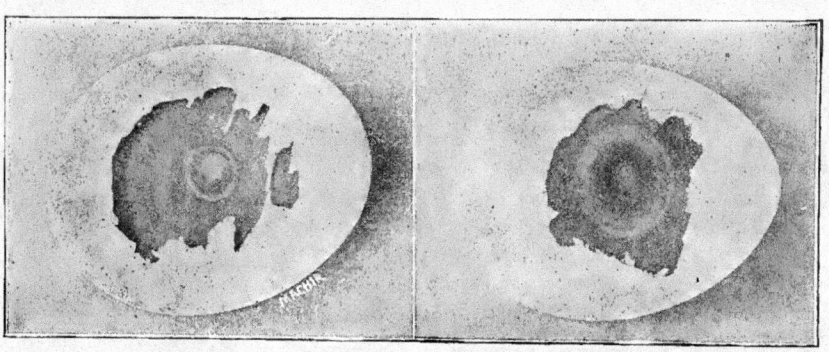

FIG. 32—APPEARANCE OF CHICK EMBRYO AFTER TWELVE HOURS OF INCUBATION
Photo from Kansas Experiment Station.

FIG. 33—APPEARANCE OF CHICK EMBRYO AFTER TWENTY-FOUR HOURS OF INCUBATION
Photo from Kansas Experiment Station.

detailed. The amniotic membrane possesses muscular fibers the contraction of which rocks the embryo, the purpose of which is believed to be to prevent adhesions.

The Chorion. This membrane is on the outside of the amnion and encloses it. It is connected with the amnion, and the allantois also connects with it at an early stage in the development of the embryo.

The Allantois. This membrane is the respiratory organ of the embryo, the blood in its vessels being aerated by air which passes through the porous shell. The allantois, being double-walled, forms a cavity or sac extending entirely around the embryo, with the outer wall coming in contact with the inner shell membrane. The cavity acts as a reservoir for the excretions of the embryo. At the end of the fifth day of incubation the allantois covers more than half of the embryo, and by the end of the sixth day it is entirely covered. By the eighth day the yolk sac is half covered and by the twelfth day the yolk is entirely enclosed, along with the remaining albumen which is wrapped in a separate sac by a special development of the chorion and allantois.

The Yolk Sac. The yolk sac is formed as a membrane enclosing the yolk and is connected with the intestine by means of a yolk-stalk. The material in the yolk is absorbed by the lining of the sac and carried to the embryo as required for its development. The inner surface of the sac is provided with numerous folds (septa)

ARTIFICIAL INCUBATING AND BROODING

FIG. 34—APPEARANCE OF CHICK EMBRYO AFTER THIRTY-SIX HOURS OF INCUBATION
Photo from Kansas Experiment Station.

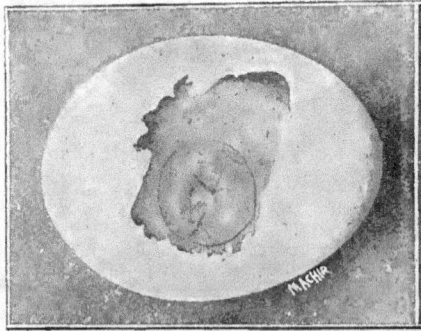

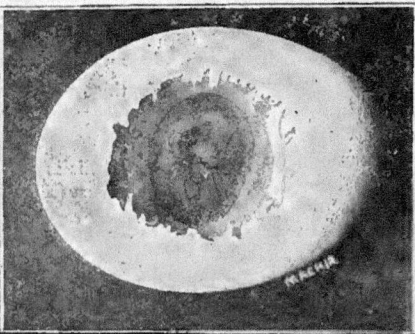

FIG. 35—APPEARANCE OF CHICK EMBRYO AFTER FORTY-EIGHT HOURS OF INCUBATION
Photo from Kansas Experiment Station.

which project more and more into the yolk substance as the embryo develops, increasing the absorptive surface. On the nineteenth day of incubation the yolk sac slips into the body cavity through the umbilicus which then closes. The inclusion of the egg is accomplished by the contraction of the inner walls of the allantois and of the amnion which definitely presses it into the abdominal cavity. What is left of the yolk then is rapidly absorbed. Its average weight is about 5.34 grains at twelve hours after hatching, and this is reduced to about .05 grains by the sixth day.

Special Conditions Affecting Eggs in Natural Incubation

The development of the embryo under the hen is affected by a number of conditions, and in learning to operate the incubator to the best possible advantage it is desirable to have a clear understanding of the practices of the sitting hen because in many details it is to her that we must look for correct methods. If allowed to follow her natural instincts the hen will seek a secluded spot for her nest and will there lay out her clutch and begin sitting. In the selection of a location for a nest she is by no means exacting, almost any secluded place may strike her fancy, from a comparatively exposed location on the ground to one high up in the barn mow, and she will bring off equally good hatches, apparently, almost regardless of location, under normal weather conditions. In dry locations and in extremely dry weather, eggs do not hatch so well and in natural incubation sprinkling the eggs or providing moist earth bottoms for the nests is believed to be helpful in getting good results. Under ordinary weather conditions no such attention is required.

The number of eggs that will be laid by hens before they begin sitting will vary widely, owing to the fact that their normal performance has been greatly modified by domestication, breeding, and heavy feeding for egg production, also by the common practice of removing all eggs from the nest each day so that there is never any accumulation in the nest. From 10 to 15 eggs can successfully be incubated by the average hen, the exact number being determined by season, location of nests, size of eggs, etc.

There are wide differences in the results secured in hatching with hens. Other conditions being similar it would seem that equal numbers of fertile eggs, placed under good sitting hens, should produce approximately equal numbers of chicks. It is common experience, however, that with hens set under the same conditions and with eggs from the same pens, some hens will bring off many more chicks than others. There may be other factors involved, but it is probable that the temperature of the hens is largely responsible for this difference, some furnishing too little heat from start to finish, to produce good hatches, while others appear to start off at the right bodily temperature, but get out of condition and fall off as much as two or three degrees during the hatch. For illustration, in a series of tests made by the writer, six hens were set at the same time and with all conditions as to eggs, environment, etc., as nearly identical as possible. The temperatures of the hens were carefully taken at the beginning and end of the hatch. There were twelve eggs in each sitting. The hatches were as follows:

Sitting No.	Eggs Broken	Eggs Fertile	No. Chicks	Temp. at Start	Temp. at Close
1	2	7	7	104	104
2	2	7	3	103	101
5	0	12	12	104¾	104½
6	1	11	9	104½	103½
7	0	6	3	103	103½
9	2	10	9	103	104¼

It will be seen that the hens that hatched practically every fertile egg (sittings 1, 5 and 9) were high in temperature, except No. 9, which started low, but finished high. No. 6 did well, though she finished a little low, while the two distinctly low-temperature hens made almost complete failures. Fertility was determined by the use of an ordinary egg tester and not by direct examination of the germ, which probably would have given different percentages of fertility, as a deficiency in heat that would result in a poor hatch of eggs known to be fertile would doubtless result in the death of some germs before they could reach a stage of development that

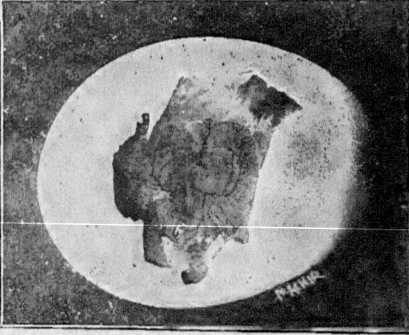

FIG. 36—APPEARANCE OF CHICK EMBRYO AFTER SIXTY HOURS OF INCUBATION
Photo from Kansas Experiment Station.

FIG. 37—APPEARANCE OF CHICK EMBRYO AFTER SEVENTY-TWO HOURS OF INCUBATION
Photo from Kansas Experiment Station.

THE CHICK EMBRYO AND ITS DEVELOPMENT

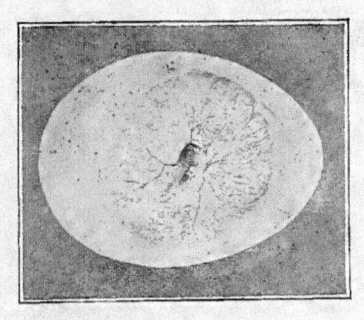

FIG. 38—APPEARANCE OF CHICK EMBRYO AFTER NINETY-SIX HOURS OF INCUBATION

would be detected by the use of an egg tester. The temperatures in this experiment were secured by placing a thermometer on top of the eggs and in direct contact with the body of the hen.

How Often Do Sitting Hens Turn Their Eggs

There is reason for thinking that sitting hens regularly turn their eggs more frequently than is generally considered necessary in artificial incubation, but the frequency no doubt varies with the stage of the hatch and with individuals. There are practical difficulties in the way of determining exactly how often the turning is done, as hens are apt to be suspicious when watched and will make no movement of any sort. Direct examination of the eggs is of no assistance, as it will be found that the hen will turn her eggs as often as she is returned to the nest, if that is every half hour.

There are several reasons why eggs must be turned more or less regularly during incubation, either natural or artificial. One is that fresh albumen may be brought in contact with the shell membrane and with the allantois, thus providing the necessary supply of oxygen for the blood. Another purpose in turning is to prevent the embryo from adhering to the shell. It is probable that turning also helps the embryo to get into proper position for normal development. There is also at least one incidental advantage realized in turning the eggs or at least shifting their position, which is the equalization of the temperature in different parts of the nest, thus securing more uniform conditions for the different eggs. There is bound to be a rather wide variation in nest temperature from center to outer edge, but the hen equalizes this by frequently shifting the eggs from the center to the outside and allowing the outer ones to roll to the center, thus giving all an equal chance and maintaining a fairly uniform rate of development in all.

Natural Cooling of Eggs

While the practice of hens differs widely, most of them leave the nest every morning with great regularity. In cold weather they absent themselves only long enough to secure necessary food and to evacuate the bowels, and then return at once to their duties. In warmer weather they will stay off for a longer period, sometimes for an hour or so. And it is to be noted that the hens that are most regular in coming off the nest daily are apt to have the best hatches, though no one has ever successfully proved that the cooling that results from their doing this has any direct connection with the better results secured. As regards artificial incubating, regular turning has some incidental advantages which are explained in the following chapter.

Moisture in Eggs

The egg contains 70 to 76 per cent of water when first laid, but this percentage is gradually reduced by evaporation from day to day. This fact is taken advantage of in one common method of determining the freshness of eggs by observing the size of the air cell through a tester or candling device, the air cell increasing in size as the moisture evaporates. This method is only relatively accurate, as the rate of evaporation is modified greatly by the conditions under which the eggs are kept. However, while eggs that are far from fresh may have small air cells, as in the case of storage eggs, large cells are never associated with strictly fresh eggs. The requirements of incubation, either artificial or natural, demand that, at the beginning of the hatch, the egg shall be as nearly normal as possible with respect to percentage of moisture contained. Hence, if they are not set at once it is desirable to keep them where they will not be unnecessarily dried out.

Loss of Weight During Incubation

Evaporation of moisture from eggs during incubation is essential to the proper development of the embryo. If evaporation progresses too rapidly the chick will be deprived of the amount of moisture needed in its development, and the difficulty of its getting out will be greatly increased. If on the other hand there is too little evaporation as a result of high humidity in the air, either natural or artificially produced, there will be a "waterlogged" chick that will not be normal, even if it succeeds in escaping from the shell. Generally such chicks do not hatch at all, but either drown in the excess moisture present at the time they break through into the air cell and begin breathing through their lungs, or the space provided by evaporation and represented by the air cell is so small that there is not room for them to get into right position for breaking out of the shell after pipping.

The chick embryo developing under a hen appears to be able to accommodate itself to a rather wide range in percentage of moisture present at hatching time, and will get out successfully whether evaporation has reached 18 to 20 per cent of the total weight of the eggs, or goes no higher than 10 per cent, and there appears to be no noticeably unfavorable effect produced by either extreme. However, chicks that have been dried down excessively are not apt to be as strong as those that have their normal percentage of moisture. Excessive drying down under hens is more or less common in extremely

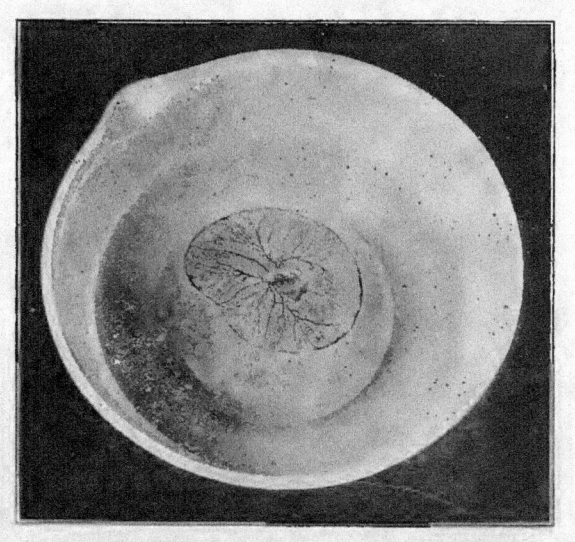

FIG. 39—CHICK EMBRYO AT 72 HOURS
Egg with embryo at same stage as in Fig. 37, emptied into a dish to show the vena terminalis—the "belt line" for the circulatory system. Photo from U. S. Department of Agriculture.

FIG. 40—CHICK EMBRYO AT SEVEN DAYS
At this stage of development, yolk is almost entirely enclosed in network of blood veins. Embryo at right. Photo from U. S. Department of Agriculture.

dry weather, but there are few instances in which there is insufficient drying down under such conditions. Methods of exact determining and regulating the rate of evaporation in artificial incubation, are given in Chapter V.

Oiling Hatching Eggs

Eggs under sitting hens are always coated with a thin film of oil as is shown by their appearance and accurately determined by chemical analysis. Whether this coating of oil, which results from long contact with the fowl's body, is an accidental condition with no direct bearing upon the development of the embryo, or whether it plays an essential part in incubation, is not known. The fact that incubators are successfully operated without any substitute for this natural oiling would seem to indicate that it is not important. However, there are some known differences between eggs incubated the natural way and those artificially incubated, which have never been satisfactorily explained, and until these are clearly understood there is always the possibility that further refinements in methods may bring about still better results or greater certainty in securing them. So far as known, efforts to reproduce the oil film artificially have not as yet proved successful.

Warming Eggs Daily While Holding for Hatching

Under normal conditions the hen that steals her nest and lays out her clutch and then incubates the eggs, is apt to hatch practically every one, almost regardless of the length of time that may have elapsed between the laying of the first and the last one. There is no evidence to show that the oldest eggs are at any disadvantage, or are any slower in hatching than those that are laid first, or that the chicks are any less strong when hatched. This is altogether different from general experience in artificial incubation where the oldest eggs are always several hours later in hatching, and the chicks from such eggs generally are believed to be less vigorous than those from eggs that have been kept only a short time.

Under the conditions of natural incubation as just described, the first eggs laid are subject to a daily warming up when the hen returns to lay on successive days, and it would seem that her well-known tendency to remain on the nest for a considerable time each day, either before or after laying, may be something more than incidental to the laying operation. It has previously been explained in this chapter that the germ already has undergone some development before the egg is dropped, and there is a possibility that the daily warming the first eggs receive prior to the time the hen begins sitting may, in a manner, vitalize the germs and thus enable them better to maintain their existence during the long wait while the rest of the eggs in the clutch are being laid.

To determine this point the writer conducted a series of experiments in which eggs, kept for various periods, were subjected to a daily warming. In all such tests, without exception, it was found that eggs warmed for about an hour daily hatched better than eggs kept for the same period without warming. In tests to establish the proper length of time for the warming it was found that one hour gave better results than 30 minutes or two hours. Eggs up to 18 to 20 days old that have been warmed for one hour daily appeared to hatch as promptly as comparatively fresh eggs, and before the egg tester the germs of these warmed eggs were plainly seen to be more active than those that had been held for an equal length of time, without warming. The warmed eggs began hatching before those not warmed, and the oldest were among the first to hatch. There are difficulties in the way of applying this principle to practical hatching operations, but it is important at least as giving addi-

FIG. 41—EGGS SHOWING DIFFERENT STAGES IN HATCH
In the egg on the left pipping has just begun. The second egg shows the normal progress of pipping as the chick turns itself in the shell, and breaks through the shell near the base of the air cell. In the third egg the shell is broken away to show the chick in position for pipping with the point of the bill against the inner surface of shell. Photos from Kansas Agricultural College.

THE CHICK EMBRYO AND ITS DEVELOPMENT

tional light on the condition of the germ when the egg is laid, and its physical requirements during the holding period.

How Long May Eggs Be Held for Hatching

The length of time for which eggs may be held without injury to their hatching qualities depends upon a number of factors, and no general rule can be given except the always safe statement that they should be set as soon as possible after they are laid. The writer has kept eggs for 26 to 30 days with a 29 per cent hatch of all eggs set, and at other times has been able to secure practically no chicks at all after the eggs were 18 days old. Much depends upon the season of the year, the temperature at which the eggs are held, and still more, probably, upon the condition of the breeding stock. Speaking in averages, there will be a marked falling off in fertility after about the 14th day, and the percentage of hatch in eggs over 21 days old usually is too low to make it worth while to waste eggs or space in the incubator in testing them out.

Position in Which to Keep Eggs

Within the limit of 8 to 12 days it does not appear to matter much what position the eggs are held in, or whether they are turned or not. In a series of tests eggs were held for varying periods up to 30 days, and in different positions as follows:

Flat, without turning.
Flat and turned daily.
Large end up not turned.
Small end up not turned.
On end and turned daily.

Different tests gave slightly contradictory results, but in general there appeared to be no difference due to position, except that the eggs laid flat, whether turned or not, generally hatched a trifle better than those on end. Since the natural position for eggs is flat, that would seem to be the safest way to place them, though the difference is so slight that there can hardly be any practical objection to standing them on end, as in shipping-cases, when it is more convenient to do so. Other tests indicated that there is no advantage in turning the eggs daily, provided they are not held over 10 to 12 days. If kept for a longer time than this better results will be secured by turning.

Washing Eggs

Experiments have shown that washing eggs will affect their hatching, the difference between washed and unwashed eggs averaging about 7.5 per cent. However, eggs that have been soiled under hens, also valuable eggs that have much foreign matter on them, doubtless will hatch better if washed than would be the case if incubated with the dirt adhering to them. This is especially true in the case of eggs that have been smeared by breakage of other eggs in the nest or during shipment. Since washing definitely reduces the percentage of the hatch, however, special pains should be taken to prevent the eggs from becoming soiled, and if they are only slightly so it is better to let them go without washing.

FIG. 42—SIZE OF CHICKS IS DETERMINED BY SIZE OF EGGS
Eggs weighing 20 ounces to the dozen. Chicks from them will be undersized and weakly.
Eggs weighing 24 ounces to the dozen. Standard-sized eggs and satisfactory for hatching.
Eggs weighing 30 ounces to the dozen. If normally this size, are extra desirable.

Resting Eggs After Shipment

It is commonly believed that resting shipped eggs for a period of 24 hours after they are received is advisable in order to give the yolks time to settle into their normal position. Some recorded experiments indicate that there is no advantage in doing this, but since the loss of time is slight and the general opinion is that such resting is beneficial, it is the part of wisdom to follow custom in this respect until some definite proof is offered one way or the other.

Size of Eggs to Use

Other things being equal, large eggs will give better and stronger chicks than small eggs. Whether this is directly due to the size of the eggs or to the fact that the best, most mature, and most vigorous hens and the ones that are best fed usually are the ones that lay the largest eggs, is not clear. Whatever the exact cause may be, it is an established fact that the largest eggs, within the limits of normal size, give the best and strongest chicks, and for this reason all small, under-sized eggs should be discarded. Discrimination in favor of large eggs should not be carried so far as to include double-yolk eggs or those that, while single-yolked, are conspicuously abnormal in size.

CHAPTER V

Operation of Incubators

How to Buy Incubators—What Size to Get—How to Set Up the Incubator and Adjust It—Complete Instructions in All Details of Management Throughout the Hatch—Latest Information on Temperature, Moisture, Ventilation, and Other Special Problems.

NUMEROUS styles and grades of incubators are offered for the use of poultry keepers, and those who are not familiar with their respective merits sometimes find it a difficult matter to select the machine that they really need, or that will most nearly meet their requirements. Naturally many mistakes are made—mistakes that involve serious disappointment and loss and that might readily have been avoided with a clearer understanding of the subject. Anyone who intends to purchase an incubator, large or small, can well afford to give careful thought to its selection, instead of "going it blind," or making price alone the basis of comparison.

Among lamp-heated incubators there are two general classes — those that are heated with hot air, and those heated with hot water. While each method of heating has advantages peculiar to itself, choice between them is based mainly on personal preference. The advantages claimed for hot-air machines generally are greater durability; more exact regulation under sudden changes of outside temperature; quicker heating up after cooling down; and as ventilation generally is associated with the heating system, the air circulation is positive and ventilation is adjustable over a wider range, and therefore has greater adaptability. For hot-water incubators it is claimed that they are less quickly affected by changes in outside temperature, and for this reason may give good results in reasonably favorable locations even when built with little insulation, which is impracticable with hot-air machines. This probably is the chief reason why most cheap incubators are of the hot-water type.

The commonly observed fact that hot-water incubators are most in demand in some localities while in others practically nothing but hot-air machines will be found, appears to be accidental, in part at least, and due to the good impression made locally by the first ones to be successfully used, of whichever type. There is a common belief that hot-water incubators furnish a moister heat than hot-air machines which, in connection with their lower average price appears to explain much of their special popularity in arid and semi-arid sections. While the idea that moisture in the egg chamber is directly affected by the nature of the heating medium is erroneous, hot water incubators probably do have less air circulation on the average, than the more adjustable hot-air machines. The practical effect of this is to reduce the evaporation from the egg in hot-water machines, thus giving the impression that more moisture is present in them.

Where gas is available, practically all lamp-heated incubators may readily be adapted to the use of this convenient fuel. Under suitable regulation, gas is entirely dependable, it requires little attention, supplies a uniform heat, and as there are no lamps to fill, the labor of caring for the machines is greatly reduced.

Electric Incubators

In the last few years electrically heated incubators have been developed to a good degree of efficiency, and where current can be obtained at a reasonable rate they are thoroughly practical and may be used as successfully as lamp-heated machines and much more conveniently. The freedom from fire risk and from lamp fumes makes it practical to operate electrics where lamp-heated machines would not be considered, and the saving in time required in caring for them will offset a decided increase in the cost of the current as compared with the cost of oil or gas. A reasonably uniform current is desirable. No harm will be done by having the current turned off occasionally, even though it may be off for several hours, but electric incubators are not recommended where the current is subject to frequent and long-continued interruptions. High-grade electrical machines should give satisfactory service for many years if properly cared for. They are subject to rapid deterioration, however, when exposed to dampness, and for that reason should be thoroughly dried out at the end of the hatching season, and stored in a dry place.

FIG. 43—A PROFITABLE HATCH

Mammoth Incubators

Of late years the use of "Mammoth" incubators has become general where chicks or ducklings are hatched in large numbers. There are several styles of mammoths on the market, but all are more or less alike in their general outlines. They are heated by means of hot water pipes supplied from a furnace or boiler which burns hard coal, as a rule, though gas is used when available. Mammoths usually are divided into compartments of varying sizes and are more or less sectional in construction, so that the machines when set up resemble a series of lamp-heated incubators without the lamps. The use of mammoth incubators saves labor and operating cost since there are no lamps to fill, and a single furnace or boiler will provide heat for a great number of sections; the cost of fuel also is reduced. They are not adapted to the requirements of small operators, and small-sized mammoths are not generally regarded as economical, unless bought with the expectation of adding more sections at an early date. The cost of such a mammoth is equal to or greater than the cost of the same egg capacity in lamp-heated machines, and the saving in cost of operation is hardly noticable. Where several thousand eggs are to be incubated at one time, however, mammoths are regarded as indispensable.

OPERATION OF INCUBATORS

The Cost of a Good Incubator

Consideration of price ought not to figure too greatly in choice of lamp-heated incubators, and the common tendency to buy the cheapest machine obtainable is the cause of much disappointment and loss. It would not be correct to say that there are no good incubators but high-priced ones, but it should call for no special argument to convince any one that durable machines of the best design and construction cannot be built to sell at extremely low prices. The manufacture of incubators is a plain business matter like the manufacture of any other kind of machinery or equipment. Some incubators cost more, simply for the material and the labor employed in them, than the retail price of others, and if practical, economical buyers in great numbers chose the higher-priced makes in preference to the cheap ones there must be sound business reasons for their doing so.

The reasons for the general preference among experienced operators for standard high-priced machines will be found in their greater durability on account of better material and workmanship used in their construction; greater adaptability to conditions generally because of better insulation; more exact regulation and consequently greater uniformity of temperature. The plain truth of the matter is that the buyer who wants the most nearly automatic machine—one that will give best results under a wide range of conditions, that will last indefinitely without expensive repairs, and that has the endorsement of expert operators generally, will have to buy one of the higher-priced makes.

This fact does not, however, eliminate low-cost incubators from practical consideration. If the machine is to be operated under favorable conditions; if the buyer wants a hatcher that will give good results for the time being, without asking too much in the way of durability; if the machine is to be used only for hatching in the natural breeding season when vitality in the breeding stock is at its highest, and when climatic conditions are most favorable; if only one or two hatches are to be made each season so that it is not desirable to have much money locked up in equipment, then the purchase of a low-priced machine may be not only permissible, but the most practical thing to do. It is for the individual to consider carefully his own conditions and plans, and see that he gets the machine that will best meet them, chosing it neither because it is cheap, nor because it is high-priced, but because it is what he needs.

What Size to Get

Large incubators are cheaper to buy and to operate than an equal capacity in small machines, and for that reason it is desirable to get as large sizes as can be used to good advantage. There is no serious objection to running a large machine without a full quota of eggs, but there is no way of making a small one hold more than its actual capacity. Therefore, in case of doubt always get the next larger size. Attention, however, should be called to the fact that incubators are designed to be operated approximately at capacity, and when large machines are run with comparatively few eggs in them there may be complications with respect to moisture and ventilation that would not be met with when the machine is operated with full trays. For this reason, also because it takes more oil to heat a large machine than a small one, it is unwise to get incubators that greatly exceed average requirements.

The proper size for the incubator is determined chiefly by the size of the breeding flock or the number of eggs produced by it. Eggs should be incubated as soon as possible after they are laid—within 10 to 14 days at the outside, and it is better to have two or three small machines that can be filled every 7 to 10 days rather than to have a large one that cannot be filled without holding the eggs for a much longer time in order to get the required number. Where this is done the percentage of the hatch will be greatly reduced on account of the low average of the older eggs. Another indirect disadvantage in the use of unnecessarily large machines is the tendency to set unsuitable eggs, such as would be discarded in filling a small machine, but which are apt to be used in order to make up the full number in the large one. It seldom is desirable to buy a machine smaller than 150-egg capacity, and even that size should not be selected unless the breeding flock is so small as to make this clearly the proper thing to do.

Where to Place the Incubator

The best place for the incubator usually is in a well-ventilated cellar. This is true because such a location provides a more uniform temperature than an above-ground house or room; there is more natural humidity in the air; the ventilating system of the machine works more certainly, especially in warm weather; and there is less danger of the hatch being tampered with by meddling hands. Of course, a cellar can be a very poor

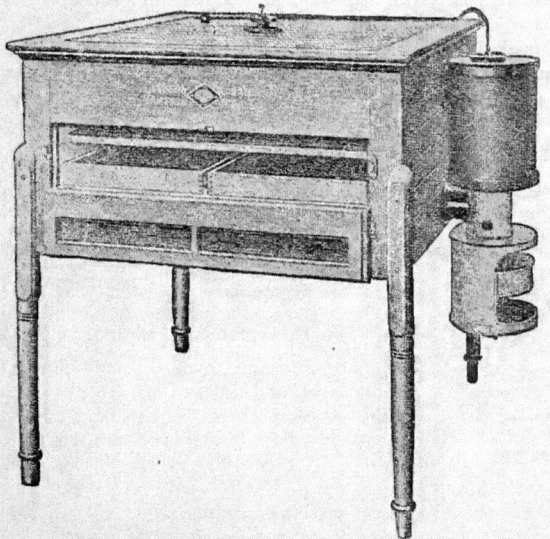

FIG. 44—HOT AIR INCUBATOR WITH CLOTH DIAPHRAGM

In this type of incubator the warmed air is diffused through cloth diaphragms, one of which is here dropped below natural position in order to show it. Courtesy Cyphers Incubator Company.

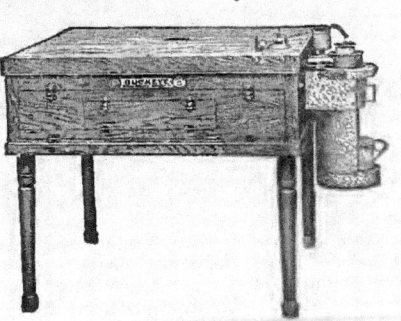

FIG. 45—POPULAR HOT WATER INCUBATOR

In this machine heat is provided by means of hot water which circulates through coil of pipe in upper part of the machine. Water is heated by lamp at end. Courtesy of Buckeye Incubator Company.

place for the incubator if it is not what a cellar ought to be. To be suitable for hatching purposes it must be well ventilated, reasonably uniform in temperature, not wet, or moldy, or otherwise unwholesome.

Incubators are successfully operated in aboveground rooms of various sorts, but unless especially constructed for the purpose, machines in them require more attention and are less easily regulated. Also, in warm weather the room temperature is liable to be so nearly that of the egg chamber that the circulation of air through the machine is sluggish and will require a great deal of helping out by frequently opening the door, cooling the eggs for long periods, and other aids to ventilation. Wherever it is placed, be sure it is not in a draft or a current of air and that it is not exposed to direct sunlight. For plans for incubator houses and suggestions for adapting to incubator use rooms or buildings already constructed, see Chapter VIII.

Setting Up the Incubator

It is not wise to take even the best incubator too much for granted, and new ones should be carefully inspected and tested in every working part to be sure that everything is as it should be before entrusting valuable eggs to them. Examine everything carefully when the machine is uncrated and test with especial care the regulator and all its connections. Do not depend upon the machine coming all set up and ready to fill with eggs as soon as the legs are screwed on and the lamp filled. Presumably that is the way every manufacturer desires to have it delivered to the purchaser, but there necessarily is a good deal of handwork about making and assembling an incubator, and errors are bound to occur no matter how carefully the machine may be inspected at the factory. Moreover, it is liable to get rough usage in shipment and may be so badly jarred that its working parts will be disarranged or broken.

Look the machine over carefully, therefore, in setting it up, and DON'T put the eggs in until it has been successfully operated for some time while empty. This injunction will stand almost any amount of emphasis. It would seem that any one sufficiently in earnest to buy an incubator, would be practical enough to be sure that it is in proper working order before filling it with valuable eggs. As a matter of fact, however, one of the most frequent causes of complaints among beginners is their practice of putting eggs in the machine when they KNOW that it is not properly adjusted. If the operator cannot maintain a uniform temperature before the eggs are put into the machine, he can depend upon it that he cannot do so afterward.

How the Regulator Works

The regulation of the temperature in practically all lamp-heated incubators is determined by the position of a damper over the heater or lamp flue which determines the temperature of the warmed air or water entering the heating system of the machine. The position of this damper is controlled by a thermostat which is connected with the damper in such a way that, when the heat increases beyond a certain point, the damper will be lifted and the surplus heat from the lamp allowed to escape. If the temperature drops too low, the thermostat releases the damper which then closes down over the flue, thus directing more heat into the machine. There are various types of regulators in use (see Fig. 51), all taking advantage of the fact that metals and liquids expand when heated and contract when cooled. The thermostatic bars and wafers are so made as to utilize this expansion and contraction by operating a regulator arm, on one end of which the damper is carried, and on the other a counterweight to balance the damper.

FIG. 47—LAMP-HEATED INCUBATOR WITH ENCLOSED FLUE
Courtesy of Reliable Incubator Co.

The regulator and its correct adjustment are fully described by each manufacturer in his book of directions, and this description should be studied until the operator thoroughly understands its construction and operation. The regulator is the heart of the incubator and if it is not correctly adjusted and kept in proper working order, exact temperature control is out of the question. The regulators used in standard incubators are so sensitive that the correct temperature can be maintained with great accuracy, and with remarkably little attention from the operator, once the proper adjustment has been secured. It is extremely unwise however, to attempt to operate the machine until the working of the regulator is understood.

The Incubator Must Stand Level

Incubators are built to stand practically level, and unless they are placed in this position there is danger that the hot air or hot water will not circulate properly, especially in the larger-sized machines. Use a spirit level, if possible, and test the machine from side to side and from front to back. If a spirit level is not available, proper adjustment can be secured by placing on top of the machine a broad, flat pan or tray with a little water in it, and leveling the machine until the water in the pan stands

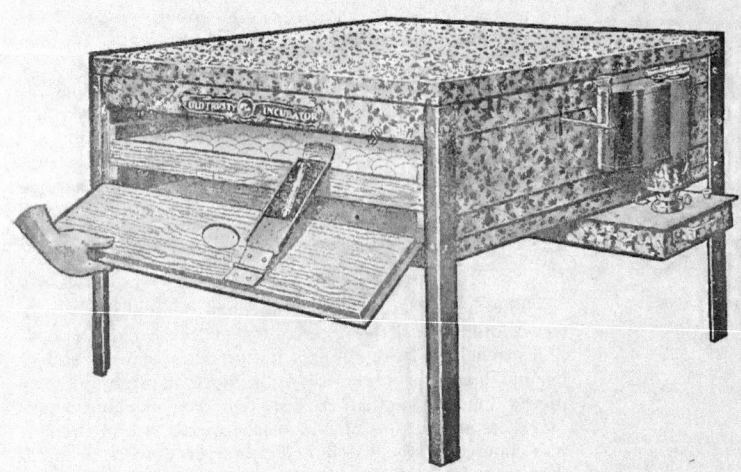

FIG. 46—METAL COVERED INCUBATOR
Courtesy of M. M. Johnson Company.

at a uniform depth. See that the machine stands firmly on the floor or on the blocks used in leveling, so that it will not move or rock when touched.

As a rule, when the machine is level the temperature in the different parts of the egg chamber will be uniform. In some cases, however, especially with hot-air machines that are longer than they are wide, it may happen that, after levelling, the end next the lamp will be warmer or colder than the opposite end. If this proves to be the case the machine will have to be readjusted to meet this condition. The right thing to do is first to level exactly and then test the temperature, using two or more thermometers of known accuracy, and testing both ends, also front and back. If any difference is noted transpose the thermometers to be sure that the variation is not in them. When certain that there is an actual and constant difference between the ends, or the front and back, the cold section may be raised sufficiently to equalize the temperature. In the case of machines having the heat flue enclosed, the difference in temperature between the two ends sometimes is more than it is wise to attempt to take care of by this method, the better plan in such cases being to secure the needed adjustment by raising the cold tray by means of strips of wood on the tray supports.

The necessity for adjustments of this sort is especially marked in cold weather; later in the season when it grows warm it may be necessary to readjust the machine again. It seldom is desirable to throw hot-water incubators out of level, as this is apt to interfere with the circulation of the water. If a serious variation is detected in such machines it is better to take care of it by the use of strips under the tray, as above described. If the front is colder than the back, look to the fitting of the door and if necessary tack strips of felt or similar material around the edges so that it will shut tight.

Care of the Lamp

Keep the lamp clean, and fill it and trim the wick strictly according to the directions of the manufacturer. Some machines are provided with large lamp bowls that only require filling now and then. Wicks generally need trimming once a day, and when the flame is turned quite high it may be necessary to trim twice daily. It is never safe to leave a heavy char on the wick; to do so is to invite smoky flames, accumulations of soot in the chimney or heater, and more serious troubles. Do not trim with shears, however, unless it is found really necessary to do

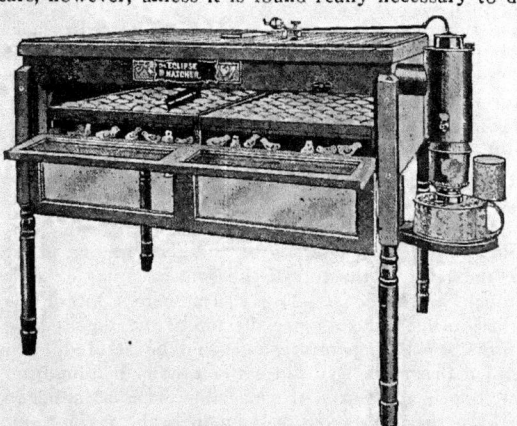

FIG. 48—INCUBATOR WITH THERMOMETER IN POSITION
This illustration shows position of standing thermometer as usually recommended—bulb about on level with top of eggs. Courtesy of Des Moines Incubator Company.

so. The easy way is to brush the char off with a match and smooth the edge down with the finger. Usually no other treatment will be needed. If this does not give a clear, even flame like the one shown in Fig. 74, then use the shears, but confine the trimming to the blackened portion of the wick. When putting in a new wick, always burn it off instead of trying to trim it with shears. Light the dry wick with a match and burn it until it goes out at the wick tube, which generally will give just the right shape to the flame. If not, the corners may be trimmed slightly (see Fig. 73). Incorrect trimming will produce irregular, smoky flames like the one shown in Fig. 75.

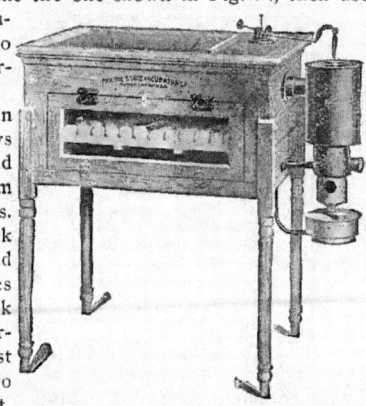

LAMP-HEATED HOT AIR INCUBATOR
This popular incubator is heated by a current of warmed air and has a sand tray under the eggs for supplying moisture. When the hatch is coming off, sand tray is removed, and a burlap screen substituted, providing a comfortable nursery compartment for the chicks. Courtesy of Prairie State Incubator Company.

Keep an old toothbrush handy for brushing off the burner, especially the gauze screen. If this screen gets clogged with dirt the lamp will smoke. In placing the lamp in position under the heater, be sure that it properly engages the heater collar or chimney, whichever is used. Failure to do this may cause serious trouble. After lighting the lamp leave the flame turned a little low until the burner gets warmed up, and never leave it for the day or the night until certain that it is properly adjusted. Any lamp flame is liable to "creep" up a little after it has burned for a short time and many complaints of smoking lamps are due to this cause.

Starting the Hatch

When everything is in proper working order and the temperature can be exactly controlled, the machine may safely be set. The best time to do this is in the morning, when the eggs will have the entire day in which to warm up, thus making certain that the machine will reach the proper temperature and will stay there, before it is necessary to leave it for the night. Frequently, after the machine has been accurately adjusted to the desired temperature with the trays empty it will be found that, with the trays full of eggs, the temperature will go up a little, necessitating a slight readjustment of the regulator. The flame also may need a little attention, as there is no advantage in running it higher than is necessary to provide the required amount of heat with enough over for emergencies.

The eggs with which the trays are to be filled should be carefully selected, discarding every one that has any serious defect. There is no necessity for filling the trays exactly full if there are not enough suitable eggs for the purpose, and it is a wasteful practice to use eggs that cannot reasonably be expected to hatch. In case the trays are not full it is a good plan to have narrow strips of wood that may be laid across the trays confining the eggs to one place and preventing their rolling about.

In case there are more eggs than the trays will accommodate in the regular way, they may be crowded somewhat by standing them nearly on end, with the large end up. Repeated tests have shown that the capacity of the trays may be increased about 20 per cent by this method, without any unfavorable effect on the hatch. The eggs may safely be left in this position until the third day, when they must be tested and the infertile ones taken out, which will leave sufficient room to lay the rest in their proper position. As it is not possible to test brown-shelled eggs with much accuracy until they have been in the incubator for four or five days, this method is not practical with them. Under no condition should the attempt be made to put a double layer of eggs on the tray. To do so will be to lose all those on top through overheating unless the temperature is adjusted to the top layer, in which case the under ones will suffer on account of too little heat.

Correct Incubator Temperature

As has already been pointed out in Chapter IV, 70 degrees is about the "physiological zero" of the chick embryo. At temperatures above this point cell division begins, but proceeds very slowly and never progresses beyond an extremely limited stage of development unless normal incubation temperature is approximated. Above this temperature, growth proceeds at an abnormally rapid rate as the temperature rises and places a severe strain upon the embryonic organism that it cannot long endure. For this reason it is highly important that the temperature of the egg chamber be maintained within comparatively narrow limits, though reasonable variation probably is in no way objectionable. There is little doubt that eggs under the sitting hen are subject to marked variation in temperature—greater in fact, than in any well-managed incubator.

The exact temperature of the embryo during incubation—that is, the temperature at which it will grow at a normal rate and will reach complete development and hatch out at the exact time intended by nature, is 99 to 100 degrees at the beginning, gradually increasing to about 103 at the end of hatch. These temperatures are the same under all conditions and at all seasons. Incubator thermometers, however, are more or less affected by outside conditions and in order that the embryo shall receive the exact degree of heat required it is necessary to take into consideration the style of machine used, the position of the thermometer in the machine, the outside temperature, whether cold or warm, the stage of the hatch, etc. It is, therefore, impossible to fix on a certain degree of temperature which is to be maintained at all times.

In a general way the manufacturer prescribes the temperature at which his particular type of machine should be operated, and it is unwise to take liberties with his instructions, particularly in the way of substituting a different style of thermometer for the one regularly sent out, or changing its position in the machine. There sometimes are special reasons why certain thermometers and certain temperatures are recommended for particular machines and no changes should be made in these details. However, it should be understood that the manufacturer's instructions are necessary more or less general, and because these advise to "run at 103 degrees," it must not be assumed that this temperature is to be adhered to under any and all conditions. There are a few general principles that must be kept in mind in operating any machine, and some discrimination must be used in meeting unusual conditions.

As has already been stated, the correct embryo temperature in the first days of incubation is 99-100 degrees. There is no practical way of taking that temperature, however, and in ordinary incubator operation, the thermometer may be located at any convenient point, if due allowance is made for the corresponding difference in temperature. This fact has resulted in the adoption of various styles of thermometers, two of which are illustrated in Figs. 82 and 83. The inovo thermometer (now rarely used) was designed to give the temperature of the interior of the eggs, or the exact embryo temperature, but for various reasons it probably does no more than approximate that ideal, and is not convenient in practical use. Some contact thermometers are mounted so as to lie on the top of the egg almost exactly over the embryo, and in that position will show a temperature somewhat higher than that of the germ itself. A practical objection to this style of thermometer is that if it is placed in contact with an infertile egg or one containing a dead or weak germ, after the eighth day of incubation, the temperature indicated will be lower than that of live embryos. Owing to the fact that this thermometer easily slips out of position, also because the eggs on which it rests vary more or less in size, the bulb is not always on the same level, leading to slight but undesirable inaccuracies in temperature readings.

Standing thermometers give the temperature at or below the level of the top of the egg, and may or may not touch it. Some standing thermometers locate the bulb half an inch or so above the top of the eggs, giving about the same temperature as would be secured by a suspended thermometer. The latter usually is hung from a wire loop in the top of the machine and is so adjusted as to keep the bulb about half an inch above the eggs, so that it will be practically unaffected by animal heat.

So far as the hatch is concerned it matters little what style of thermometer is used if the temperature is maintained at the point necessary to secure the correct embryo

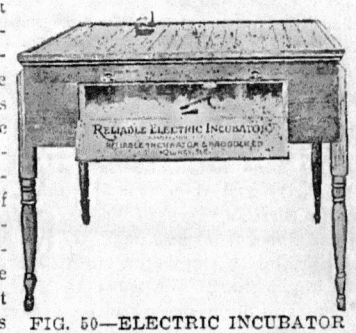

FIG. 50—ELECTRIC INCUBATOR
Courtesy of Reliable Incubator Co.

FIG. 49—ELECTROBATOR
Courtesy of Cypners Incubator Company.

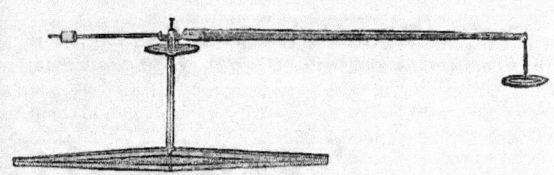

FIG. 51—METAL-BAR REGULATOR FOR INCUBATORS
Courtesy of Cyphers Incubator Company.

temperature. The degree of heat required in incubation depends to some extent upon the stage of the hatch. The following table showing the internal temperature of eggs incubated under hens, for each day of incubation, is from Lillie's Development of the Chick:

Day of incubation	1	2	3	4	5	6	7	8	9	10
Temperature of hen	102.2	103.0	103.0	104.0	103.8	105.0	104.6	104.5	105.0	105.0
Temperature of eggs	98.0	100.2	100.5	100.4	101.0	101.8	102.5	101.6	102.0	

Day of incubation	11	12	13	14	15	16	17	18	19	20
Temperature of hen	104.8	105.2	104.5	105.0	105.2	105.0	104.6	104.8	104.5	104.5
Temperature of egg	101.8	102.2	102.0	102.5	102.0	103.0	102.4	103.0	103.0	103.0

In a series of tests by the writer with incubators running at approximately the correct theoretical embryo temperature, the following results were secured—the figures given representing the average temperature recorded by each thermometer, for four 5-day periods:

	First Period	Second Period	Third Period	Fourth Period
Inovo	98.89	99.21	99.79	100.91
Contact	101.56	101.60	101.52	102.42
Suspended	103.90	104.22	103.64	103.06

It will be seen by this that the variation between thermometers in different positions is not the same at all stages of the hatch. While the suspended thermometer maintained approximately the same temperature throughout, the inovo and contact thermometers were decidedly lower at the start but gradually approached that of the suspended one. There was a difference of nearly five degrees between the inovo and the suspended thermometer during the last period, with the contact thermometer about midway between them. The Indiana Experiment Station definitely recommends a temperature of 101-102-103 degrees for the first, second, and third weeks respectively, using a standing thermometer on a level with the top of the egg but not touching them. In the experiments leading to this conclusion it was found that the standing thermometer regularly registered one-half a degree lower than contact thermometer.

This graduation of the temperature for different periods of the hatch is secured by the occasional adjustment of the regulator, in the case of inovo, contact and standing thermometers, but with the suspended type with the incubator temperature maintained at practically the same point throughout the hatch, the animal heat of the growing embryo itself providing the desired increase, as is shown by the experimental data previously quoted.

How Outside Conditions Affect Incubation Temperatures

The recommendation to run at any given temperature necessary is subject to some modifications, however, as determined by outside conditions, type of machine, whether or not the eggs are cooled, color of shells, etc. The attempt to run throughout the season at a uniform 101-102-103 temperature, for example, will almost certainly lead to dissatisfaction.

Most practical operators allow a difference of nearly a degree between cold and warm weather hatching temperatures, this being provided to offset the greater cooling down that the eggs receive in a cold room, and possibly for other reasons. There is a common belief that high altitudes call for a somewhat higher temperature than is generally recommended, though there does not appear to be any actual proof of this. Brown-shelled eggs are supposed to require more heat than white-shelled ones. It is not likely that this is due to any difference in the actual degree of heat registered by brown and white eggs under exactly the same conditions, as some seem to suppose, but it is probable that brown-shelled eggs actualy have a slightly longer incubating period and hence require a higher temperature to bring them out in the time required by white-shelled eggs. Whether it is desirable that brown-shelled eggs be given extra time, or instead should receive additional heat in order to bring them off earlier, does not seem to have been carefully investigated, but in general practice the latter plan usually is followed.

The normal period of incubation for hen eggs is stated as "21 days," but the actual time required is somewhat less than that. The incubation period can be shortened or increased by several hours without any apparent ill effects. It is general experience that chicks may come out on the 20th day and be quite strong and vigorous, while they may be delayed until the 22nd day without injury. The development of the chick is more or less under the control of the operator who can hasten or retard progress by the degree of heat supplied, or the length of the cooling periods.

Effect of Too Much Heat

In considering excess heat it is necessary to distinguish between short-time exposure to temperatures high enough quickly to endanger the life of the embryo, and longer exposure to temperatures only little above normal. The effect of high temperatures is to quicken cell division and stimulate more rapid growth in the embryo, and if the heat is not too high the embryo will live and develop, but will hatch prematurely or before it has had time to "ripen." At higher temperatures the heart and arteries will be overtaxed and hemorrhages will result, producing what is commonly known as "blood rings" in early stages of development. Any temperature above 104 degrees with a contact thermometer is "high" and if

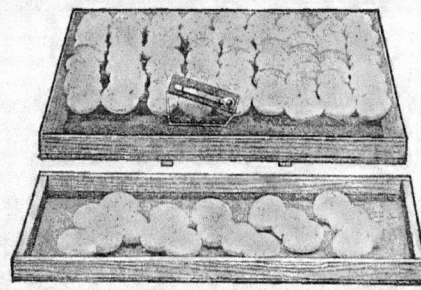

FIG. 52—SMALL TRAY, USEFUL IN TURNING EGGS
Where eggs are turned by shuffling, a small tray holding 15 to 18 eggs should be provided to avoid breakage. Courtesy of Buckeye Incubator Company.

continued for any length of time will injure or kill the embryo. The further the development of the embryo has progressed the better able it is to stand excessive heat, so that in late stages of the hatch temperatures as high as 110 degrees can be endured for a very short time. In all cases when eggs have been overheated, they should be removed from the machine at once and cooled in order to reduce the blood pressure as quickly as possible. In addition to the direct injury to the embryo, overheating is believed to bring about unfavorable changes in the yolks, causing one form of "white diarrhea" in the newly hatched chicks.

Effect of Too Little Heat

It is not probable that moderately low temperatures, unless too long continued, do any real harm aside from delaying the hatch, which is harm enough of course, but not apt to be so disastrous as overheating. Low temperatures during early stages of the hatch can be offset to some extent by operating at a higher temperature later on. Up to a certain point it does not appear to matter whether the heat is maintained at the exact normal temperature throughout the hatch or is subject to moderate fluctuation, provided the total number of required heat units is supplied. From a practical viewpoint, however, irregular temperatures greatly increase the difficulty of operating the machine and bringing the hatch off at the right time. It is desirable therefore that the temperature be kept as uniform as possible, that all extremes be avoided, and that every departure from correct temperature be followed by prompt correction. It should be remembered that too much cooling or cooling to too low temperatures, and leaving the eggs out for a long time in warm weather even though they are not cooled down noticeably, will delay the hatch just as certainly as low temperatures in the machine.

Every one who runs an incubator should keep a daily temperature record or chart like the one shown on page 47. A seemingly slight variation, if frequently repeated, may appreciably affect development of the embryo, but with a record of temperature variations from day to day, a tendency to run too low or too high can readily be detected and correction made before harm is done. The importance of doing this is all the greater from the fact that the average beginner generally regards whatever temperature is recommended for his machine, as the maximum rather than the average to be maintained. In other words, if the instruction book says that the temperature should be kept at 103 degrees he is apt to feel that he dare not go above that, but that no harm will result if it drops below, now and then. So, to be on the safe side, he runs a little low most of the time, and as a result the hatch is seriously delayed. A daily record should help to overcome this tendency.

Turning the Eggs

Turning should begin on the morning of the third day and should be continued thereafter until the chicks begin to pip. Sometimes directions are given to discontinue turning on the 18th day, regardless of the stage of development. This is correct only when the chicks come out on schedule time, in which case they will begin pipping on the 20th day. In the case of delayed hatches, however—and there are many such, especially early in the season—much better results will be secured if the turning is continued until pipping actually begins, even though this may not be until the 21st day.

When the trays have flat bottoms and the sides are of proper height, the eggs may all be turned at the same time, by placing an extra tray over the full one and, holding the trays firmly in the hands, simply flop them over. This cannot be done with trays with sloping bottoms, and even where it is practicable many operators prefer to turn by shuffling, believing that better results are secured by that method. In turning this way, 12 to 18 eggs are removed from one end of the tray and the rest then are pushed over into the empty space, using the flat of the hand and shifting the eggs about more or less at the same time so as to change their position in the tray, after which the eggs that have been removed are returned to the empty end. This method keeps the eggs shifting about and equalizes any slight irregularity in temperature that may exist at different points on the tray, thus giving all the eggs an equal chance.

It is a good plan to provide a small tray in which to place the eggs that are taken out, as they are liable to be cracked in laying them on a hard surface, such as the top of the work table or the incubator. Make the tray about 5x15 or 18 inches, with a bottom of fine wire or duck, and have the sides extend at least an inch below the bottom so that the latter will not touch whatever the tray may be resting upon. One or more of these small trays will be found convenient for a variety of purposes in handling hatching eggs.

Some extra conscientious persons mark the eggs so that they can be certain that they have been turned completely over each time, but there is no necessity for doing this and it consumes a good deal of time. It is important, however, to see to it that the eggs always lie with the large end up. The experienced operator places a little pressure on the eggs in turning and with slight effort keeps the small end down without paying any special attention to the matter. In order to be sure that they are in this position, however, it is advisable for the beginner to look the trays over, carefully turning down any eggs found with the small end up.

It is not meant by this that the eggs are to stand on end, but simply that the small end should be lower—the position they naturally take in the nest. The purpose of doing this is to fix the air cell in the large end of the egg, which is essential to the normal development of the embryo and its successful exclusion. Especially during

FIG. 53—A THREE COMPARTMENT MAMMOTH INCUBATOR
Courtesy of Newtown Giant Incubator Corporation.

OPERATION OF INCUBATORS 41

ing at all, a good hatch under such conditions is purely a matter of luck, and no one who really wishes to be successful will follow this slipshod method. The opportunities which testing affords for checking up on fertility of the eggs, and on the temperature, moisture, and ventilation of the machine, are invaluable.

With a good tester the first test for the removal of infertile eggs may be made as early as the third day in the case of white-shelled eggs, while those with brown shells can be tested on the fourth or fifth day. The beginner, however, will do well to wait for another day or two, as he will find it much easier to detect fertility then, and there is no practical advantage in extremely early tests. While the careful operator will make it a practice to test a few eggs every day or so after the first few days, two or three general tests are all that are really necessary to the proper operation of the machine. If the rate of evaporation is to checked up by weighing the eggs (see page 43) it will be found convenient to divide the hatching into three 6-day periods, weighing on the sixth, twelfth and eighteenth days, doing the weighing and testing at the same time.

On the sixth day the germ should be plainly seen, even in brown-shelled eggs. At this time there will be a central opaque spot about a quarter of an inch in diameter with blood vessels reaching out from it on all sides, the embryo being sufficiently developed to give the yolk a distinctly different appearance from that of an infertile egg, though the yolk will not be entirely enclosed by the net work of blood vessels until about the 8th day.

Embryos that die during the first few days usually are "blood-ringed," the germ spot being surrounded by a more or less clearly defined ring the size of which will depend on the stage of development at which the germ died. Sometimes the dead germ will show as a dark

FIG. 54—APPEARANCE OF FERTILE EGG BEFORE TESTER AFTER SEVEN DAYS OF INCUBATION
At this stage of development, the germ should be plainly seen toward the upper end, and usually will be in motion, appearing and disappearing in a regular, pulsating movement.

the early stages of incubation, permitting the small end to remain uppermost will cause many air cells to form in that end, with serious consequences to the embryo.

Numerous mechanical egg-turning devices have been introduced from time to time and have enjoyed varying degrees of popular favor, but many operators feel that the advantages of hand turning fully compensate them for the time required in doing it. In all cases, regardless of how the eggs are turned, the position of the trays in the machine should be changed from day to day, turning them end for end, and shifting from side to side if the machine has more than one tray, in order to equalize inequalities in temperature.

The frequency with which eggs should be turned is largely a practical question. Twice a day is as often as the average operator feels that he can afford to do it, though it is probable that the hen turns her eggs much more frequently. Twice a day appears to be sufficient, so far as the actual requirements of the embryo are concerned, but under special conditions there is reason to believe that more frequent turning will prove advantageous. Especially in warm weather, when the temperatures of the room and the incubator are so nearly the same that the ventilation of the machine is sluggish and uncertain, it is probable that opening the door and taking the eggs out for an extra turning or two each day will give better ventilation and may prove directly beneficial to the embryo.

How to Use the Egg Tester

The object in testing eggs is to remove the infertile ones, to follow the development of the air cell, and to watch the growth of the embryo. While some operators do not remove infertile eggs or do any systematical test-

FIG. 55—APPEARANCE OF FERTILE EGG BEFORE TESTER AFTER TWO WEEKS OF INCUBATION
At this stage the egg will be almost entirely opaque, showing only a narrow transparent edge along the lower side.

spot with indistinct outlines and no ring. Since a weak or undeveloped germ may have the same general appearance, such eggs should be marked and put back for a few days more when, if dead, their development will be so far behind that of the living germs that there will be no danger of confusing them with the latter.

Infertile eggs will be practically as clear at this test as when they were first placed in the machine. For that matter, they will remain so throughout the hatch if left in. It is not desirable to do this however, if for no other reason than that their presence in the tray adds to the time required to turn the eggs, while in case a contact thermometer is used the correct temperature will not be secured after the first few days, unless the operator is careful to see that the thermometer always rests on a fertile egg. The air cell on the seventh day should be about as shown in Fig. 63. If it is noticeably smaller or larger, the ventilation or moisture, or both, will need attention. In determining the extent of evaporation by the size of the air cell, it is important to be sure that a correct average is taken, since when eggs of different ages are set together, or those having shells of varying degrees of porosity, there will be a good deal of irregularity in the size of the cells.

In testing it is desirable to use as strong a light as is available for the purpose. The small lamp testers that generally are sent out with the machine serve fairly well to determine the presence of the germ and the size of the air cell, but to do early testing and to follow the development of the germs, strong light is necessary. Sunlight is excellent for testing purposes and there are various ways of utilizing it. As an emergency measure a roll of stiff paper can be used, simply holding one end to the eye and placing egg at other end and directing it toward the sun.

FIG. 56—APPEARANCE OF INFERTILE EGG BEFORE TESTER
An infertile egg examined before the tester should be almost clear, the yolk showing but faintly even after having been in the incubator for two weeks, as was the case with egg here shown.

Different Styles of Testers

For day testing the incubator room may be arranged so that it can be darkened, and a window facing the sun provided with a covering having one or two 1¼-inch holes, in front of which the eggs are held. Sunlight testing is frequently inconvenient and for cloudy days and night work artificial light must be used. Electric light is best, using "Mazda" bulbs. Ordinary incandescent bulbs give a yellow light which is not desirable. If electricity is not available acetylene may be used, also gas, or kerosene—with mantles if possible, to avoid yellow flames. All of these lights (except electricity) generate a great deal of heat which may prove uncomfortable in the small, close quarters in which eggs often are tested, and the enclosures provided for the lights must be of good size and well ventilated to avoid broken mantles and chimneys. There are a number of high-grade egg testers on the market and it generally is better and cheaper to buy these than to experiment with home-made contrivances.

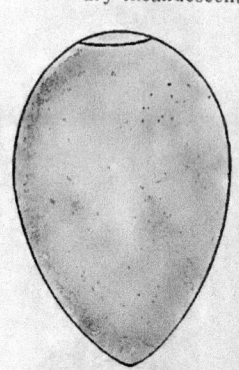

FIG. 57—EGG WITH SPIRAL SHELL
When examined before the tester, eggs frequently will be found in which the shell is marked by dark spiral rings as indicated above. Such eggs rarely hatch.

When the eggs are tested on the twelfth to fourteenth day, any doubtful ones may be removed, also any infertiles that may have been overlooked in the first test. At this time the air cell should be about the size shown in Fig. 63, and proper changes should be made in the ventilation or moisture, if the air cells are not developing normally. The fertile egg will appear as in Fig. 55 and the embryo will be more or less active, regularly rising and falling, or appearing and disappearing, before the tester. The egg generally will be opaque below the air cell but there may be a bright edge along the underside of the egg as shown. This should be of limited extent however. If there is a large bright area, the development of the embryo is not progressing in a normal manner.

Dead germs may be found in various stages of development, but they are not easily distinguished unless they have died during the first few days. It is not usual for dead germs to decay in the incubator, but they sometimes do so. In case the odor on opening the machine indicates the presence of rotten eggs they should be removed at once. It usually is not necessary to test all the eggs to find them, as they can be more quickly discovered by their outward appearance, or by holding the nose close to the eggs.

On the eighteenth day the final test will be made. At this time the embryo should fill the shell with the exception of the air cell and the eggs before the tester will have throughout a plain opaque appearance. The chick may even have broken through the membrane into the air cell, filling it also, though not unless development has been little too rapid. This final test enables the operator to determine whether or not the chicks may be expected to come out on time and whether ventilation and moisture have been correct. It affords the last chance of making adjustments to correct errors in this respect, also in temperature, but such final changes can only be slight.

Ventilation and Moisture

The purpose of ventilation is to provide the growing

OPERATION OF INCUBATORS

embryo with a constant supply of fresh air, and while its requirements in this respect are limited, they are by no means negligible. As a rule, ventilation and moisture are the manufacturer's problems and he can safely be assumed to have solved them in a general way, so far as his machine is concerned, though there is always some opportunity for the operator to help in final adjustment. Incubators that are intended to meet any and all conditions under which they may be operated, generally are provided with comparatively large adjustable openings so that sufficient ventilation can be secured to meet all requirements of location and season. Some machines permit only the slightest adjustment in this respect, the amount of ventilation being fixed by the manufacturer at the point where best results will be secured under average conditions and during the natural hatching season. This plan has the advantage of simplifying the management of the machine and prevents extreme adjustments either way (a common mistake among beginners), but does not afford opportunity for meeting extreme or unusual requirements.

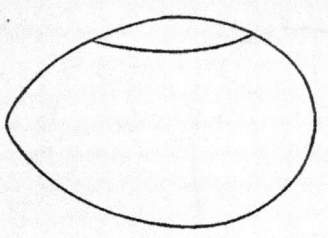

FIG. 61—AIR CELL ON SIDE OF EGG
This frequently occurs where the eggs have not been properly turned.

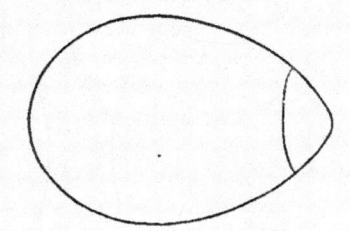

FIG. 62—EGG WITH AIR CELL IN SMALL END
When the air cell develops in the small end, the chick rarely hatches.

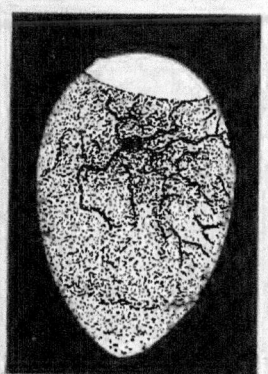

FIG. 58—APPEARANCE OF EMBRYO AFTER SEVEN DAYS OF INCUBATION
This diagram indicates the appearance of normal embryo after seven days, with outlines of germ center and blood vessels distinctly brought out. Compare with Fig. 54. Reproduced from Cornell University Reading Course, Bulletin No. 80.

As has already been explained, the egg contains all the moisture needed for the development of the embryo and for successful exclusion, and a liberal additional allowance to meet the natural loss from evaporation. It is essential that the normal rate of evaporation be maintained, and as this depends upon the circulation of air in the machine and the degree of moisture which the air contains, moisture and ventilation are closely associated together. Evaporation during the hatch varies rather widely with the season, and there is some disagreement among investigators in regard to what the normal loss of moisture should be. However, a reduction of about 13 per cent in the weight of the eggs from the first to the eighteenth day, may be taken as a safe average. While the degree of evaporation may be approximated by observing the development of the air cell, as already described, it may be followed much more accurately by weighing the eggs at regular intervals.

The beginner who has a reliable set of scales at hand and will weigh the eggs at regular intervals, for example on the 1st, 6th, 12th, and 18th days, will find it an easy matter to control the evaporation and keep it just where it should be, either by adjustment of ventilation or by supplying moisture. The evaporation from the eggs proceeds a little more rapidly as the hatch progresses, and should average about 3½ per cent the first 6 days, 4 to 4½ per cent from the 6th to the 12th day, and 5 per cent from the 12th to the 18th day. To get the percentage of evaporation, the net weight of the eggs without the tray should be used, and care must be taken that at the first weighing the tray shall be thoroughly dry, otherwise the evaporation from it will lead to error. The tray should be weighed before being filled with eggs, and its weight regularly deducted from each subsequent weighing.

By way of illustration, if 100 eggs weigh 200 ounces net, when placed in the machine, their weight at the end of the 6th day should be 192-3 ounces. At this time the eggs probably will be tested and the infertile ones removed after which they should be weighed again. If 20 infertiles are taken out this will reduce the net weight to perhaps 155 ounces. At the end of the 12th day the eggs should weigh about 6½ ounces less, leaving the total weight about 148½ ounces. If no eggs are taken out there will be a further loss of 5 per cent, by the end of the 18th day, or 7½ ounces, leaving the net weight about 141 ounces. If a few eggs are broken or removed for any cause, deduct their average weight to get the net weight of the remaining eggs, before taking the percentage.

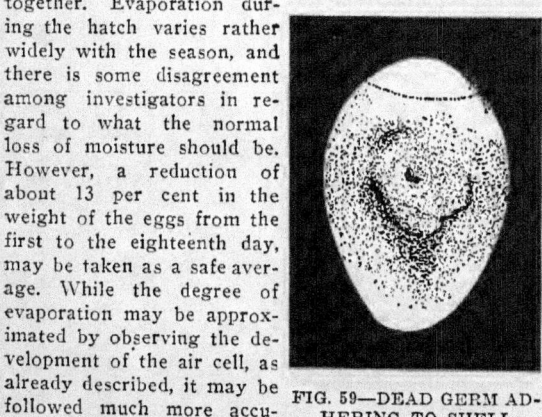

FIG. 59—DEAD GERM ADHERING TO SHELL
Germs that stick fast to the shell will develop for a short time but soon die, presenting an appearance similar to the above, when examined through the egg tester. Cornell University Reading Course, Bul. 80.

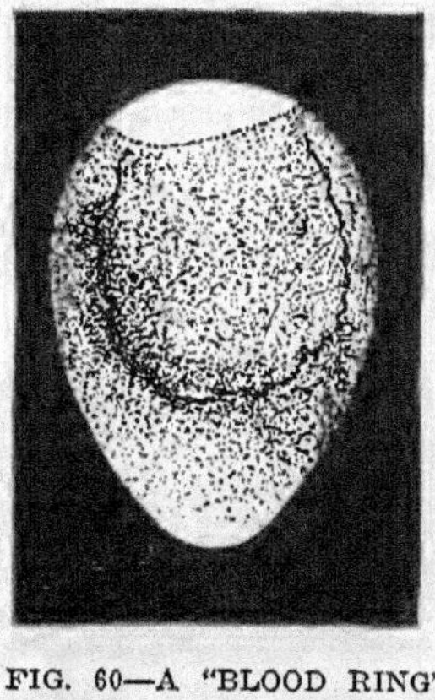

FIG. 60—A "BLOOD RING"
Germs that die during the first few days of incubation, particularly as the result of overheating, show more or less distinct "blood rings" when tested. Cornell University Reading Course. Bul. No. 80.

How Evaporation May Be Controlled

If at any stage of the hatch the evaporation is found running below the percentages just given, it must be increased by providing more ventilation and, if necessary, a slightly higher temperature in the machine, also by longer cooling periods. If the evaporation is running too high, it may be checked by reducing the ventilation or, if that is not desirable, by supplying moisture. The easiest and simplest way to do this, when it is possible, is to sprinkle the floor of the cellar in which the machine is being operated, or place pans or tubs of water under the

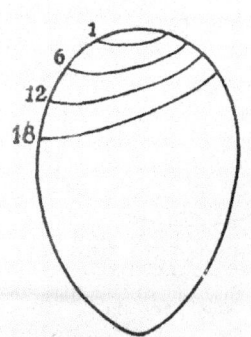

FIG. 63—DEVELOPMENT OF AIR CELL DURING INCUBATION

The average size of air cell at various stages of incubation is indicated in above diagram. Line marked 1, indicates average size in fresh eggs. Lines marked 6, 12 and 18 represent average size after a corresponding number of days of incubation. Size of air cell is controlled by ventilation and moisture.

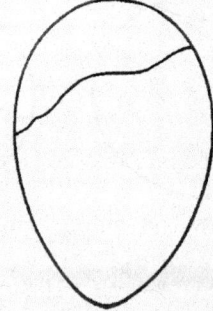

FIG. 64—EMBRYO READY TO BREAK THROUGH INTO AIR CELL

When the embryo has practically completed its development, or about the 19th to 20th day, it breaks through the membrane, separating it from the air cell, and occupies this space. The irregular line here shown is characteristic of appearance of egg before tester just before this occurs.

machine, using hot, steaming water if conditions demand it. Be governed in this by the directions of the manufacturer. If he specifies a particular way in which to supply moisture, be sure that there is a good reason for it and follow directions exactly. One method of regulating the evaporation of the eggs is by the use of a hygrometer (see Fig. 77). This instrument is designed to indicate the relative humidity of the air in the machine.

Ventilation is considered but little in the practical operation of incubators, aside from its influence on evaporation and moisture. When there is sufficient air circulation to dry the eggs down at the normal rate, there is little danger that there will be any deficiency in meeting the needs of the developing embryos for oxygen. Recent investigations at the Storrs (Conn.) Experiment Station indicate that while the amount of carbon dioxide (which is the usual basis of comparison in determining the purity of the air) is 3 parts in 10,000 volumes of fresh air, it is decidedly higher under the sitting hen and increases to 50 to 60 parts toward the end of the hatch.

In commercial incubators the proportion runs well below that found under hens. Even when the proportion of carbon dioxide is artificially increased much above what is regularly found in incubators or under hens, it does not appear to have any marked influence on the hatch until it reaches about 150 parts, so that the purity of air in the incubator need hardly concern the practical operator. As a matter of fact, the average incubator, instead of being deficient in ventilation, is more likely to afford too much, which is the chief reason for supplying moisture, this being done to offset the excessive evaporation that naturally accompanies a too rapid change of air.

As a rule, the danger of excess ventilation in incubators applies only to their operation in cold weather. In warm weather or in heated rooms the circulation of air is apt to be quite slow unless the machine is provided with unusually large ventilating openings.

Cooling An Aid to Ventilation

The necessity for cooling the eggs down each day during incubation is a much-debated point about which we have surprisingly little accurate information, considering how energetically the subject has been discussed. It is doubtful whether there is any advantage in cooling early in the season, and the practice generally results in a low average temperature, thus delaying the hatch. The general tendency is for early hatches to fall behind the normal rate of development at any rate, and cooling simply means further delay.

When the eggs are cooled down until they are cold to the touch, which may happen in a very short time in winter hatching, it will take two or three hours to bring them back to the right temperature again, and as a result the embryos will not get the required number of heat units unless the deficiency is made up by running the machine at a higher temperature. Merely turning the eggs probably gives them all the cooling they need under such conditions.

If cooling is to be practiced because it is the "natural way," it must be remembered that when the hen returns to the nest she can warm the eggs up in a very short time, through the application of contact heat, while the incubator is much slower, taking from one to three hours to do what the hen will do in half an hour or less. For this reason, cooling in artificial incubation must either be for a decidedly shorter time than under natural conditions, or the machine must run at a higher temperature in order to offset the slower heating up after returning the trays to the machine.

In warmer weather or where the machine is operated in a heated room there probably is a distinct advantage in regular daily cooling as a means of improving ventilation. In this case cooling may begin about the 6th or 7th day and should continue until the 18th. In a cool room the rule should be to leave the eggs out until they are lukewarm or neutral to the touch—that is, feeling neither cold nor warm. This rule will not apply in a warm room, however, where it might be necessary to leave the eggs out for an hour or two to bring them down to such a temperature, which is not at all desirable. In this case, cool for a few minutes only, at first, gradually increasing the time until the eggs are out 20 to 30 minutes near the end of the hatch. It seldom is desirable to leave them out for a longer time than this unless they have been overheated or are developing too rapidly as a result of a general high average temperature. In all cases keep the door of the incubator closed while the eggs are out, and do not expose them to drafts or currents of air. Under no condition should eggs be cooled if they are known to be underdeveloped for the stage of the hatch.

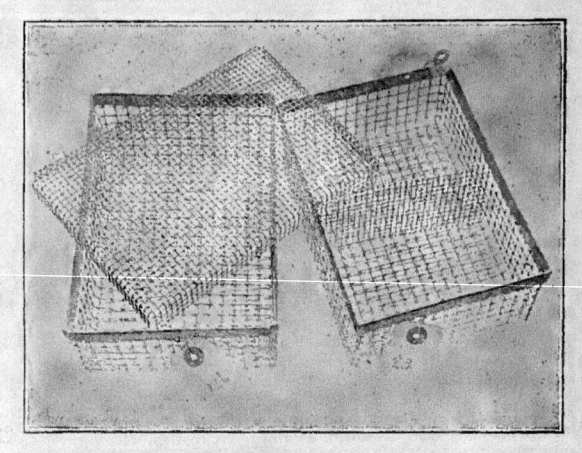

FIG. 65—PEDIGREE HATCHING BASKETS
Courtesy of Maine Exp. Station.

OPERATION OF INCUBATORS

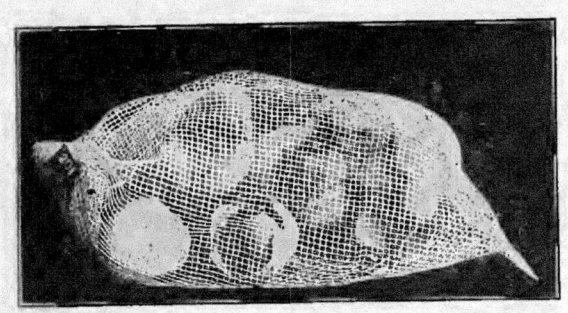

FIG. 66—MOSQUITO NETTING BAGS FOR PEDIGREE HATCHING
Courtesy of Kansas Experiment Station.

On the other hand, if they have been accidentally overheated, cool them down at once.

Bringing Out the Hatch

After the eighteenth day there is little that can be done by way of favorably influencing results. If at this time it appears that too much ventilation has been given, moisture may be supplied, and in most machines it is customary to use moisture regularly from this time until the end, doing this in the exact manner recommended by the manufacturer. No amount of supplied moisture can restore what has been taken from the eggs, but with plenty of humidity in the machine at hatching time, even chicks that have been dried down too much during the earlier stages of the hatch will have a fair chance to get out. If the eggs have not been dried down sufficiently, more ventilation can be supplied for a short time, but this must be done cautiously and promptly reduced to meet the manufacturer's instructions when the chicks begin to come out, otherwise there is danger that the air in the machine will be lacking in moisture. If the temperature has been too low, resulting in a delayed hatch, more heat may be given, and less if there appears to be danger of the chicks coming off too soon.

These last-minute adjustments however, offer at best only a choice of evils, and there is strong probability that more harm than good will be done by them. No matter how desirable it may appear to have provided more or less heat, moisture, ventilation, cooling, or whatever detail may have been improperly adjusted, it now is too late to do much by way of correcting conditions. Only slight changes may be made at this time; for the rest, it is necessary to accept the result, whatever it may be, and learn the lesson so well that there will be no danger of making the same mistake again.

The beginner must learn to keep cool in the face of poor hatches, and not let an obvious error, such as bringing off the chicks too soon, drying down too much, or any of the mistakes that may be made, lead him to go to the other extreme in the next hatch. He should remember that he is working with extremely narrow margins all along the line, and the result of any hatch is determined by comparatively slight adjustments or differences continued throughout the hatch. The common tendency to extremes in method must be avoided, whether applied to changes made during a single hatch, or in successive hatches.

In the case of pedigree hatching or where the chicks from different pens are to be hatched separately, the eggs, properly marked, may be mixed indiscriminately in the tray during incubation, but at the last turning they should be separated and placed in pedigree egg trays such as are supplied by the manufacturer of the incubator, or in small wire baskets such as are shown in Figs. 65 and 67. A still cheaper way is to use small bags of "mosquito bar" like those shown in Fig. 66. With any of these appliances the eggs must not be crowded, but must have plenty of room—much more than is necessary in regular hatchings, or the chicks will not be able to get out properly or will smother after they are out. If the trays are full of fertile eggs to be divided into different lots in this way, it will be necessary to have an empty machine warmed up and ready to help out at this time. It is useless to attempt subdividing eggs in full trays unless this is done. Where pedigree hatching is practiced it is not possible to use the nursery of course, and more careful attention must be given to the chicks, removing and marking them when they are well dried, and transferring them to baskets or other warm comfortable quarters. They must not be kept too long in the close quarters in which they were hatched.

When the eggs begin to pip or when the chicks are heard, which may be before pipping is observed, the machine must be put in order for the hatch and arranged so that it will not need to be opened again until the hatch is over, or practically so. If it has a nursery compartment the trays should have the trap side turned to the front, though the trap is to be left closed until the hatch is well underway. If the thermometer is of the contact type or is fastened to a loose stand it should be permanently fastened in place so that it cannot be knocked over. If the machine is regulated properly there will be little danger of the temperature getting far out of the way at this time, but it always is desirable to have the thermometer in position to refer to. With the chicks coming out lively, the temperature may run up to 104 or 105 degrees, but this will do no harm, and the regulator should not be interfered with unless the temperature goes above 105 degrees.

In incubators with nursery compartments the chicks may be allowed to drop down after about one-third of them are out, but until then they should be kept up on the trays. Nurseries are always lower in temperature than the egg trays, and the chicks are liable to get chilled if they are allowed to drop down before they are dry, and before there are enough of them out to keep each other warm. Many epidemics of so-called "white diarrhea" are caused by the chicks getting chilled in the nursery. Always keep them up, therefore, until the hatch is at least one-third over, then open the trap and let them find their way down gradually.

Avoid Overcrowding in the Nursery

It seldom is necessary or desirable to disturb the chicks while they are coming off, and opening the door and fussing with them should be avoided. In case the hatch is extra good, however, it may be necessary to remove some of the first chicks hatched, after they are thoroughly dry, in order to give the later ones a chance,

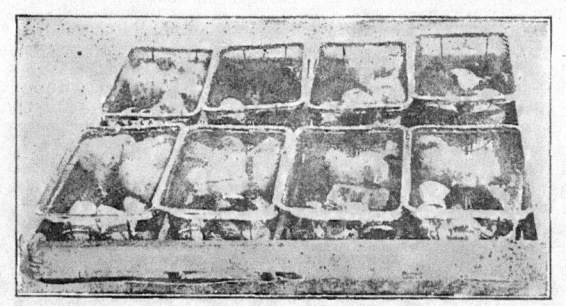

FIG. 67—CORN POPPERS USED IN PEDIGREE HATCHING
Courtesy of American School of Poultry Husbandry.

also to avoid injury to those that are out. If the machine is plainly overcrowded and the chicks are panting seriously (a little panting need not cause uneasiness), provide a warmly lined basket or tray such as is shown in Fig. 80, and remove enough to relieve the congestion. If the chicks are carefully covered and placed in a warm place they will in no way be injured, and the conditions in the machine will be much better for the chicks that are left and for those that are not yet out. Where this is done however, it should be remembered that removing a large number of chicks is liable to result in lowering the temperature, and the regulator may need to be readjusted to keep it up to normal.

In extra-good hatches, if none of the chicks are removed it will be necessary to throw the ventilators wide open, and possibly wedge the front door slightly open also, in order to supply sufficient air. It should be remembered that the requirements of chicks are greatly in excess of unhatched embryos. This extra ventilation will save those that are already hatched, but may make it increasingly difficult for the later ones to get out, as it will lower the temperature and dry the air, causing the chicks to stick in the shell. It is a good deal better to relieve the situation by taking out some of the strong-

When the incubator can be spared, it is better to leave the chicks in it for 24 hours, removing the trays as soon as hatching is over, to give the chicks more room and better air. At this time it generally is wise to give all the ventilation that the machine can supply. If the incubator must be reset at once the chicks can be taken out as soon as they are thoroughly dry and placed in baskets, trays, or day-old-chick shipping boxes, where they should remain for about 24 hours, or they can be taken directly from the incubator to the brooder if it is ready, thoroughly warmed, and regulated.

Burn or bury all dead chicks, kill the cripples, if any, and include them in the burning, also the eggs that did not hatch. The empty shells, however, may be pounded up and fed to the laying hens. Clean and disinfect the machine thoroughly before resetting it. Brush out all dust and down, scrub the trays and burlap frames, if any, using a good disinfecting solution, with which also the entire inner surface of the machine should be sprayed or scrubbed. Any good coal tar disinfectant may be used for this purpose, or a home-made preparation if preferred. The regulator must be reset and the machine operated long enough to be sure that it is correctly adjusted before it can be considered ready for next hatch.

PURDUE UNIVERSITY EXPERIMENT STATION
DEPARTMENT OF POULTRY HUSBANDRY
INCUBATOR REPORT

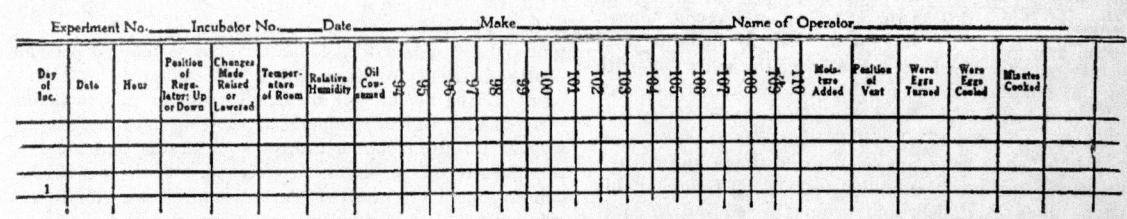

Experiment No.____ Incubator No.____ Date____ Make____ Name of Operator____

FIG. 68—A WELL PLANNED RECORD BLANK FOR THE INCUBATOR OPERATOR

The temperature record on the sheet is kept by drawing a line from reading to reading, giving a "curve" that shows in the plainest manner the fluctuations of temperature. The sheet—only a part of which is here shown—provides for 23 numbers, three lines being allowed to each number. After figure 6 are the words "Test eggs first time," after 13, "Test eggs second time," after 20, "Note hour when first chick hatched," after 21, "Note hour when through hatching," after 23, "Date and hour when chicks were removed from machine." Below that are blanks for final report, as follows:

FINAL REPORT

No. eggs put in ____ —Per cent fertile eggs to total eggs____
No. eggs infertile ____ —Per cent dead germs to fertile eggs____
No. eggs with dead germs ____ —Per cent dead-in-shell to fertile eggs____
No. eggs broken ____ —Per cent crippled chicks to fertile eggs____
No. chicks dead in shell ____ —Per cent vigorous chicks to fertile eggs____
No. crippled chicks ____ —Per cent vigorous chicks to total eggs____
No. vigorous chicks ____ —Per cent vigorous chicks to egg in machine
Remarks: after second test ____

est, doing this as quickly as possible, however, without keeping the incubator door open long or permitting the chicks that are removed to get chilled. Those that are taken out in advance of the rest of the hatch must be kept covered (not too closely) and in a warm place. As a rule they will do better if treated in this way than when placed directly in a brooder, no matter how comfortably it may be heated.

Cleaning Up the Hatch

When the hatch is about over the eggs should be examined, and if any are covered by large sections of empty shells these should be removed to be sure that no chicks are thus imprisoned and prevented from getting out. If a few are stuck in the shells, they may be helped out. Chicks that are not able to get out without assistance seldom are worth bothering with, but there are sufficient exceptions to the rule to encourage some to give the little extra attention which may be sufficient to save them. The best way to help chicks out of the shell is first to raise the temperature, which nearly always drops below normal when the chicks are practically all out and down in the nursery. Then get the "stickers" together and cover them with a flannel cloth wrung out of water about as hot as the hands will stand it. Do not cover the eggs tightly, but lay a single thickness of cloth over them. If they have stuck on account of a lack of humidity in the machine this will enable them to get out. If their failure to hatch is due to actual weakness it is not worth while to do anything more for them, as they will not live even if they do get out.

Day-to-Day Details of Incubator Operation

By way of putting the everyday details of incubator management in simple consecutive order, the following daily schedule is suggested. With such a definite schedule before him the beginner will be able to plan ahead a little and to know what is coming before he reaches it. In this schedule it is assumed that the hatch will be so handled as to have it come off on the morning of the twenty-first day. If for any reason the hatch is earlier or later than this the details of operation must be modified accordingly.

First Day—Set the machine in the forenoon, adjusting the ventilation exactly as directed by the manufacturer. Always test new thermometers before using them, and old ones at the beginning of each season. If a suspended thermometer is used, measure the distance between the bulb and the bottom of the egg tray, and if this is not as the manufacturer says it should be, stop right there until the error is corrected. Do not go to bed the first night until certain that the temperature is stationary at the right point. Sometimes the thermometer will register accurately for days with the machine running empty, but when the eggs are put in it may run up a little.

Second Day—Look at the thermometer a few times and fill and trim the lamp in the evening, doing this, if possible, about six or seven o'clock, so that when the last inspection for the day is made at bedtime the final adjustment of the flame can be safely made for the night. If there is reason to believe that the room temperature will drop much, turn the flame a little higher than would

OPERATION OF INCUBATORS

be necessary to maintain the temperature at time of adjustment, depending on the regulator to take care of the surplus heat until it is needed along towards morning.

Third Day—Turn the eggs in the morning, and put them back into the machine without any unnecessary delay. From this time on turn regularly morning and night till the chicks begin to pip.

Fourth and Fifth Days—No special attention required on these days aside from the regular daily care.

Sixth Day—This is the best time for testing when the machine is filled in the regular way with either white or brown-shelled eggs, especially if the eggs are to be weighed to determine the percentage of evaporation. Eggs with rings around the embryos are dead, the cause being either weak germs, or too high temperature in the machine. Take out the infertiles and feed them to young

rect mistakes along these lines if not too serious. If the hatch is progressing as it should, it will do no harm to begin cooling down once a day, even if the weather is cool, unless there is reason to believe that the germs are a little behind in development, in which case do no cooling at all. Never cool more than once a day under ordinary conditions.

Thirteenth to Seventeenth Days—Nothing but regular duties for these days, but watch for the temperature to creep up as animal heat increases and readjust the regulator accordingly. Test a few eggs every day to keep in touch with the development of the embryos.

Eighteenth Day—This is about the last chance to correct any conditions that may need attention. Test the eggs again, unless the chicks can be heard peeping in the shell or some of the eggs are pipped. If appearance

INCUBATOR RECORD

INCUBATOR No.......... MAKE .... SIZE ....DATE SET .... OBSERVER............. ....

TEMPERATURE OF INCUBATOR

DATE / DAY OF INCUBATION	0	1	2	3	4	5	6	7	8	9	10	11	12	13	14	15	16	17	18	19	20	21	22
MORNING																							
NOON																							
EVENING																							

TEMPERATURE OF ROOM

MORNING																							
NOON																							
EVENING																							

HUMIDITY OF INCUBATOR

MORNING																							
NOON																							
EVENING																							

HUMIDITY OF ROOM

MORNING																							
NOON																							
EVENING																							

EGGS COOLED—MINUTES

MORNING																							

FERTILITY AND HATCHABILITY

NO. SET	INF.	FERT.	% FERT.	DEAD 1ST TEST	DEAD 2ND TEST	DEAD 3RD TEST	DEAD HATCH	CRIPPLED CHICKS	EGGS BROKEN	STRONG CHICKS	

FIG. 69—COMPLETE HATCHING AND BREEDING RECORD AS USED AT OHIO STATE UNIVERSITY
Incubator operators who keep accurate records as are provided for on this sample blank, will have at the end of the hatching season information in regard to their hatching and brooding operations that should prove invaluable to them. Record keeping requires some time and attention, but the operator will be amply repaid for his pains by the better and more certain results that he will be able to secure.

chicks or adult hens. They are just as good for the fowls as so much meat scrap.

Seventh Day—In mild weather begin cooling now, leaving the eggs out until they are lukewarm—that is, neither warm nor cold to the touch. In warm weather leave them out about 10 minutes and then return them to the machine whether they are lukewarm or not.

Eighth and Ninth Days—No special attention aside from cooling and regular daily care.

Tenth and Eleventh Days—About this time, if the embryos are developing as they should, look for the temperature to run up a little. This is due to the increasing animal heat in the egg, and the regulator must be changed to take care of it. Turning the flame a little lower will not answer. From this time on it will be necessary to be on the watch for rising temperature and readjust the regulator from time to time to take care of it.

Twelfth Day—Weigh the eggs or test them, to determine whether they are drying down as they should; also note whether the germs are developing properly. If too much ventilation has been given, begin supplying moisture according to the book of directions that accompanies the machine. If the air cells are too small, give more ventilation, and if the germs are a little behind in development, increase the heat. There is time yet to cor-

of the embryos as observed through the tester, indicates that the temperature or ventilation has not been correct, a little can be done to remedy matters, but not much. It is unwise to attempt to make any marked change at this time.

Nineteenth Day—Turn as usual, if there are no chicks pipping, but do no more cooling. Turn the eggs and get them back into the machine as quickly as possible. If pipping has begun, do not disturb the eggs at all, but be sure that the trap in the egg tray is next the door.

Twentieth Day—The chicks should be coming out briskly about the end of the twentieth day. Keep the flame up to normal and don't worry about the temperature. If the machine has a nursery compartment do not open the trap to let the chicks down until at least a third of them are out.

Twenty-First Day—The chicks should be all out and down in the nursery dry, before the end of the 21st day. If they are a little late coming out give them more time. Chicks may be lively and strong even if a day late, though generally they are not. As soon as the chicks are all out remove the trays to give them more room. Clean up the incubator as soon as the chicks are taken out and thoroughly disinfect it, whether it is to be reset at once or not.

CHAPTER VI

Mistakes in Artificial Incubating

Common Mistakes Made in Buying, Setting Up and Operating Incubators—Mistakes Made in Taking Off the Hatch— Special Details of Operation That Should Prove Helpful to All Incubator Users in Preventing Serious Errors and the Losses Occasioned by Them

SUCCESSFUL operation of incubators is a comparatively simple and easy matter as long as the beginner confines himself to the general directions accompanying his machine, coupling with these a careful consideration of the detailed information in Chapter V. of this book, which is designed to meet special conditions and to make it possible for the operator, however inexperienced, to have an intelligent understanding of the reasons for doing or not doing certain things, rather than blindly to "follow directions." As a rule, trouble is experienced only when the operator commences to experiment, to listen to the suggestions of local advisers who have had little or no experience with his particular type of machine, or to indulge in the common practice of "taking chances" and "cutting corners."

It is not the purpose of this chapter to try to point out all the mistakes that the beginner may make, when he embarks upon this course. That would be an endless task. It is much simpler and easier to learn the few, essential details of correct operation than to attempt to learn the innumerable incorrect practices that must be avoided. Experience has shown however, that there are some particular errors into which the beginner is very apt to fall, even when trying hard to do things right, and to these it seems that some special attention should be paid or added emphasis be given regarding their danger, even though they may already have been mentioned briefly in the preceding chapter.

Getting the Incubator Too Late in the Season

The best and most profitable chicks, and generally the easiest ones to raise, are those that are hatched early. For this reason the incubator should be on hand well in advance of the time when it will be needed. There are almost certain to be delays in getting the incubator if it is ordered direct from the manufacturer during the busy season. If bought from an agent he may not have the right kind or size in stock unless arrangements have been made well in advance. There may be some missing or broken parts when the machine is uncrated, or various things may happen to interfere with getting it set up and properly adjusted.

All of these possible sources of delay should be considered, and discounted by ordering in ample time. One of the commonest causes of disappointment and loss among beginners is this delay in getting the machine and the consequent haste to get it started which results in setting it before it is properly adjusted, or without giving it a thorough preliminary tryout. Keeping the eggs waiting while the empty machine is being tested and adjusted, appears to be too much for the average person's self-control. Avoid this danger by getting the machine early.

Failure to Set Up and Adjust Correctly

A surprisingly large number of persons fail to meet the conditions of success in this obviously important detail. Some do not read the instructions in regard to setting up, and try to "puzzle out" for themselves the use and location of parts, the assembling of which is fully explained in the directions that accompany the machine and on whose exact adjustments its proper working depends. Many do not read the description of the machine with sufficient care to know whether it is set up right or not. And others may even know that it is not correctly adjusted but blindly hope to operate it successfully any way.

The various parts of the incubator MUST be connected up properly and adjusted to work exactly as they should, or trouble is bound to ensue. This is not a thing that should call for argument or explanation; it is an imperative requirement. It is not necessary to take chances or to guess, and there is no excuse for doing so. The operator can readily know whether his machine is set up correctly or not, and unless he does know this before placing eggs in it he has only himself to blame if results are not satisfactory.

Locating Incubator Where Ventilation is Poor

It is useless to expect good results if the machine is located where ventilation is deficient and where lamp fumes cannot be got rid of. A cellar with tightly closed doors and with the windows banked to keep things from freezing, also rooms that are small and close, are not suitable locations for incubators. The actual requirements of the embryos for fresh air are quite small, but the incubator lamp uses a great deal of oxygen in a day's

FIG. 70—A "FAIR" HATCH
The difference between a fair hatch and a first-class one, such as is illustrated in Fig. 71, is chiefly a matter of careful attention to details all along the line from the selection of the fowls in the breeding pen to the management of the incubator.

FIG. 71—AN EXCELLENT HATCH
There is no mystery and but little "luck" about getting good hatches. The careful, painstaking operator with a standard machine and good eggs can regularly get large hatches, and his profits will be much greater than with the merely "fair" kind such as shown in Fig. 70.

MISTAKES IN ARTIFICIAL INCUBATING

time and gives off a large volume of poisonous fumes which are certain to cause trouble unless ventilation is free enough to reduce the proportion of lamp fumes to a harmless percentage. Incubators can be operated in comparatively small rooms or where there is only a limited amount of ventilation if the lamp fumes are conducted out of the room by means of suitable pipes.

FIG. 72.
A SIMPLE EGG TESTER

Operating Without Instructions

This mistake is especially common among those who purchase used or second-hand incubators with which they have had no previous experience, and attempt to run them without the manufacturer's book of directions. No matter how successful the operator may have been with other makes he needs the manufacturer's instructions for each type of machine used, and it is simply inviting trouble to attempt to operate without them. No one need hesitate to write to the manufacurer for directions, when these are missing for any reason, and if a charge is made for supplying them the sum demanded will be but a small one and should be cheerfully paid.

Irregular Hours for the Work

There should be regular hours for caring for the machine, morning and evening, and these should be rigidly adhered to. The two periods should divide the day as evenly as possible without interfering with other duties. A good time in the evening is just before or after supper. At this time the eggs should be turned and the lamp filled and trimmed, giving time for the eggs to get warmed up before the last visit at bedtime, when the flame can be finally adjusted for the night. In the morning there will be nothing to do but turn the eggs, as a rule, and if the thermometer is looked at again at noon there will be little danger of the temperature getting much out of the way between times.

Lack of Conveniences for the Work

Wherever the machine is located, it pays to fix things up conveniently for doing the work. The chief function of the incubator is to save time, either directly or indirectly, and the practical operator will try to save all he can by installing suitable facilities for tending it. If the machine is of the type that does not have a clear top on which to place the trays, provide a table or large box of proper height. If the eggs are turned by shuffling, the small tray illustrated in Fig. 52 will be found a real necessity. Arrange a convenient place for the oil can and a funnel for filling the lamp, and do this work over a small box or pan containing planer shavings or other absorbent material so that if any oil is spilled it will not soil anything or saturate the floor. It is much more convenient to use an oil can with a faucet in the bottom, than one from which the oil must be poured.

Using Undesirable Eggs

One of the reasons why the sitting hen often has more chicks to her credit proportionately than the incubator is that when there are only a few eggs to be set they are carefully selected and only the ones that are most suitable for the purpose are used. In filling incubators however, especially when there is room in the machine for the entire available supply, many eggs are used that cannot possibly hatch. All eggs that are abnormally large or small, or that are rough, thin-shelled or otherwise defective, such as those having spiral marks (see Fig. 57), transparent spots, etc., should be discarded, even if it is necessary to operate the machine with the trays partially filled. It is better to waste space than eggs.

Flame Too High

When leaving the machine for the night the flame ordinarily should be turned high enough to provide an excess of heat that will hold the damper open a little—usually about one-eighth of an inch, though this will depend somewhat on the style of machine. With this excess heat the regulator can take care of a sudden drop in the temperature or if it should get warmer instead, will still be able to dispose of the extra heat without trouble. Too much should not be demanded of any regulator, however. This delicate device as made for practically all standard machines is remarkably efficient, but should not be expected to control wide extremes in temperature. When the flame is turned entirely too high the surplus heat will exceed the regulator's capacity to divert or waste it, resulting in the egg chamber becoming overheated, and this may happen with the finest regulator made. Another objection to an extremely high flame is that it is a wasteful use of fuel, adding unnecessarily to the cost of operating the machine; also, with a high flame the danger of a smoking or overheated lamp is greatly increased.

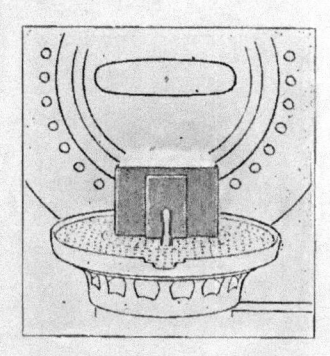

FIG. 73—HOW TO TRIM LAMP WICKS
The corners of the wick must be rounded off as here indicated, to get an ideal flame. Wicks will burn this way naturally with a little attention.

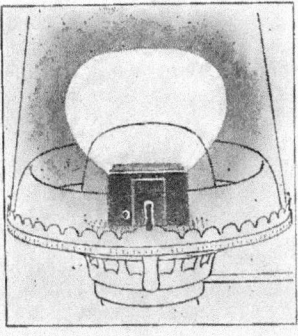

FIG. 74—IDEAL LAMP FLAME
Flame shaped as here illustrated will give the greatest amount of heat and may be turned quite high without danger of smoking. Such a flame is secured by trimming the wick as shown in Fig. 73.

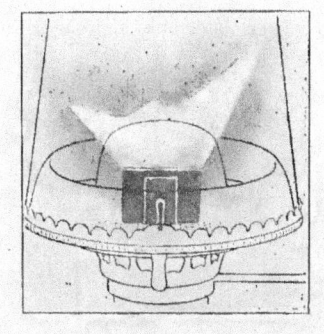

FIG. 75—IMPROPER TRIMMING OF WICKS
If the corners of the wicks are not properly rounded off, the flame will be sharp cornered and will smoke and form dangerous deposits of soot. Such a flame will supply comparatively little heat.

Flame Too Low

With a low flame there will not be sufficient heat to keep the temperature up to the desired point if there should be a marked drop in the room temperature, which is especially apt to occur during the night. Unless there is a certainty of a rising temperature there should always be some surplus heat. In a good cellar, and with a well-insulated machine, it often is possible to run through an entire hatch without any special adjustment of the flame, the regulator being depended on to take care of all variations in temperature that may arise. In above-ground rooms where the temperature fluctuates widely from day to day, and with imperfectly insulated machines, frequent readjustments of the flame will be required.

Making Changes in Equipment of Incubator

A good deal of trouble grows out of the too common practice of making changes in the equipment of the machine, or using nonstandard parts, such as thermometers, lamps, burners, diaphragms, etc. Sometimes this is done as a matter of convenience, the regular parts not being at hand, and sometimes merely to save a few pennies when the standard parts happen to cost a trifle more than substitutes. This practice is usually a most short-sighted kind of economy, the losses in a single hatch often amounting to more than the entire cost of every regular part needing replacement.

It is safe to assume that the manufacturer has chosen the equipment for his machine with the greatest care, and after most expensive tests. He often has good reasons for using certain articles, and it is the part of wisdom to take advantage of the other fellow's experience. Especially in the case of incubators using diaphragms, it ought not to be necessary to explain that the manufacturer uses certain materials because he finds it important to do so, and the substitution of other fabric having different properties, may result in highly unsatisfactory results.

Using Untested Thermometers

The average incubator thermometer is accurate and reliable, but there are enough of the other sort to make it important that every one be tested before being placed in active service. Once in a while a defective thermometer may get past the inspector; still more frequently they are damaged in shipment through the breaking or separating of the mercury column in the tubes, and any thermometer that has stood for some months is apt to change through the seasoning of the glass. Take no chances, but be sure that the thermometer registers correctly before starting the hatch.

Thermometer Not in Correct Position

A great deal depends upon having the thermometer in the position in which it is designed to be operated, and as there are several types with directions necessarily modified for each, there is more or less confusion here. A suspended thermometer is intended to hang with the bulb at a certain specified distance from the bottom of the egg tray. If the wrong hanger is used or it is not hooked properly in place the bulb may be too low or too high, the wrong temperature at the egg level being secured in either case. Such thermometers are apt to be pushed up when the trays are removed or replaced, and if they do not swing freely may remain in this position and, of course, will not then register correctly. It is immaterial what style is used, provided the thermometer is operated in the position intended and the temperature adjusted accordingly.

Contact thermometers can be placed with the bulb on top of an egg, but are more apt to slip down so that they rest between two eggs and touching both, with a corresponding difference in

FIG. 76—KEROSENE LAMP AND PASTEBOARD BOX FOR EGG TESTING
Anyone who has a small handlamp can readily arrange a homemade tester in the manner here indicated. Provide a good-sized opening in the lid (on the back) to admit air to lamp, and at top to let hot air escape. Reproduced from Bul. 172 of Oregon Exp. Station.

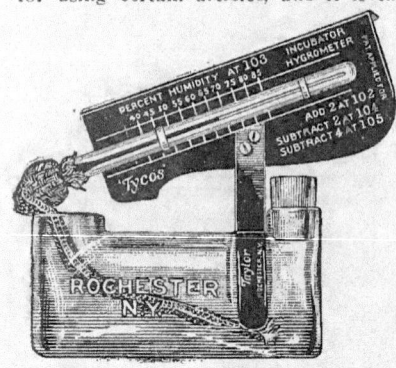

FIG. 77—HYGROMETER
This instrument is used in measuring the degree of humidity in the egg chamber. Courtesy of Taylor Instrument Companies.

FIG. 78—ELECTRIC LIGHT AND PASTEBOARD BOX USED AS AN EGG TESTER
Reproduced from Bul. 172 of Oregon Experiment Station

MISTAKES IN ARTIFICIAL INCUBATING

temperature. There also are three distinct positions for standing thermometers; between and touching two eggs; on a level with top of egg but not touching; half an inch above top of egg. There may be as much as two degrees difference in the reading of the thermometers in these different positions—which fact ought to make it clear that the manufacturer's directions and the particular style of thermometer for which the directions are given, should be rigidly adhered to.

Too High Temperature At Start

It is quite important to avoid too high temperatures at the beginning of the incubation period. The practice of starting at a relatively low temperature and gradually increasing as the hatch progresses, has the indorsement of most practical operators, where contact or low standing thermometers are used. There is no question about the fact that the embryo is much more apt to be injured by high temperatures during the first few days, and if the incubator cannot be depended upon to maintain exactly the desired temperature it is better to be on the safe side by running a trifle low. But do not forget that any departure from the correct temperature, either high or low, must be offset by an equivalent increase or decrease later on.

Failure to Average the Temperature

Attention has been called in the preceding chapter to the error that the careful operator is liable to fall into, of regarding the normal incubation temperature as the maximum rather than the average which he should secure. This results in many persons habitually running a little below the proper temperature, or while they may hold to the exact temperature, as a rule (103 degrees for example), they are slower about correcting the temperature when it falls below that point than when it happens to exceed it, and in any case they fail to offset low temperatures by running correspondingly higher later on. Either way the practical result is an average temperature just that much below the correct one, which means a delayed hatch. This is one of the principal reasons why most hatches made by beginners are slow in coming off, often disastrously so. There is danger in high temperatures, it is true, but the cumulative effect of running a trifle below normal for long periods, may prove to be just as unfavorable in the final result.

FIG. 79—EGG CARTON SUITABLE FOR KEEPING HATCHING EGGS

Failure to Adjust for Animal Heat

If there were no animal heat generated by the developing embryo, any good incubator favorably located and properly adjusted should run through the hatch without the slightest variation. As the embryo develops however, it begins to generate heat, and about the tenth day the thermometer is liable to take a jump upward as a result of this. This rise is not as sudden as it appears, but it takes close watching to detect it at first and the average operator is apt to be conscious of it for the first time when he finds the thermometer running a degree or so above what it should be. The animal heat will continue to increase in a normal hatch right up to the end, and must be taken care of by readjusting the regulator as often as necessary.

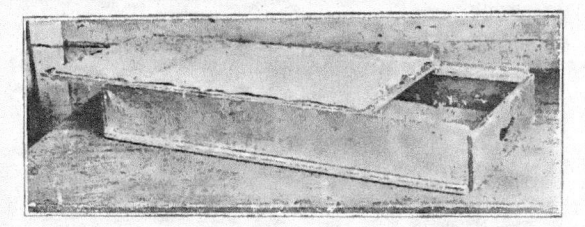

FIG. 80—BOX FOR MOVING CHICKS FROM INCUBATOR
Photo from Cornell University.

Failure to Test the Eggs

The beginner may find it difficult to learn much at first about the development of the embryo, but if he will persist in using the tester, examining all the eggs at regular periods as directed in the previous chapter, and making almost daily tests with a few, he will find that it is possible to follow the growth of the embryos with a good degree of certainty, and the ability to do this will prove of great value to him if he is going to produce chicks in large numbers. It is scarcely worth while to go through the motions of being a chick raiser if such opportunities for making oneself proficient in the work are to be ignored or neglected.

Failure to Examine Eggs During the Hatch

The beginner can make no better use of some of the eggs in his first hatches than to break a few for examination from time to time during the hatch, after first having examined them through the tester. Do this not only with infertile eggs and dead germs, but with some containing live germs also. It may be possible to get good hatches without having a clear understanding of how normal incubation progresses, but the chances of uniform success are greatly improved by such knowledge, and no earnest operator will neglect any reasonable opportunity to learn all that he can. A few living embryos sacrificed in this way will be repaid a hundred times over in the better hatches realized later on. It will prove especially helpful if, in doing this, a careful record is kept of the appearance of the embryos at different stages of incubation, both before the tester and when the shells are broken.

Neglecting the Lamp

When the lamp has been running along for several

FIG. 87—A CASE OF HATCHING EGGS
Where eggs in large number are to be held for hatching, about the most convenient way of handling them is to put them in regular shipping cases. So packed they will be protected from evaporation, mold, etc., and can readily be turned if necessary.

days without any irregularity, as incubator lamps often will do, the beginner is apt to feel that he can safely take some liberties with it, such as letting it run an extra day without filling, omitting to trim the wick, neglecting to wipe the oil off the top of the lamp bowl, etc. It is just this slacking up in care that makes nine-tenths of all lamp troubles. The work of caring for the lamp should be arranged in a regular schedule, to be followed day after day with unfailing regularity. With a lamp bowl of sufficient size it will not be necessary to fill it every day, or even every other day; but there must be some regular period for doing so, otherwise it is only a matter of time until it will be neglected one day too long and a spoiled hatch may be the result.

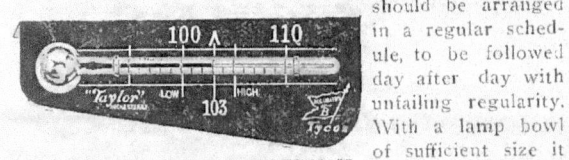

FIG. 82—SUSPENDED THERMOMETER
Designed to be suspended by a wire loop and as a rule is located with the bulb about one-half inch above the top of the eggs. Courtesy of Taylor Instrument Companies.

Importance of Daily Trimming

With practically all oil-burning lamps, the wick must be trimmed every day, and in cold weather it often is necessary to trim twice a day. It is never safe to let the wick get covered with a heavy scale. Especially where low-grade oil is used, a heavy scale or char will cover the end of the wick and the air tube in a comparatively short time, and an attempt to adjust the flame with the wick in this condition is liable to result in a smoking flame. It does not require much attention to keep the wick clean and the flame burning brightly, and failure to do this is inexcusable.

Using Defective Burners

The average brass burner is made of pretty thin material and is easily bent out of shape. It requires but a small dent in the top of the burner or in the wick tube, to make the flame burn unevenly or to have the wick stick or drag on one side. Do not try to repair burners

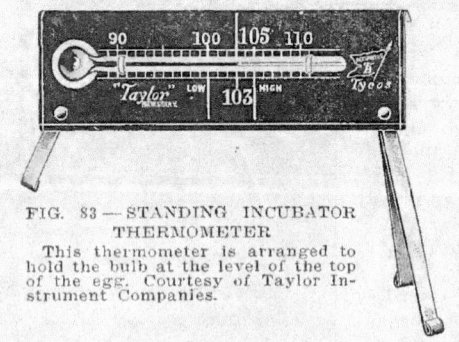

FIG. 83—STANDING INCUBATOR THERMOMETER
This thermometer is arranged to hold the bulb at the level of the top of the egg. Courtesy of Taylor Instrument Companies.

that are seriously damaged. They are not expensive, and it is cheaper to buy new ones than to take chances with an old one that is not working right. In all cases of smoky lamps the burner should be carefully examined.

Extra Parts Should Be Kept On Hand

One of the most common and least excusable mistakes made by beginners is failure to keep a supply of extra parts on hand for emergencies. It costs only a small sum to provide an extra thermometer, a burner, a lamp bowl, a few wicks, and an extra set of cloth diaphragms for machines requiring them. It is a good plan to have an extra connecting rod for the regulator, also, and a wafer for the thermostat if the machine uses that type of regulator. With these extras on hand there will be no danger of spoiling a hatch while waiting for a new part to replace one that has been accidentally broken or otherwise damaged.

Turning the Eggs Must Not Be Neglected

From the time turning begins until it is discontinued the eggs should be turned twice daily. Not once, nor three times, nor now and then, but twice, and at regular hours. Nothing should be allowed to interfere with this. More frequent turning will do no harm, it is true, and in warm weather, when the circulation of air in the machine is liable to be sluggish it may prove decidedly helpful. But under all ordinary conditions twice a day is sufficient, and regularity is about as important as the turning itself.

Turning Eggs With Oily Fingers

A very little kerosene on the shell will kill the embryo and fingers that are oily from handling the lamp will soon supply enough to do this. It usually is most convenient to turn the eggs in the evening at the time

FIG. 84.—MAGIC EGG TESTER
This device is intended to indicate the hatching strength of eggs before incubation—doing so by specific gravity test. Egg is slipped into the wire holder and placed in water, as above illustrated. The manufacturer states that first-class hatching eggs will always pull the tester down as in No. 1, while those of inferior quality will float higher in the water, as in No. 2. Courtesy of Magic Egg Tester Company.

the lamp is filled and trimmed, and to be on the safe side it is advisable to make it a rule always to turn the eggs before the lamp is touched.

Neglecting to Turn and Shift the Trays

The trays should be turned end for end each day and if there are two trays in the machine they should be shifted from side to side daily. There is no machine made that will not show some variation in temperature in different parts of the egg chamber, and some of them show a good deal. If this variation is not too great, and if the trays are turned and shifted as suggested, the inequality will be equalized and the eggs should hatch uniformly in all parts of the machine.

Opening the Door After the Chicks Begin to Hatch

Opening the incubator door causes changes in temperature, moisture, etc., in the egg chamber, and should be avoided as far as possible. With a little forethought

MISTAKES IN ARTIFICIAL INCUBATING

FIG. 85—STANDARD-BRED PEN OF WHITE WYANDOTTES
To secure hatching eggs of uniform character—an important factor in successful incubation—the fowls that lay the eggs must be uniform in breeding. With high-class standard-bred fowls like the pen illustrated above, good results are practically insured. This pen of White Wyandottes won first prize at Madison Square in 1919, and is the property of J. S. Martin.

everything that will need to be done from the time the chicks begin to pip until they are practically all out can be attended to at the last turning. At this time, if the machine has a nursery the trays should be placed with the traps next the door. If moisture is to be supplied during the hatch, the thermometer fastened in position so that it cannot be overturned by the chicks, or any other changes made, now is the time to attend to it. Then when the chicks begin to pip the door can be shut and the chicks left alone.

Get the Chicks All Out

As contrasted with the person who is so anxious to help that he does much harm by untimely interference, there is the other extreme in the operator who leaves the chicks entirely to themselves, in the belief that any that cannot get out without help are not worth saving. This is true when the inability to get out is due to inherent weakness, but not when the chick sticks for some purely accidental reason. It often happens that some fail to get out for some simple reason, though they would live and grow as well as any of their fellows if they could have a little timely assistance. The practical incubator operator will see to it that if any are stuck in the shell toward the end of the hatch, they have a chance for their lives, supplying some added moisture or heat or possibly helping them to break the shells.

Overcrowding in the Incubator

The average incubator does not have sufficient room for all the chicks that can be hatched in it if the trays are practically full of fertile eggs and they nearly all hatch. A chick requires more room than the egg from which it comes and when an extra good hatch is secured they are liable to be overcrowded. It is highly injurious for chicks to be packed in the incubator to the point where they become overheated, and half suffocated, and when there is danger of this condition existing it is necessary to remove some of the first arrivals. It is better to do this than to try to afford relief by excessive ventilation which will dry out the air and make it impossible for the last chicks to hatch at all.

Taking Chicks Out Too Soon

Removing the chicks from the incubator as soon as hatched may be necessary for the reasons already suggested, but this step should be regarded as the lesser of two evils and should be taken with great care. Never do it unless it is clearly necessary. There is no better place for chicks the first day after hatching than in the nursery of the incubator. In any event, never take chicks from the machine that are not thoroughly dry, and do not remove too many at one time. As soon as the hatch is over and the chicks dry the trays should be removed, which will give the chicks more room and better air, and then supply all the ventilation possible. If the regular ventilation of the machine is not sufficient to keep the chicks from panting, wedge the door open—but be governed in this by the instructions of the manufacturer. Some machines are apt to be drafty with the door open.

Letting the Chicks Get Chilled in Moving Them

In removing chicks from the incubator, extreme precautions must be taken to prevent their getting chilled, which may happen even in comparatively warm weather. Directions for taking off the hatch are given in the preceding chapter and these instructions should be carefully followed. In cold rooms, only a few should be taken out at one time, not only for their own sake but for the protection of those left in the machine, as the temperature will drop quickly when the door is open. If the brooder is not ready, or if it does not have a reliable regulator, it will be better to leave the chicks in a basket or in day-old-chick boxes for a day or so. If they are kept in a warm place they will be comfortable and will get hardened a little before they are transferred to the brooder.

Leaving the Machine Without Cleaning

Immediately after the hatch is taken off the machine should be thoroughly cleaned, whether another hatch is to be started at once or not. Never store a machine away at the end of the season until it is cleaned and disinfected. Empty the lamp bowl, throw away the old wick and put a new one in the burner, and if there are any parts on top of the machine that are liable to be disturbed, such as regulator arm, connecting rod, etc., these should be removed and placed inside the machine. Then it will be in condition to go over to the next season without suffering any injury, and be ready for use again on short notice.

The Biggest Mistake of All

Right here, after all serious mistakes of the incubation period have been successively avoided and a big hatch of sturdy, vigorous chicks secured, the biggest mistake of all often is made. This is the failure to provide suitable brooding facilities for the chicks. By "suitable" is meant a brooder that is well made, that will supply enough heat to keep the chicks warm under any condition that must be met, that can be regulated with a good degree of accuracy, and that provides sufficient capacity to brood the chicks without crowding. It is useless to hatch chicks at all unless they can be kept under reasonably favorable conditions afterwards. Poor brooders, or not enough of them, cause the loss of enormous numbers of chicks every season. Whatever other mistakes are made, at least let somebody else make this one.

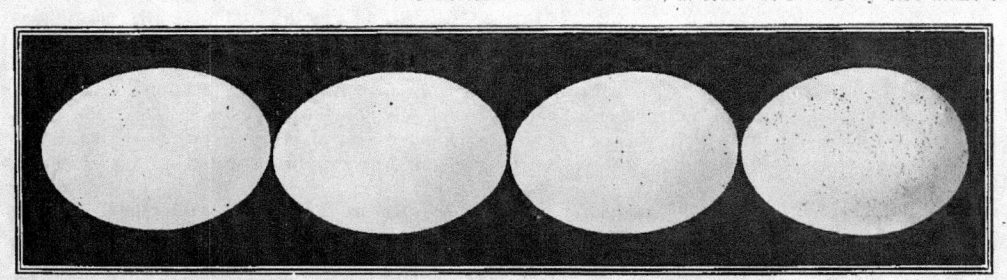

FIG. 86.—EGGS OF NORMAL SIZE ARE BEST FOR HATCHING
Eggs that are of good average size, weighing two ounces each or over, and of ideal egg shape, will hatch much better than eggs that are abnormal, either in size or shape.

CHAPTER VII

Day-Old Chicks and Custom Hatching

Origin and Development of This Unique Industry—Who Should Hatch Day-Old Chicks and Who Should Buy Them—Hatching With Lamp-Heated Incubators Profitable as Well as With Mammoth Machines—How to Build Up a Profitable Business in Custom Hatching.

PRODUCTION of day-old chicks has developed into a great industry within a comparatively short space of time, and countless "hatcheries" have been established in all parts of the country, ranging in size from the modest and inexpensive home "plant" of a few lamp-heated incubators in the house cellar, to corporations operating batteries of huge mammoth incubators, each with a capacity of many thousands of eggs.

The following historical summary of the development of this industry was prepared by Herbert H. Knapp, president of the International Baby Chick Association. Writing in 1918, he says:

"It has been just twenty-six years since Joseph D. Wilson, of Stockton, N. J., sent 50 baby chicks from Stockton to Chicago. After he was satisfied that chicks could be sent successfully on long trips without being fed, he undertook to advertise this fact and solicited business, believing he had made a great discovery, though his hopes fell somewhat, when he was visited by a post-office inspector and accused of using the mails for fradulent purposes.

"Mr. Wilson, however, continued his experiments undaunted. He shipped to nearby points, gradually reaching out and extending his business until no one could accuse him of advertising a fraud. His customers were living witnesses that the shipping of baby chicks was a success. They bought from him season after season. They didn't want to hatch their own chicks. Wilson's chicks grew even better than the ones they hatched themselves. They didn't know why, but the fact remained. Now we know that it was because they did not get that dose of wet cornmeal the day they were hatched. While they were absorbing the food nature had provided for the first two or three days (the yolk of the egg) they could be carried many miles from the place of birth. In truth, every hour of the trip they were getting larger and stronger.

"While they were resting comfortably in a well-ventilated box they could not be pampered and overfed by an over-solicitious owner during those first two or three important days of their lives. The hen that steals her nest, hatches chicks and is not discovered for two or three days invariably raises more and hardier chicks than the one carefully attended and whose chicks are promptly fed as soon as they hatch out.

"Mr. Wilson had the field to himself for practically ten years. Then a few more took it up. Possibly Howard Davis, also of New Jersey, was the second man to begin shipping. Now New Jersey is one of the great centers of the industry with numerous plants ranging in capacity from fifty to two hundred and fifty thousand eggs.

"The industry was started in Ohio by Michael Uhl, of New Washington, 18 years ago. Michael was a young man of about 25 years at that time who—it is said—refused to become interested in his father's farming operations. He would not do anything but 'fuss with hens.' His chief delight seemed to be setting the hens and seeing how many chickens he could raise on his father's supply of grain. This did not suit the elder Uhl, so he set 'young Mike' off on a piece of land by himself, where he could raise chickens to his heart's content. He saw the necessity of getting some revenue before the chicks grew to marketable age and began to sell baby chicks to his neighbors, sending them farther away each year, until he ventured to put them into wooden boxes and send by express to neighboring towns, and thus the day-old chick business in Ohio was started.

"Both Mr. Wilson and Mr. Uhl began with very crude hatching machines. Mr. Wilson used machines in which the eggs were placed on sawdust and heated with pans overhead, filled twice daily with hot water. These were followed by lamp machines until hundreds were in use, and every lamp had to be filled and trimmed daily. Mr. Wilson at one time had 135 Cyphers Model incubators of 360-egg capacity each. Later he began to build 'mammoth' hot water machines, using Candee coal burning heaters, continuing this style of machines to his present capacity of one hundred and twenty-five thousand eggs.

FIG. 87.—A SHIPMENT OF DAY-OLD CHICKS

"Mr. Uhl built small, lamp machines of 200-egg capacity until he had 250 in one cellar. He saw the necessity of larger units and about eleven years ago constructed his first mammoth machine. His entire plant is now equipped with this type and has a capacity of 200,000 eggs. Lawrence and George Uhl, who are brothers of Michael, also operate large hatching plants. The Uhls were closely followed in Ohio by Dr. S. B. Smith, who has invented several types of machines, his present hatchery being a novel heated-room system having a capacity of 665,000 eggs.

"The one feature that has been responsible more than any other for the development of the day-old chick industry is the recent great improvement in brooding systems. The old type of mammoth hot water brooders was expensive to install and lately has given way to the coal and oil burning brooders—this style being more efficient and requiring comparatively small space. Brooders with rated capacities of 300 to 1200 chicks are being purchased very generally by farmers, who find it to their advantage to be able to buy a sufficient number of chicks to arrive in one shipment to run the brooder at full capacity.

"We hereby warn amateurs not to place too many chicks under one hover. Five hundred should be the limit for the best success. A thousand or more chicks might get along very nicely for a few days in open weather, but remember that the chicks should grow, and they need plenty of room in which to thrive. If you wish to start a thousand chicks you would better buy two or three colony brooders. Those who wish to purchase only twenty-five to one hundred chicks may purchase small lamp-heated brooders that are easy to operate, thus making it practical for all classes of poultrymen to buy their chicks already hatched—doing away with the bother and inconvenience of incubating by hens."

Both Lamp-Heated and Mammoth Incubators Used

This branch of the poultry industry is especially attractive to persons with limited capital, since it can be started profitably even on an extremely small scale. The large operators with their huge mammoth machines have important advantages over the small producer with his few lamp-heated incubators, but the latter also has some advantages over the former and need have no fear that he is going to be crowded out of the business. The person who hatches chicks by the hundred only can sell his total production locally at good prices and with little expense for advertising and shipping. And he has the satisfaction of knowing that as his reputation grows (and the man who can uniformly supply first-class, livable chicks to his customers does not have to wait long for a "reputation") he can rapidly build up his plant until he too may be turning chicks out by the tens of thousands.

It is not necessary, therefore, to have a mammoth incubator to engage successfully in the production of day-old chicks. Many persons, both men and women, have found that with a few lamp-heated machines in the house cellar they could turn out large numbers of chicks in a season, in this manner marketing at good prices the eggs produced by their flocks, and laying the foundation for increasing trade in following years. Where the hatching is on a large scale, mammoth incubators are conceded to be a necessity, as they are more economical in operation and require much less time in attendance. Each operator must determine for himself which type he needs.

Mammoth incubators now are made in comparatively small sizes though, for the average operator, there is little advantage in buying these. In starting on a small scale it usually will be better to buy lamp-heated machines which can be operated fully as efficiently and economically as "baby" mammoths, changing over to a large mammoth after sales have reached the point where it is desirable to do this. It may be necessary to take some loss in making this change but there is always a demand for second-hand machines in good condition, so that the loss is not great, and a good portion of it should fairly be charged off as rental. In starting with lamp-heated machines however, it is important to get standard makes. These are easier operated and require much less attention than second-class machines and will soon repay their extra cost in the economy in labor which they will effect. Moreover, high-grade incubators have a definite replacement value or can readily be sold as "used machines," while inferior makes are practically worthless after a few years' use.

Who Should Buy Day-Old Chicks

Day-old chicks can be secured in almost any desired grade or quality, with respect to breeding, and nearly every one engaged in poultry production, from the backyard grower to the larger breeder and the commercial egg producer who count their fowls by the thousands, finds it desirable from time to time to purchase chicks. The person who wishes to start in poultry keeping in the spring, doing so on a small scale and at little expense for equipment, usually finds day-old chicks the cheapest and most convenient way of securing his stock. Those who require great numbers of chicks either for starting large plants or in order to replace their old flocks, find that by ordering baby chicks from some large hatchery they are able to get all they need, of the desired grade and at just the date when they want them, without providing expensive incubating equipment, and without any trouble or uncertainty about hatching.

The purchase of chicks would seem to offer special advantages to beginners, or persons who wish to try things out before investing extensively in any sort of equipment, also those who are only taking up poultry keeping in a small way. Speaking generally, the poultry keeper who is trying to breed up his flock, to improve the laying qualities of his fowls or their standard value must, it would seem, do his own hatching, using eggs from his own fowls. Even the commercial poultry keeper

FIG. 88—TYPE OF MAMMOTH INCUBATOR EXTENSIVELY USED IN DAY-OLD CHICK HATCHERIES

While great numbers of chicks are hatched in lamp-heated incubators, mammoths are almost invariably installed when large hatching capacity is desired. Their use results in greatly decreased labor, and fuel cost is lower. Courtesy of Candee Incubator Company.

usually will find that he will have better stock and will secure it at less expense if he utilizes the pick of his flock in the production of eggs for hatching.

However, there are numerous exceptions to this general rule. Some who would naturally be expected to do their own hatching may not have sufficient help to operate a good-sized poultry plant and look after the added work involved in the production of good hatching eggs and their incubation. Others on account of limited funds may find it necessary to purchase chicks instead of providing their own hatching facilities. The commercial egg farmer who wishes to raise each year a certain number of pullets to keep up his flock can place his order with a responsible hatchery with the certainty that the entire number of chicks needed will be delivered to him on the date which will insure the pullets coming into laying at the right time in the fall. This also greatly simplifies the work of caring for the chicks since they can be brooded in large flocks with colony hovers—the saving in brooding cost possibly covering the extra expense of buying the chicks instead of hatching them in numerous small broods at home.

FIG. 89—CHICK BOXES WITH WOODEN STRIPS TO INSURE VENTILATION
Shipping boxes provided with narrow wooden strips on top and sides cannot be piled together closely enough to interfere with the air supply of chicks in inside boxes.

Who Should Produce Day-Old Chicks

Almost any person who has a moderate-sized breeding flock and a suitable place for a few incubators, can embark in this branch of the industry with excellent prospects of success, almost regardless of location. There is no fixed limit in equipment required for profitable operation, or in size of breeding flocks. The thing to do is to start with whatever good-quality stock is on hand or may readily be obtained, providing as many lamp-heated machines as are needed to take care of the eggs produced, doing this with the assurance that any volume of production, no matter how small, may readily be disposed of at a profit.

While the advantages possessed by large operators are important, there are distinct limits as to distance or time required for delivery which make it impossible for the large concerns to reach out for trade beyond a certain radius, no matter how low they may make the price within their natural territory. Moreover, there will always be many who will prefer to buy near home; who will want to buy from breeders whom they know and trust; who will want the better stock that it is reasonable to expect from the small operators who hatch only the eggs produced by their own carefully mated breeding pens; and there is not the slightest doubt that, other things being equal, the shorter the distance the chicks have to travel the greater the certainty that they will arrive at their destination in prime condition. For these and other equally good reasons there is scarcely a locality in this country where it is not practicable for a competent breeder or incubator operator to develop a profitable trade in baby chicks.

In many instances hatcheries are operated by persons who have little or no breeding stock, but who depend upon getting their hatching eggs from other breeders or from farmers who have flocks of standard fowls from which they are willing to sell hatching eggs at only a slight advance over the market price. This practice is especially common where large numbers of eggs are required and where the operation of the hatchery alone demands all the owner's time and attention. It has proved entirely practicable to maintain hatcheries in this way, and the farmers in the surrounding territory, with a little encouragement and expert advice, develop well-bred flocks and come to take a good deal of pride in them. It is generally conceded that there is no better source of hatching eggs than a flock of fowls having the range of a farm, where their health and vigor can be maintained at a high level by free range and the generally favorable conditions under which they are kept. Sometimes the hatchery operator reserves the right to provide the males for these farm flocks, selling them to the owner usually at only nominal prices. He can well afford to do this in view of the improvement in the quality of the chicks that may thus be secured, and the consequently better prices that may be realized for them.

Keeping faith with the customer is important in the day-old chick industry at all times and under all conditions, but it is imperative in the case of the small producer with a local market. The opportunity of dealing more or less personally with customers, of establishing a positive reputation for competency as a breeder and for fair dealing, is the small producer's greatest asset, and one that the distant, impersonal large concern cannot take from him. This reputation ought to cover the breeding of the chicks, their strength and vigor as determined both by the character of the breeding stock and the skillful management of the incubator, also the delivery of chicks exactly when promised, and in prime condition. The wise operator will lose no opportunity to win and keep a reputation for doing all this. It is betraying no secret to say that not every one who attempts to furnish day-old chicks is successful in producing strong, vigorous stock; and a sickly lot of chicks is the poorest advertisement that the seller can have. On the other hand the person who supplies strong, lively chicks that thrive and grow, and show that they are of good breeding as they develop, need have no fear of not being able to sell all that he can produce, and at profitable prices.

What Breeds to Keep

With a comparatively small plant, chicks of any of the popular breeds and varieties will find ready sale. If larger numbers are to be produced it is wise to consider the local demand thoroughly before determining what kind of fowls to keep. It is better to sell people what they want than to try to influence their choice. By all means avoid comparatively unknown breeds or varieties. No matter how desirable a particular breed may appear to the producer, it is not his preference but the customer's that is going to determine sales, and the day-old chick business is largely limited to a few popular breeds such as White Leghorns, Plymouth Rocks, Wyandottes, R. I. Reds, Orpingtons, etc.

Leghorn chicks generally are produced more cheaply than others, owing to the fact that the average operator is able to get better hatches and better chicks from Leghorn eggs than from eggs of the larger breeds. If sales are to be made mainly to farmers, it usually is necessary to supply chicks of the general-purpose breeds mentioned in the preceding paragraph, as there are many agricultural communities where Leghorns are not considered desirable. The latter, however, usually are demanded by commercial egg producers. Much that is said in regard to choice of breeds in Chapter I applies with full force to selection for the day-old chick trade.

Prices That May Be Realized

It is an unfortunate fact that the day-old chick business was started on a scale of too low prices, and the effect of this is still felt, though much has been done lately to raise the general average of the chicks sold, and to educate the public to pay the better prices which must be realized if well-bred stock is to be furnished. It is safe to assume that hatcheries that sell chicks at a price low enough to enable the 5 and 10 cent stores to retail them at ten cents apiece, are not losing money, but the buyer who expects to get anything but "just chickens" at that price is about certain to be disappointed. The average hatchery, especially when operating on a large scale, at minimum cost for both fuel and labor, can make out very well if it can sell chicks at an advance of $4.00 per hundred over the cost of the eggs. This means that with chicks selling at 10 cents from the incubator, the eggs must be bought at around 4 cents apiece, assuming that the two-thirds of all eggs set will hatch saleable chicks.

This illustration is given for the double purpose of showing the buyer how unexacting he must be regarding the quality of chicks purchased so cheaply that they necessarily are hatched from eggs but one degree moved from ordinary market eggs; also of showing the small operator that he cannot afford to cater to this low-priced trade. This is true not only because he is bound to suffer disproportionately in reputation from the sale of inferior stock, but because he must, with his small hatching capacity and correspondingly increased cost of production, get a greater margin of profit than would satisfy the large-scale operators—either this, or he must place a valuation on his own time too low to make the business really attractive. It is true that educating the public to pay higher prices is a task that calls for a good degree of salesmanship. The individual operator must decide for himself just how far he can afford to go in meeting the demand for cheap chicks, and how strong a stand he wishes to take in holding prices at a point that will make it possible to hatch eggs produced by genuinely good breeding fowls. But there should be an especial effort to have a clear understanding regarding the stock that is supplied at the price, whatever that may be.

In making prices on stock of better quality the operator must learn to figure for himself, but he should learn to figure accurately. If the eggs are produced by fairly good breeding stock and are valued as low as $10.00 per hundred, then in hatching operations that should be considered the cost price, and the operator cannot afford to sell chicks from such eggs unless he gets this "cost price," plus an additional sum that will cover labor, interest on the investment, overhead charges, and a reasonable profit. A price for chicks that does not provide such a margin simply means that the operator is underselling himself. And absurd as it may seem, there is reason to believe that a good many are doing just that thing. In a general way most operators charge about double as much for chicks as they would be willing to accept for the eggs, though where fertility runs high this margin can be reduced somewhat, if it is found desirable to do so.

How Day-Old Chicks Are Handled

Owing to the peculiar provision of nature by which the newly hatched chicks are supplied with a store of food in the form of unabsorbed yolk which enables them to go for several days, if necessary, without drawing on any other source of supply, it is practicable to ship them over considerable distances. The U. S. Post Office Department will accept parcel post shipments of chicks that can be delivered within 72 hours after they are received at the postoffice. A great many instances are on record where chicks have been on the way for a longer time than this, without suffering any apparent injury.

Chicks generally are shipped as soon as possible after they are dry, and in order to avoid delay, every detail of their shipment is attended to in advance of their hatching. The shipping boxes, which are bought flat or knock-down, are set up, labels pasted on, and the bottom of the box covered with suitable litter. The shipping tags also are made out and the number for each order is marked on the tags, so that when the chicks are ready to be

FIG. 90—PASTEBOARD CHICK BOXES
Packed in these substantial but light-weight boxes, chicks may be shipped by express or parcel post and will travel comfortably and arrive in practically as good condition as if hatched right at home.

taken from the incubator, there will be no necessity for referring to the original order, or the correspondence. The chicks are simply removed from the machine, counted into boxes, the tops tied on with stout cord or sealed with a strip of gummed paper, and they are ready for the express or mail train.

Shipments usually are made in corrugated pasteboard boxes, which are quite light in weight, and their construction affords fair insulation so that the chicks' bodily warmth keeps them comfortable under all ordinary conditions, and they suffer no ill effects whatever from two or three days' confinement if adequate ventilation is provided. This is done by cutting or punching holes in the top and sides of the box, the number and location being left to the judgment of the shipper, who is guided in these respects by his knowledge of the conditions under which the chicks are to travel, the weather, etc. Shipments in cold weather, or over routes which involve long, cold waits at junction points, should have less ventilation than those made in warm weather or where they are to go through without delay and will be kept in heated cars or offices most of the time.

After careful deliveration the International Baby Chick Association, in 1918, decided upon a standard style and sizes for boxes to be used in the shipment of chicks, which boxes are illustrated in Figs. 89 and 90. These boxes are of double-faced, waterproof corrugated board, and the sizes are as follows:

```
100 chick box, 22x18 in. x 5½ in. deep—4 compartments
 50 chick box, 18x11 in. x 5½ in. deep—2 compartments
 25 chick box,  9x11 in. x 5½ in. deep—1 compartment
 12 chick box,  6x 8 in. x 5  in. deep—1 compartment
```

Extreme delays due to neglect, freight congestion, or bad connections, and chilling through excess ventilation or exposure to severe cold, are the most serious dangers that have to be considered in day-old chick shipments, and it is unavoidable that there should be some disappointments and some injured, weakened chicks. Every possible precaution should be taken to prevent these misfortunes or to minimize their effects. There should be the clearest possible understanding between shipper and purchaser as to when the chicks are to be shipped and how, so that the latter can be on hand to receive them as soon as they arrive. The seller must give safe delivery his careful attention, as a single lot of dead or weakly chicks may mark the end of his business relations with the customer or the entire community. He can afford to do everything in reason and a few things out of reason to insure complete satisfaction.

Whether he should guarantee safe arrival and replace damaged shipments free or at a reduced price, must be determined individually; practice varies in this respect. Guaranteed shipments undoubtedly contributed to the purchaser's satisfaction, but complaints are always much more frequent under guarantees than where chicks are shipped at customer's risk. Whatever plan is adopted in this respect there should be a clear understanding in regard to it, and both seller and buyer must fairly meet the terms of the agreement, the obligations of which rest with equal weight on each. One thing that the buyer can and should do is to place his order with the nearest hatchery that can fill it acceptably. The shorter the distance the chicks have to be transported and the fewer changes they must make en route, the better chance they will have to come through in first-class condition.

The provision that the customer makes for the reception and care of the chicks may be no direct concern of the seller, but it is common knowledge that great numbers of chicks are lost each year through improper brooding, and this always reacts more or less seriously upon the person who supplied them. The average inexperienced buyer of chicks often fails at this point, either through not providing adequate brooding facilities, resulting in overcrowding, or through employing cheap, unreliable brooders, particularly the "fireless" kind, the use of which in cold weather, by persons inexperienced in the handling of chicks, is almost certain to result in heavy losses and epidemics of so-called "white diarrhea."

The buyer of day-old chicks must keep in mind that this industry is conducted mainly on the basis of advance orders, and if he sends in his orders, especially during the busy season, expecting immediate delivery, he is apt to be disappointed. The only way to insure delivery of chicks at a certain time is by getting the order in early enough to insure one's "turn" coming on that date. Most operators will file orders and hold them for delivery on a specified date if a reasonable deposit is made, the balance of the purchase price to be forwarded about the time the chicks are to be shipped. To insure delivery exactly when wanted however, it usually is necessary to file orders weeks or even months in advance.

What to Do With Surplus Chicks

After chicks have reached the age where feeding and watering must begin (2 to 3 days), they cannot then be safely shipped, but must be held until they no longer require artificial heat and can be handled in the same manner as adult fowls. Since there often are hatches or parts of hatches for which there are no advance orders, every hatchery must be equipped to brood chicks so that any surplus may be properly cared for and the chicks raised to a saleable age. Do not attempt to do this by the use of lampless brooders. It can be done, but the labor cost will be out of all proportion to the value of the chicks. For large numbers there is nothing better than coal, oil or gasoline-heated colony hovers (see Chapter IX). For small lots the average operator will find good lamp-heated hovers more satisfactory, hence brooders of both types should be provided and held in reserve for emergencies. The exclusive use of colony hovers is apt to lead to putting chicks of different ages into the same flock, which is not practical and will result in heavy losses.

One feature of the chick business that is developing rapidly is the sale of "six-weeks-old" chicks, meaning chicks that have been raised to the point where they no longer need artificial heat or brooding and where the sex may be determined, the demand of course being almost exclusively for pullets. Just as there are many persons who do not want to do any hatching, so there are many others who wish to be spared the further expense of providing brooding facilities for raising young chicks, or the trouble of caring for them. They prefer to secure their stock after all the difficult work has been done, when few further losses are to be expected, and when only the slightest skill and experience are sufficient to insure raising the chicks to adult size. The day-old chick producer is in position to meet this demand to good advantage, using all chicks for which there may not happen to be a market at the time they come from the machine, and raising them to this age at comparatively little cost.

FIG. 91—A FINE LOT OF SIX-WEEK-OLD CHICKS
The trade in partially grown chicks is increasing rapidly and seems to be capable of indefinite extension. At this size, sex can be determined with a good degree of accuracy. The demand, of course, is chiefly for pullets, and good prices are paid for them at this age, when they no longer require brooding.

Custom Hatching

Custom hatching, by which is meant operating incubators on a rental basis, or hiring space in machines to persons who furnish the eggs to be incubated, is becoming increasingly popular, especially among those who keep fowls and who wish to have chicks hatched from their own stock but do not want to go to the expense or trouble of providing their own hatching facilities. Where this is done the charge is based either on chicks hatched, or on a 100-egg rate.

The satisfaction realized in this branch of the industry depends upon the fertility of the eggs and the skill of the operator, both of which should be good if complaints are to be avoided. Persons who furnish eggs for this purpose often have extreme notions as to the number of chicks that should be delivered to them, and poor hatches are a source of great dissatisfaction and may cause much more trouble than the business is worth. Experienced operators who are uniformly successful in the work, however, find it quite profitable.

The usual charge made where large hatching capacity is available, is about 4 cents per chick or $3.00 per hundred eggs. There would appear to be especially good opportunities for the development of a profitable business in custom hatching in agricultural communities where there are large numbers of good-sized flocks of fowls, and where the home use of incubators is limited.

CHAPTER VIII
Practical Incubator Houses

Convenience and Economy of Having a Practical, Well-Planned House for Incubators—Building to Save Time and Labor—Best Location and How to Build—How to Insure Thorough Ventilation—Plans for Houses Underground and Aboveground.

THE poultry keeper who has a good-sized house cellar in which suitable conditions can be maintained, and who does not expect to operate more than a few machines, may not find it necessary to provide special quarters for them. There are a number of practical advantages in having a separate, specially designed house for incubator use, however, and in the long run it usually pays to provide such where many chicks are to be hatched. Some insurance companies refuse to permit the operation of incubators in houses insured by them, and this may have a bearing on the decision regarding special quarters. However, as there are a number of companies that make no objection to the use of the better grades of incubators, which are practically fireproof, there usually is no difficulty about arranging for the transfer of the insurance to a company with a more liberal policy, if that is the only serious obstacle to be considered.

The usual practical difficulty met in utilizing the house cellar is that ventilation is nearly always inadequate, and special provision must be made for this. Neither is it desirable to operate incubators in cellars that smell musty, or that are used for the storage of vegetables or fruit, either fresh or canned, as a suitable temperature for the incubator makes the cellar too warm for such purposes. Extremely cold cellars are not desirable and if heated by the house furnace, some means will have to be provided for overcoming the dryness of the air which is a regular accompaniment of artificially heated rooms, either below or aboveground.

Where a number of incubators are operated in a cellar of ordinary construction, ventilation may be secured by installing flues of the type illustrated in Fig. 95. These, in connection with such windows as usually are provided should supply ample ventilation. If the expense of installing flues is considered out of the question it may be possible to pipe the fumes directly out of the room. Some machines are especially constructed to meet this requirement.

Incubators are used in various aboveground buildings and rooms and often with a good degree of success, though the difficulties in the way of securing satisfactory hatches under such conditions unquestionably are greater than in houses especially planned for the purpose. Incubators are capable of remarkably exact regulation within reasonable limits, but a room in which the temperature fluctuates 20 degrees or more from day to day adds greatly to the difficulty of operation. To be relieved of the necessity for watching the incubator closely, it is necessary to have the machines in a room where the temperature does not vary greatly, a condition which it is practically impossible to secure in a house or room of ordinary construction. Where such rooms must be used, much can be done to reduce temperature variations by closing with wooden shutters all windows facing the south, and shading any through which the sun can shine directly, also by looking carefully after the ventilation. In severely cold weather the room should be heated to 50 to 60 degrees, the most desirable temperature in which to operate incubators. The moisture problem generally is much more troublesome in such rooms than in cellars.

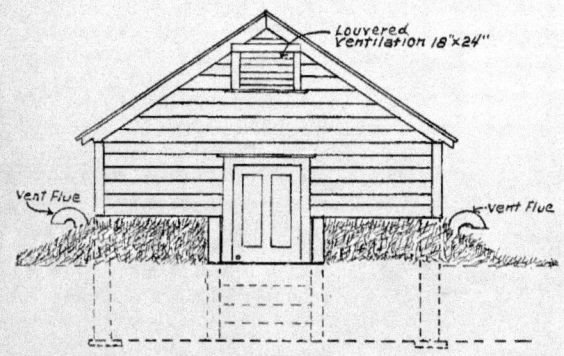

FIG. 92—END ELEVATION OF INCUBATOR HOUSE

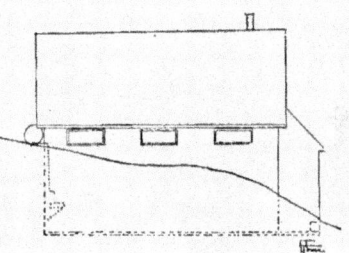

FIG. 93—INCUBATOR HOUSE ON SLOPING GROUND
This probably is the most desirable location for the incubator house, where the slope of the ground makes it possible to build in this way. Reproduced from Reading Course Bul. No. 80, Cornell University.

Location for Incubator House

With an incubator house properly designed and constructed, and with the conveniences and labor-saving facilities that can there be provided and which it seldom is practical to supply in other locations, the work of caring for the machines may be greatly reduced and most desirable conditions as to temperature, moisture, and ventilation can constantly and uniformily be maintained.

The best location for the permanent incubator house in most sections is partially underground in order to secure uniformity of temperature, but not so much below the ground level as to interfere with ventilation. Other reasons for placing incubator houses partially underground are that they usually are more economical to build than aboveground houses affording similarly favorable conditions; they are warmer in winter and cooler in summer; a more uniform degree of humidity can be maintained the season through. The house may be built entirely aboveground where it is necessary to do so, but such construction usually is more expensive if the building is planned so as to secure reasonable uniformity in temperature.

To meet average requirements the building should be four or five feet underground, and the rest above, though something depends upon the slope of the land where the house is to be located. With sufficient slope an ideal arrangement is to have all the back part of the house underground up to the eaves, and the side with the

59

entrance at or near the ground level, as in Fig. 93. On level ground the general outlines of the house shown in Figs. 92, 94, 95, and 96, will be found most desirable. The length and width should be proportioned to the size of the incubators to be used, always allowing for a passage-way of ample width between the machines—seldom less than four feet. A narrower passage can be used if testing and most other work is to be done in a separate workroom, but the convenience of the wider passage will amply repay the slight additional cost. Making the ceiling of the incubator room so low that only comfortable headroom is afforded is a grave mistake. To secure proper ventilation it should be fully 8 feet high, and it will be better still if higher.

The incubator house should have a gable roof with plenty of space between the ceiling and rafters. The roof is the point which, after the windows, is apt to cause most variation in room temperature, and if this is entirely cut off by a tight ceiling and the gable ventilated by large openings that permit free passage of air, heat from the roof will make little trouble. Gable ventilation should be adjustable, or the openings should be more or less tightly closed in cold weather by covering with muslin or burlap to conserve heat.

The floor and the underground walls should always be of concrete. This not only gives greater permanence, but wood used underground is apt to be quickly covered with mold on exposed surfaces, which may prove a source of trouble. If possible, the floor should have a drain so that the room can be conveniently flushed and scrubbed. Do not neglect providing a trap in the drain even though the latter may have an open outlet.

All walls that are above the ground level should be doubled, with dead air spaces or packed with insulating material. Ordinarily the walls above ground level should be boarded on the outside with matched siding, using ceiling boards or a heavy coat of wall plaster on the inside walls and ceiling. The best grades of waterproof plasterboard would seem to be well adapted to this use, as they afford little chance for the accumulation of dust, and can be washed down when necessary. Good wooden shingles make the best roofing, as these do not absorb heat like ordinary prepared roofing. The latter, however, is cheaper and for that reason is most generally used.

Every incubator cellar of whatever size should have a separate vestibule and workroom where the trays are filled, the eggs tested and weighed, the lamps filled, and where all desirable conveniences for doing the work can be provided. A good workbench should be installed at a convenient height. The oil supply should be kept in a tank or barrel on the outside of the building and piped into the workroom. A cupboard or shelves should be provided for the storage of burners, thermometers and all extra parts and accessories. If large numbers of lamps are to be filled it may be well to have a sink under the oil faucet, to carry off any oil that may be spilled, and

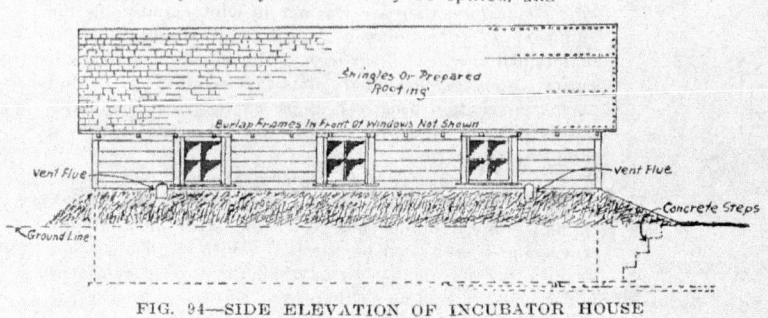

FIG. 95—CROSS SECTION OF INCUBATOR HOUSE

with a water tap for flushing if possible. For the small cellar, a more practical plan is to have a box or tray of suitable size to be kept under the drip and partially filled with shavings or other absorbent material which can be emptied from time to time, thus preventing the floor from becoming saturated with oil. These oil-soaked shavings make excellent kindling for fires.

If available, running water should be piped into the workroom. If this cannot be done there should be a water tank with a faucet, or at least a good-sized bucket, so that there will always be a supply of water on hand for various uses. A convenient place for washing hands is desirable. In one end of the workroom provision may be made for storing eggs while awaiting their turn in the incubators.

If the eggs are to be tested in daylight the workroom should be provided with shutters or tight curtains so that it can be made dark for the purpose. It often is possible to arrange for one or two holes in one of the window shutters or curtains so that the eggs can be tested by direct sunlight. It is desirable to have electric light in the workroom if possible; if not, a permanent light of some other kind should be installed, if only to discourage the tendency to keep the incubator lamps burning while they are being filled, which is more or less dangerous, and fills the room with smoke.

Incubator House for Lamp-Heated Incubators

The house illustrated in Figs. 92, 94, 95 and 96, will accommodate eight good-sized machines, and can readily be changed to meet larger or smaller requirements, simply increasing or reducing the length. There seldom is any necessity for changing the width. The outside dimensions of the house are 13 feet, 4 inches, by 26 feet, 2 inches, or 12 by 25 feet, inside measurements. The ceiling is 9 feet, 4 inches high.

This house has a 5-foot concrete wall, extending 3 feet below ground level and windows in the framed wall as indicated. With these windows so located and protected by outside burlap screens, also by wide eaves, they will admit little direct sunlight, and all incubators will be equally well located as to ventilation, provided proper attention is given to the adjustment of windows, those on the side from which the wind comes always being closed, or practically so,

FIG. 94—SIDE ELEVATION OF INCUBATOR HOUSE

PRACTICAL INCUBATOR HOUSES

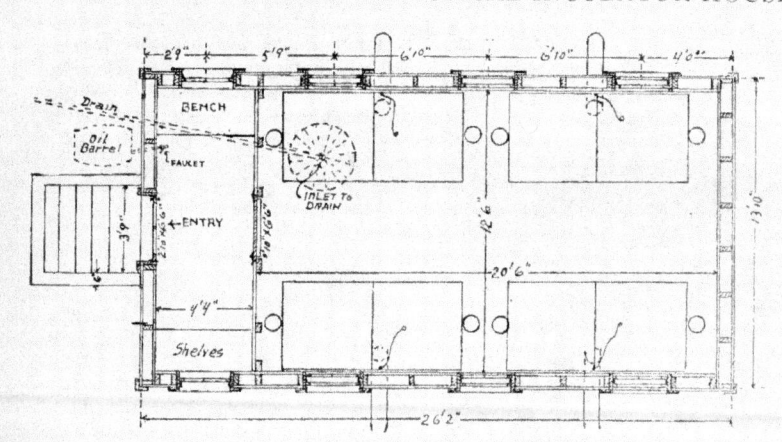

FIG. 96—FLOOR PLAN OF INCUBATOR HOUSE

except in warm weather. If the house is built with the door facing in the direction from which severe storms are to be expected, it will be necessary to protect the steps with a vestibule, hood, or sloping doors.

As will be seen in Fig. 95, this house is to be provided with ventilating flues. These may be made of galvanized iron as indicated in the plan, or heavy sewer pipe may be used. Many prefer to build the flue into the concrete wall, which in most cases is the better and cheaper way. These flues are to be 8 inches in diameter or must provide an equivalent amount of flue space if made in some other shape. There should be one flue for every 100 square feet of floor space and in connection with the windows in the upper part of the wall these will supply adequate ventilation for the room under practically any condition. A damper or check must always be provided so that the air circulation will be under control.

If this system of ventilation is not installed it will be necessary to provide some means for piping the lamp fumes out of the room, though it is difficult to do this with most machines. The circulation of air in such pipes is a somewhat uncertain factor in windy weather when back drafts often are set up which return the fumes to the room unless the outlet pipe is connected with a flue in which forced air circulation is maintained by heat. In general, it is much better and simpler to provide for the removal of the lamp fumes and the renewal of the air in the room by the use of correctly designed ventilation.

In building this house remember that the forms for a five-foot concrete wall require heavy bracing. Whatever the thickness of the wall, it is desirable to have the bottom extended for footing, as shown in Fig. 95. If soft spots are found in the ground at this depth, which is not probable, the excavation at these points must be carried down to solid ground to prevent cracking and settling of the walls. The side walls at the steps may be four to six inches thick, and the steps should be solid.

The frame of this house is to be of 2x6-inch timbers, with the sills anchored to the foundation wall. The walls above the ground are to be double-boarded with heavy sheathing paper nailed to each side of the studs and the boards laid over this. The ceiling of the room should also have an insulating covering of sheathing paper tacked to the lower face of the joists before the boards are nailed on.

Note that burlap frames are to be provided outside of all windows, screening the windows from the sun and preventing direct air currents when the windows are open. In warm weather or when the wind is not blowing, the burlap screens may be opened outward admitting more air, but still screening the windows from direct sunlight which, if unobstructed, is liable to raise the room temperature several degrees in a short time, and interfere with the regulation of the machines. A shingle roof is recommended for this building as shingles give a more even temperature than prepared roofing. Both gables should have louvered ventilators, as shown.

BILL OF MATERIAL FOR INCUBATOR HOUSE

Use	Size Inches	Length Feet	No. of Pieces	Remarks
Sills, side	2x6	14	4	
Sills, end	2x6	14	2	
Plates, side	2x6	14	4	
Plates, end	2x6	14	2	
Studs, front & back	2x6	10	7	1 piece cuts 2
Studs, ends	2x6	8	12	Cut to fit
Rafters	2x6	10	28	
Ties	1x6	10	13	
Partition studs	2x4	10	6	
Ridge pole	1x7	14	2	
Roof boards	1x10			500 ft. board measure
T & G siding	⅞x6			325 ft. board measure
Ceiling, partition, shelves, etc.	⅞x4			1000 ft. board measure
Frame for doors and windows	⅞x6			100 lin ft. Surfaced 4 sides
Frame for burlap shutter	⅞x2			70 lin ft. Surfaced 4 sides
Trim lumber	⅞x4			150 lin ft. Surfaced 4 sides
Barge boards	⅞x8			100 lin ft. Surfaced 4 sides

5M. shingles.
2 doors, 2 feet, 10 inches x 6 feet, 6 inches.
6 sash, 6-light 12x12-inch glass.
6 metal sash adjusters.
36 sq. ft. burlap.
6 bolts ½x12-inch with 2-inch washers.
1 pr. 5-inch butt hinges.
12 pr. 2-inch butt hinges for windows and screens.
1 metal ventilator slide 5 inches x 2 feet 3 inches.
1 door lock.
4 8-inch ventilator flues with dampers, cords and pulleys.
Nails, tacks and paint.

MATERIAL FOR FOUNDATION AND FLOOR

70 bags of Portland cement; 162 cu. ft. of sand; 325 cu. ft. of crushed stone or gravel.

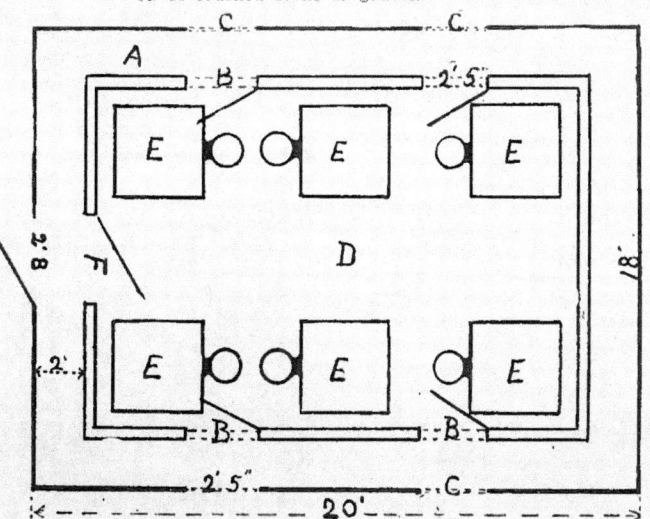

FIG. 97—FLOOR PLAN OF ABOVEGROUND INCUBATOR HOUSE
The principal feature to be secured in an aboveground house is insulation, to avoid irregular room temperatures. Note how this is provided by means of a double wall with 2-foot passageway between outer and inner walls. Reproduced from Bulletin 4, Western Washington Experiment Station.

FIG. 98—A SUCCESSFUL ABOVEGROUND INCUBATOR HOUSE
Photo from Oregon State Agricultural College.

A Small Incubator House

Where there are practical objections to building the incubator house partially underground as suggested in the preceding plan, it may be built entirely aboveground and, if properly designed, will give excellent service. Such a house has been built at the Western Washington Experiment Station and has been in successful use there for several years. It is illustrated in Fig. 97. This house can be built at comparatively slight cost where cheap lumber is available, and is large enough to meet the requirements of farmers and small producers generally. It can be located wherever convenient and requires no excavation whatever. The following description is condensed from Bul. No. 4 of the West. Washington Station:

"The house is 16 feet wide, 20 feet long, and 9 feet to the eaves, finished with No. 1 rustic, with a one-third slope, and has a shingled roof. The door is in the north end. There are two windows in each side. The south end of the building is built solid, with the exception of the small ventilator in the end near the peak, as seen in the north end above the door and just below the peak. The house was painted red and trimmed in white, giving it a neat appearance. To construct an incubator house like the one illustrated above, the following bill of lumber is required:

"The main and outer portion of the building requires:
  3 pieces 4x4-in., 20 ft. long, for sills.
  2 pieces 2x4-in., 20 ft. long, plates.
  11 pieces 2x4-in., 16 feet long, floor joists.
  30 pieces 2x4-in., 9 ft. long, studding.
  11 pieces 2x4-in., 16 feet long, ceiling joists.
  22 pieces 2x4-in., 12 ft. long, rafters.
  750 board feet of matched siding.
  600 board feet of 1x6-inch sheathing (also used for corner boards and other finish lumber).
  4M cedar shingles.
  320 board feet of matched flooring.
  320 board feet of matched ceiling.
  1 door 2 ft. 8 in. x 6 ft. 8 in.
  4 window sash 12x16-in., 4-light.

To construct the inner hatching room provide:
  22 pieces 2x3-in., 9 ft. long.
  1200 board feet of matched ceiling.
  1 door 2 ft. 8 in. x 6 ft. 8 in.

"The building is constructed on the ground with a wooden floor and stands on cedar blocks resting on flat rocks projecting above the surface of the ground. The three pieces, 4 inch x 4 inch x 20 feet, provided in the bill of materials, are used as sills, one on either side and one in the middle. Eleven pieces, 2 inch x 4 inch x 16 feet, are nailed on their edges two feet apart to the sills and covered with 1 inch x 6 inch tongue-and-groove flooring. For studding for the outer walls use 2 inch x 4 inch x 9 feet, set two feet apart, center to center. For plates use 2 inch x 4 inch x 20 feet. For ceiling joist, use eleven pieces 2 inch x 4 inch x 16 feet, and for rafters 22 pieces 2 inch x 4 inch x 12 feet. Ceil with 1 inch x 4 inch tongue-and-groove ceiling. Enclose the building with 1 inch x 10 inch shiplap. Cover the rafters with 1 inch x 6 inch sheathing laid and nailed two inches apart, and shingle. Put in on either side two 3 ft. x 3 ft. windows, placed five feet above the floor. Build the frame for the window to admit opening them by sliding. These windows cannot be hung on hinges, since the inner room would interfere in opening them. Now draw a line around the entire room two feet from the wall. On this line at intervals of four feet place 2 inch x 3 inch x 9 feet studding. Ceil both sides of the studding with 1 inch x 4 inch ceiling. Put in two ventilator windows 2 feet x 2 feet 5 inch in each side directly opposite the outer windows and close them with doors made of matched ceiling. Hang these ventilators with 4-inch strap hinges at the lower edge. To open them, tip them back from the top by the means of a cord.

"In the floor plan here shown the door in the north end leads into an air space (A) two feet in width extending around the inner room (D), which is entered through the door (F), which is directly opposite the outer door. The inner room (D) contains six 250-egg incubators (EEE). CC are the windows in the outer wall and are directly opposite and at the same height as the ventilator windows (BBB) in the inner double wall.

"As originally constructed the house proved to be too warm when all machines were running but this trouble was eliminated by the installation of a King Ventilating System and we now regard it as quite satisfactory, securing as it does an even temperature and pure air,

FIG. 99—BRICK INCUBATOR HOUSE
Brick houses are desirable, but rather expensive. This house has ventilating flues running above the roof, and chimney for stove in the workroom. It would be improved by addition of louvered ventilators in front and rear gables. Is in use at Pennsylvania Experiment Station.

both of which are indispensable in the hatching of chicks or turkeys by artificial methods."

It will be noticed that this house is described as being 16 feet by 20 feet, though in the floor plan the width is indicated as 18 feet, which no doubt is an oversight, as the proportions correspond to the printed descriptions. In the bill of material the amount of flooring, ceiling, etc., as specified, represents only the surface to be covered, and about one-fourth should be added to the estimates to cover matching and other shrinkage.

In considering this plan it should be remembered that the climate of Western Washington is comparatively mild and less provision need be made for warmth than will be found in many other sections of the country. In warm climates the plan of having the entrance door on the north side will be found desirable, but where severe winters are the rule it will be better to have it on the south side. Under such conditions, also, building the house with a single board floor will not be satisfactory. If a board floor is used at all it should be doubled, with heavy insulating material between the top floor and the subfloor, and the space between floor and ground should be tightly enclosed by banking up around the building with earth. A concrete floor however, will be much better, particularly for use in cold climates, and probably will be no more expensive than a properly constructed board floor. With these and possibly other minor changes in detail to meet special conditions, this house should prove satisfactory almost anywhere.

Other Types of Incubator Houses

Other incubator houses are shown in Figs. 98, 99 and 100, their special features being readily understood

FIG. 101—INTERIOR OF INCUBATOR HOUSE AT PENNA. EXP. STATION

with but little detail description. The aboveground incubator house shown in Fig. 98 has been in use for some years at the Oregon Experiment Station, where it has given satisfactory results. This is a frame building, shingled on the outside and ceiled on the inside with tongue-and-groove boards. It is 20x30 feet, with 6-inch foundation walls 12 inches in the ground, on a 10-inch footing, and extending about 8 inches above the top of the floor. It is provided with a 4-inch concrete floor. The incubator room is 9 feet high in the clear.

There are three double windows on each side, the sashes being 30x24 inches, hinged at the bottom to swing in. All window openings are covered with shutters having adjustable wooden slats, and there are 6 metal air-intakes, which discharge air into the room near the floor level. As will be noted, the windows are high up on the sides and the building has wide eaves which shade the windows and help to prevent the sun from heating up the interior. A double door is provided in front for ease in taking incubators in or out, and the gable has louvered ventilators.

The house shown in Figs. 99 and 101 is in use at the Pennsylvania Experiment Station. It is built of brick, with a stone foundation and concrete floor, and is provided with built-in ventilator flues in opposite corners of the room, with openings both at floor and ceiling. These flues discharge through brick chimneys extending above the roof as shown. One corner is cut off for use as a vestibule and workroom, and the entrance to the incubator room is through this. The large door shown as one side of the front opens directly into the incubator room, but is only used when incubators are to be removed, or in cleaning and sunning the room. The entrance door commonly used is at the left of the double door, being hidden by a tree in illustration. This door opens into the workroom which is provided with a small stove that not only keeps it at a comfortable temperature but, by leaving the door open into the incubator room, it will also warm that to some extent—a most desirable feature for winter use. There are

FIG. 100—CONCRETE INCUBATOR CELLAR
For incubator houses built mostly underground, solid concrete construction to the square is very satisfactory. The incubator room should be ceiled overhead and gable well ventilated so that the sun shining on the roof will not affect room temperature.

windows on all sides of this house except the south and wooden shutters are provided to prevent fluctuation of temperature due to direct sunlight. An interior view of this house is shown in Fig. 101.

The concrete incubator house shown in Fig. 101 is similar to the one shown in Figs. 92, 94 and 96, except that the walls are of concrete to the square. In place of the side ventilator flues, a center flue is provided which opens above the ridge and extends down to within a foot of the floor. This flue is sawed off just below the ceiling and hinged so that it can be hooked up out of the way when desirable. The photo from which this illustration was made was taken before the steps and banking up were completed. The house is 12x12 feet, inside measure, and furnishes ample room for the average small operator. Where gravel and sand are readily available and the work can be done without hired help, the cost of such a building will be comparatively slight.

Incubator House Floors

The statement on page 60 to the effect that incubator house floors should always be of concrete, is subject to modification under some conditions. Many operators prefer to lay concrete floors only in the passageways, the balance of the floor being left bare to insure greater humidity. There is no practical objection to doing this where the soil is sandy or gravelly. Even where the soil is clay, but where the site can be well drained, it is practical to follow the same plan, excavating the floor deep enough so that the unfloored sections can be filled in with four to six inches of sand. This arrangement materially increases the moisture naturally present in the air in the incubator room and when more is required the floor can be wet down at intervals. Supplying needed moisture to the air before it enters the incubator is the most natural way of doing so. Under ordinary conditions excellent results are secured by the above method, though it is much more difficult to keep the floor clean and sanitary.

Houses for Mammoth Incubators

Plans for mammoth incubator houses generally are furnished by the manufacturers of the machines purchased. However, the plans for a house for lamp-heated machines, shown in Figs. 92, 94, 95 and 96, will prove helpful in many cases, as they suggest some general details of practical value in any house, regardless of what make of incubator is used. Dimensions will depend on the size of the machine to be accommodated, and on whether the sections can be set up facing each other or must be tended from both sides, thus requiring a passageway all round the machine. The house illustrated in Fig. 102 is built after the general plan of the one designed for lamp-heated machines, but as there will be only one or at most two coal-burning heaters in operation and no lamp fumes discharged into the room, there is less need for special ventilators, which some omit entirely, though a few flues certainly will prove desirable. The windows should be installed as shown in Fig. 95, and provided with burlap screens in the same way.

The ventilated gables shown in Fig. 102 will answer very well for houses under 50 feet in length, but if longer, ridge ventilators should be provided. These may be of the familiar wooden louvered type spacing them 20 to 30 feet apart, or special galvanized iron ventilators may be obtained.

The floor plan in Fig. 103 shows the usual method of installing a single mammoth of the type having doors on both sides. In all cases, make the room wide enough to give a roomy passageway—a feature of much importance in the daily care of the machine. A great convenience in all large incubator rooms is a work-table mounted on easy-running, rubber-faced castors or small wheels, so that when machines or sections are to be set or hatches taken off, the table can readily be wheeled just where it is needed, and much inconvenience and loss of time avoided.

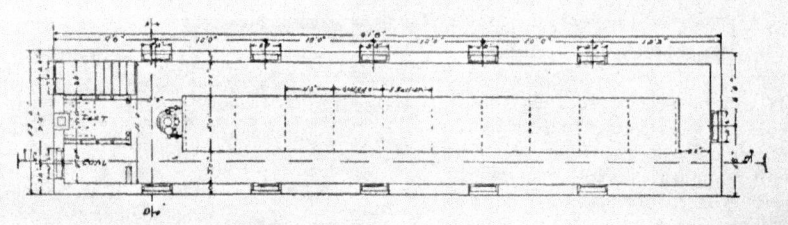

FIG. 103—SINGLE MAMMOTH INCUBATOR CELLAR PLAN
This floor plan can be adapted to any style of mammoth. In case of doubt as to dimensions, always build a little larger than seems necessary. Crowded quarters in the incubator house are annoying and add to the labor. Courtesy of Candee Incubator Company.

FIG. 102—HOUSE FOR MAMMOTH INCUBATOR

CHAPTER IX

The Selection of Brooding Equipment

Complete Description of Practical Types of Brooding Equipment—Fireless Brooders and How to Build Them—Lamp Heated Hovers—Portable Hovers—Outdoor Brooders—Colony Hovers—Hot Water Systems, Etc.—How to Select the Kind Best Suited to Individual Use.

BROODING chicks by the natural method, while practical with small flocks and as an emergency measure, is entitled to scant consideration where large numbers are to be raised, or where it is desirable to do the work in a thoroughly efficient manner. This is true largely because the labor involved in hen brooding is out of all proportion to the results secured, though there are other important objections, such as the impossibility of securing a sufficient number of broody hens when they are wanted, the inevitable heavy losses due to enemies and to a variety of accidental causes; the necessity for keeping up an everlasting fight with lice, etc. In sharp contrast with this laborious and unpleasant method is the ease and comparative certainty of artificial brooding. With proper equipment the chick raiser is practically independent of season and weather, and the number of chicks that he can successfully care for is increasing indefinitely.

Unquestionably chick raising is the most difficult part of the poultry keeper's work. To bring newly hatched broods through the danger period in good health and with minimum losses calls for some degree of skill and experience in meeting their exacting requirements. This is true without regard to the method of brooding followed. It also is true that well-selected equipment will greatly reduce these difficulties and will almost entirely eliminate the element of chance. As a matter of fact, many of the difficulties experienced in raising chicks are self-imposed, growing directly out of failure to provide the right kind of brooders or enough of them, or to slackness in methods of general care. The chick raiser now has available for his use practical, reliable, thoroughly tested brooding devices that are exactly adapted to his requirements, whether he is raising chicks on a small or a large scale, in cold or in warm weather, and so nearly automatic that even the inexperienced can operate them with practical certainty of good results.

Available brooding equipment includes the humble "fireless," which is only one remove from the natural method in point of labor, cost, and uncertainty of results. There are independent lamp-heated hovers that may be attached to almost any goods box, brooder case, or any sort of suitable building; various complete lamp-heated brooders for either indoor or outdoor use. Still more convenient are the portable lamp-heated hovers that can be used anywhere indoors without direct connection with the building where operated. Then there are electrically heated brooders, and colony hovers brooding hundreds of chicks in single flocks, using either coal, oil, gas, or gasoline for fuel. And finally, for those who wish to brood chicks under most trying winter conditions, up-to-date hot-water brooding systems are available.

These various devices are manufactured by reliable concerns and are sold at prices that bring them within the reach of every one who broods chicks. Not all of these are equally desirable under given conditions, but just as in the purchase of incubators, if the buyer will confine his patronage to reputable concerns, purchasing standard, high-grade appliances such as he can secure at reasonable but not extremely low prices, he need have no difficulty in obtaining thoroughly satisfactory equipment. The only place where he is liable to make a serious mistake is in choosing from the assortment of available styles the one best suited to his conditions.

It is quite important that this feature be carefully considered. Decision as to what to buy should in all cases be based on the adaptation of the appliance to one's particular requirements rather than on its general popularity. For example, colony hovers are in great favor at present and for the purpose of brooding large flocks of chicks they are indispensable. Many persons however, are buying these whose needs would be better served by an altogether different type of brooder about which perhaps comparatively little is heard. In this chapter practically all kinds of standard brooding equipment are described, and their respective merits explained in sufficient detail to enable the inexperienced to select just the kind and the size required to give him the service best suited to his conditions.

"Fireless" Brooders

Almost every one with practical experience in raising

FIG. 104—CHICKS LIKE THESE ARE ENTITLED TO A GOOD COMFORTABLE BROODER

chicks has had occasion at some time or other to keep small broods in baskets or boxes, without any source of warmth other than that afforded by the chicks themselves. If the box is warmly lined, and bedded with fine absorbent material like short-cut alfalfa, is located in a warm place, and the chicks covered over with a light blanket or cloth except when taken out for feeding or exercise, their bodily warmth is sufficient to keep them quite comfortable and contented.

Fireless brooders are simply these old familiar boxes or baskets made a little (and ONLY a little) more convenient for use. When they are properly designed, so that the chicks are kept snug and warm with sufficient ventilation to meet their rather limited requirements, and when used in warm weather, or at least in a warm place, and given the painstaking care and attention which brooding by this method demands, it is possible to raise chicks quite successfully in them. They represent the extreme limit in simplicity and low cost in brooding devices, but have distinct limitations. As emergency brooders or for small lots of chicks not regularly provided for, also in warm weather when the chicks require practically no brooding during the day, they serve a practical purpose, and everyone who raises chicks in numbers should keep a few on hand for such use. It is not wise to employ them in cold weather however, unless they can be kept in a heated room, and it is doubtful if they should ever be employed for anything but emergency service or where labor cost is a matter of indifference.

There are good fireless brooders on the market, or they can readily be made at home if desired. A practical, easily built brooder is shown in Fig. 106. It can be made any size from 15x15 inches (for about 25 chicks), to 24x24 inches, the latter size readily accommodating 50 to 60 chicks. The sides of the hover should be about 12 inches high and the entire top is to be covered with muslin as shown. This feature insures good ventilation. The hover may be made in various ways as convenient, the underside, next the chicks, usually being a single thickness of muslin. Over this may be placed pads of cotton batting, covered with cheese cloth to protect it and keep it from getting soiled. Use one or more pads as may be required to keep the chicks warm. A cheaper plan is

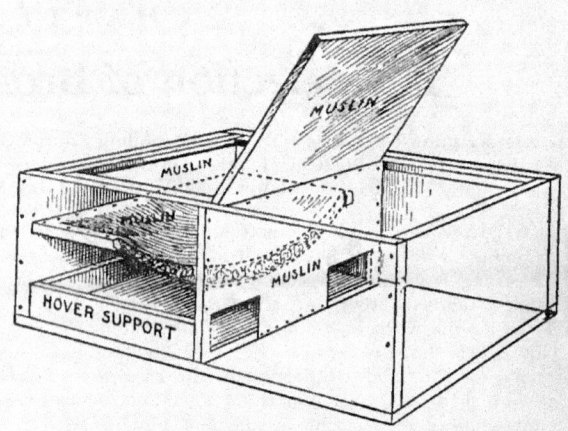

FIG. 106—A HOMEMADE FIRELESS BROODER
This brooder can be made from any suitable box. If new lumber is bought get light-weight material. Partition between hover and exercising compartment is of muslin. Box should be about 12 inches high with top covered with muslin tacked to movable frame.

to place one to three inches of clover chaff, planer shavings or similar material on top of the muslin, as in illustration.

The hover here is shown raised up, but when in use it rests upon the hover support, which consists of a strip of board extending around three sides of the enclosure. This hover support should be five to six inches wide so that when the floor is bedded down with two to three inches of fine litter, the chicks' backs will be against the underside of the pad. Pieces of board or wire cloth (not shown in illustration) should be fitted into the corners to round them out so as to prevent crowding. After the first day or two the chicks can be let out into the front or exercising compartment for feeding and exercise and after a few days, depending upon the outside temperature, they may be allowed to run out in a small pen in front of the brooder.

Chick doors should be about an inch from the floor (not at floor level as shown in illustration) in order to retain the litter with which the floor is to be kept covered at all times. In this brooder no provision is made for adjusting the height of the hover, the proper distance between it and the floor being maintained by varying the thickness of the mat of litter previously mentioned. As the chicks grow larger and require more room, less and less litter will be used, in this way increasing the height of the hover chamber.

Another type of fireless brooder that can readily be made by any person is shown in Fig. 105. In this brooder the sides of the hover compartment are heavily padded, except the front which is protected by a double thickness of felt. The hover consists of a light wooden frame, covered with felt to which can be added a light covering of cotton batting, planer shavings, or other material, if necessary.

How to Use Fireless Brooders

Owing to the danger of chicks crowding for warmth, which is especially liable to occur among those that have no source of artificial heat, it is never advisable to brood them

FIG. 105—ANOTHER TYPE OF FIRELESS BROODER
This illustration shows the simple, easily made fireless brooder in use on Poultry Plant at Wisconsin University.

FIG. 107—ONE OF THE FIRST SUCCESSFUL LAMP-HEATED BROODERS

This brooder has a lamp box underneath the brooding compartment, and was for years a popular type of brooder, until the introduction of independent hovers such as shown in Figs. 108 and 109.

in flocks larger than about 50 to 60, and as there must always be enough to keep each other warm, the flocks should not number less than about 20. The principal difficulty in the use of these brooders is to get the chicks trained to return to the hover for warmth, and this can only be done by giving them the closest attention for the first few days, letting them out just long enough to eat and then pushing them back under the hover and keeping them there. Later, a few minutes at a time, they may be allowed to run out in the exercising compartment if a hover like the one shown in Fig. 106 is used. If the brooder has only a single compartment, the chicks should have a run in front of the brooder not over a foot wide at first, and must be watched and pushed back under the hover at the slightest sign of discomfort, and at frequent intervals whether they appear uncomfortable or not.

Since the dark, heatless hover space does not offer any special attraction to chicks, the difficulty of making them "hoverwise" is greatly increased. Even after they appear to have become accustomed to the use of the hover they never can be entirely trusted, as they are more or less liable to take to huddling outside at any time, and hence must receive more or less attention during practically the entire brooding period.

Owing to the lack of artificial heat, hovers in fireless brooders quickly get damp and it is important to have them taken out daily and sunned or dried before a stove or otherwise. If this is neglected the hover will not only be unsanitary and unhealthful, but the dampness and cold will add to the difficulty of training the chicks. The floor should always be heavily covered with suitable litter and cleaned often enough to keep it dry and free from odor. General methods of care and feeding for the chicks are the same as for those kept in any other style of brooder, and are given in detail in Chapters X and XI.

Lamp-Heated Hovers

Various styles of lamp-heated brooding devices are on the market, belonging, as a rule, to one of two general types—independent hovers, or complete brooders. The former consist simply of a brooding compartment having a metal or wooden top (usually round) supported on legs at a suitable height and with the space underneath enclosed by means of a slashed hover curtain of felt or similar material. To the hover is attached a heating system, with the lamp enclosed in a separate compartment. The whole device is self-contained and more or less independent of the brooder, coop, or house in which it is to be operated. In "portable" hovers the brooding compartment and lamp box are built together and may be moved about at will. These hovers rest directly on the floor of the house or apartment in which they are operated. They have no connection with the enclosure and require no alterations of any kind to fit the building for their use.

Lamp-heated hovers of the type designated by such trade names as "Adaptable," "Universal," etc. (see Figs. 108 and 109), are in great favor among successful chick raisers, especially where chicks are to be brooded in moderate-sized flocks. Hovers of this type have a detachable lamp box, the bottom of which is several inches below the floor on which the hover stands. The lamp box is intended to be located on the outside of the house or compartment in which the chicks are confined, and requires an opening of suitable size in the brooder case or house wall to admit the heat pipe. These hovers may be operated indoors if desired, in which case an elevated floor must be provided for the hovers, the height being adjusted to the particular make of hover used.

Hovers of this type may be used in connection with regular indoor or outdoor brooder cases, ready-made or homemade, or they may be attached to any suitable coop or house. They are moderate in cost and afford almost ideal conditions for brooding chicks in flocks of 100 or less. Equipped with regulators, a reasonably uniform temperature can be maintained, and they probably are as safe from fire as any lamp-heated device can be made. No matter how small the compartment in which the hover is confined the chicks are always sure of a constant supply of fresh air which is drawn from the outside and passes through the heater where it is thoroughly warmed, afterward being forced gradually down among the chicks and finally out through the slits in the hover curtain.

Since the lamp discharges its fumes on the outside, as the hovers are regularly installed, the air in the brooder is kept pure at all times. When the lamp box is located inside the house, the fumes must be discharged indoors but this is not a serious matter in a room of good size. Lamp-heated hovers are used extensively in compartment

FIG. 108—HOVER WITH OUTDOOR LAMP BOX

This hover is designed to be attached to any suitable brooder case, coop, or house. The lamp box is located outside the house and the lamp fumes are discharged on the outside through a specially designed fume pipe which keeps the lamp flame from blowing out. Courtesy of Prairie State Incubator Company.

brooder houses, with or without auxiliary heat. Where this method is followed each brood has separate pen or compartment and may be given just the temperature required for best results, regardless of the others. A long

FIG. 109—HOVER WITH MUSLIN COVERED ENCLOSURE
With lamp-heated hovers of usual size this enclosure should be about 3 feet square and 18 inches high. This enclosure confines the chicks near the hover and prevents floor drafts from striking them. The muslin-covered top will keep the chicks warm under the hover even when the outside temperature drops quite low.

brooder house equipped with hovers of this type is illustrated and described in Chapter XII.

Hover Enclosure for Cold Weather

For cold weather use it frequently is desirable to enclose these hovers, using the convenient form of enclosure shown in Fig. 109. At the Maine Experiment Station where more or less cold weather is regularly experienced at the brooding season, a special type of enclosure has been developed. This is illustrated in Figs. 111 and 113, and is described as follows in Bulletin 471 of that institution:

"In planning this brooder the primary point aimed at was to make a "fresh air and pure air" brooder. With this idea in mind it was thought advisable to make the walls of the brooder in some degree permeable to air. To meet this requirement the walls and cover of the brooder are made of cloth. Essentially the brooder is a cloth box containing a hover, of the type in which the lamp fumes are conducted outside of the building by an exhaust pipe.

"These brooders are built as a constituent part of the house which they occupy. Two brooders are placed in each colony house, one in each of the back corners of the building. In this way one end wall and the back wall of the building form two of the sides of each brooder. The remaining side and cover are made of cloth tacked on light wooden frames as shown in the working drawings.

"The floor of the brooder stands 10 inches above the floor of the house. From the front of the brooder a sloping walk extends down to the house floor, reaching in width clear across the front of the brooder. The cloth front and side of the brooder are not permanently fixed in position but are removable panels held together and to the frame work by hooks and eyes. The cover is hinged in the middle in such a way that it can either be half opened, or entirely opened and folded back out of the way. In consequence of this arrangement it is possible to regulate with great nicety the amount of air which shall be admitted to the brooder. Either the front or the side panel may be tilted out as much as desired at the base, thus admitting air there. Furthermore, by partly opening a panel and the cover it is possible to insure that there shall be a circulation of air through the brooder at all times.

"The hover used in this brooder is the "Universal," modified for present use so that the lamp is inside the house underneath the brooder rather than in a box outside the house, as in the usual arrangement of this hover. The reason for this modification is that in this climate, where bad weather is likely to be experienced during the early part of the hatching season, with heavy winds, snow, and rain, it is much easier and more satisfactory to take care of the lamp inside the house than from a small box outside. Another modification is that in the hovers which are installed in these brooders an especially heavy insulation is put on top of the drum to reduce the loss of heat by radiation in extremely cold weather early in the spring.

"One of the essential points about the brooder is its compactness in storage, and the fact that all the parts may be stored in the base of the brooder itself. In this way the labor expense of carrying parts back and forth from a storage house each year is avoided. To bring about this result the size of the base is so calculated that all parts of the brooder may be enclosed in it. It will be seen that the end of the brooder base containing door is removable, being held in place by buttons at the top. When the end of the brooding season is reached and there is no further use for the brooder that year, the side and front end panel of the brooder are removed, the canvas cover folded back and tacked to the wall of the building and the hover dismantled. All of the parts are then shoved under the brooder floor and the end put back in place again. The floor of the brooder is removable so that it and the floor underneath may be cleaned and disinfected. By removing its legs the hover may be stored in the brooder base along with the other parts, or if one does not desire to do this the hover may be suspended close up to the roof of the building. In that position it will be impossible for the birds to roost on it. Of course, all

FIG. 110—LAMP HEATED HOVERS IN COMPARTMENT BROODER HOUSE
These lamp-heated hovers are the same as the one shown in Fig. 108, modified to permit placing the lamp under an elevated hover floor. For plan of compartment house equipped with ten hovers, see Chapter XII. Courtesy of Prairie State Incubator Company.

movable parts should be taken from the hover before it is hung up in this way. These parts may be stored in the brooder base."

Portable Lamp-Heated Hovers

Portable hovers are quite similar to the lamp-heated hovers previously described, but are so designed that the

THE SELECTION OF BROODING EQUIPMENT

lamp box rests directly upon the brooder or house floor and hence can be set up in any kind of house or apartment where it is practicable to brood chicks, and without the necessity for cutting holes for the heat pipe, providing raised floors, or making any other alterations. Hovers

FIG. 111—MAINE STATION INDOOR BROODER
This illustration shows how hovers like the ones shown in Figs. 108 and 109 may be enclosed, for use where the chicks are to be brooded in cold weather and where unprotected hovers would not afford sufficient warmth without turning the flame extremely high. Courtesy of Maine Experiment Station.

of this type are intended strictly for indoor use and give excellent service under reasonably favorable conditions. The lamps however, are rather closely confined, and when the flame is turned high there is danger of the lamp smoking or becoming overheated. For this reason portable hovers are not recommended for use in severe weather unless they are operated in warmed rooms or are provided with heat-retaining enclosures. A brooder house with auxiliary heat is a most desirable place in which to operate them, and if it is the intention to use these appliances early in the season such a house should by all means be provided.

In moderately cold weather portable hovers may be enclosed in muslin-covered cases as shown in Fig. 124 (illustrated without top in order to show hover in position). This enclosure consists of four frames, which should be about 18 inches wide and 36 inches long, for hovers of average size. Use inch or inch-and-a-half strips of white pine, spruce, or similar light-weight wood that does not split readily, and cover with a good grade of muslin. The panels thus formed are hinged together at three corners, the fourth having a hook instead, so that the frame can be folded compactly for storage when not in use. A small door should be provided in the front panel. The top may be a simple frame covered with muslin, with a hole for the waste-heat pipe from the hover, or better still may be made as shown in Fig. 109.

As long as the temperature of the house or room is 60 degrees or over, it will not be necessary to enclose the hover, but when it goes below that point it is better to do so, especially for newly hatched broods. Even though the hover may be able to furnish sufficient heat to keep the chicks comfortable at lower temperatures, it will be necessary to keep a high flame in order to do it, involving the risk of overheating the lamps and also using a great deal more oil than would be required with the hover suitably enclosed. If it is desired to make this enclosure ratproof it may be done by covering the panels on the inside with wire cloth. Placing the wire on the inside also protects the muslin from the chicks which are apt to pick holes through it.

While it is practicable to brood chicks successfully where there are wide extremes between hover and room temperatures this cannot be considered a favorable condition. It unquestionably increases the attendant's troubles, and the chicks are apt to be stunted and injured by the alternate chilling and overheating. They also are liable to spend more time under the hovers than is good for them when they cannot go outside without instant discomfort. In continuous cold weather much better results will be secured if portable hovers are operated in a house with some form of auxiliary heat. A good-sized room may be warmed to a fairly comfortable temperature with a coal stove or water boiler, doing so at comparatively little expense, and greatly reducing the consumption of oil in brooder lamps. It may not be necessary to provide a hover enclosure under such conditions and it is much more convenient to care for the chicks without it. However, it always is desirable to surround the hover with some sort of guard for the first few days.

It will be clear from the illustrations of portable hovers here shown, that they regularly discharge their lamp fumes inside the apartment in which they are operated. So long as the room or house is of good size and well ventilated, no harm will be done. When the hover is installed in a small building however, such as the average portable colony house, some provision must be made for conducting the fumes outdoors. A practical way of doing this is to provide a galvanized iron pipe about 2 inches in diameter running it straight up or out through the side wall. The lower end of the pipe should be funnel-shaped and must be held securely in place an inch or two above the waste-pipe of the hover so that wind will not affect the lamp, and so that the increased draft caused by the long pipe will not "draw" the flame. Do not neglect providing a T on the outer end as in Fig. 108; it helps greatly in keeping the wind from blowing out the flame.

FIG. 112—PORTABLE HOVER WITH ENCLOSED LAMP BOX
This illustration shows a small lamp-heated portable hover with the lamp box under the hover. Courtesy of Prairie State Incubator Co.

The lamp in a portable hover should be tended regularly and kept scrupulously clean. The lamp bowl should not be filled more than about two-thirds full and should never be allowed to burn empty. A lamp either full or almost empty is more liable to smoke than one moderately full. If the lamp bowl is of limited capacity it is desirable to fill it at least once a day, and when the flame is turned high it may be necessary to do this twice daily. The flame usually gets its supply of air through screen-covered openings and it is highly important that these be kept clean and free from dust which otherwise will clog the screen and cause the lamp to smoke. As to capacity, the rule given on page 80 applies regularly to all sizes of portable hovers. Those most generally in use, such as are shown in Figs. 112, 114 and 124, are designed to accommodate about 100 newly hatched chicks or 65 to 75 older ones.

Hovers Installed in Colony Houses

While the cheapest method of providing comfortable brooding accommodations for small or medium-sized flocks is by the use of hovers installed in homemade brooder cases, the most satisfactory method for general use, especially for early hatches, is to install them in small colony houses, or houses especially designed for the purpose, such as those illustrated and described in Chapter XII. Where this is done the chicks will have plenty of floor space and when they must be confined indoors for days at a time, as is often necessary early in the season, they will continue to grow and thrive almost as well as when able to be outdoors all the time. Such houses may be built in various sizes to meet the needs of the individual chick grower, providing for one or more hovers as preferred.

In a colony house 6x6 feet, which is about as small as it is practical to build them, it seldom is desirable to install more than one hover, but two can be used quite conveniently in houses 6x8 feet or larger. When operated in compartment brooder houses each hover should have a space 4 to 5 feet wide and 8 to 10 feet long. In permanent houses the hovers can either be located on a raised floor or the floor of the passageway may be sunk 6 or 8 inches below the main floor. With colony houses the usual plan is to set the house on runners, or block it up

FIG. 113—MAINE STATION BROODER ENCLOSURE PARTIALLY DISMANTLED
This illustration shows enclosure dismantled. Hover and parts are in lamp box. Top of enclosure is folded back against rear wall of house and fastened by wooden buttons. Courtesy of Maine Experiment Station.

a few inches off the ground so that the hover can rest directly on the house floor.

Indoor and Outdoor Brooders

Complete brooders, to be operated either indoors or outdoors, have been in use for many years. Indoor brooders are not now in much demand, as their place is largely filled by the independent hovers already described, used either with or without enclosures or cases, which, if required, usually are of homemade construction. Outdoor brooders, however, are used in great numbers, particularly where colony houses or permanent brooder houses are not available.

FIG. 114—PORTABLE HOVER WITH OUTSIDE LAMP BOX
This portable hover is similar to the one shown in Fig. 112, except that the lamp box is entirely outside of the hover whereas in the other it is underneath. Courtesy of Watson Manufacturing Company.

One of the first really successful brooders adapted to outdoor use is illustrated in Fig. 107. In brooders of this type the lamp was located underneath the brooder. The floor occupied by the chicks was about ten inches from the ground, and reached by means of an incline in front of the brooder. The lamp or brooder stove used to provide heat had a chimney which came up close to, but did not touch, the underside of a metal sheet which was thus made quite hot and in turn warmed a current of air which was introduced from the outside, passing over the top surface of the metal and beneath the brooder floor. After being warmed the air passed up through a flue or pipe and was discharged under a hover, and forced down around the chicks afterward passing out through slits in the hover curtain, substantially as in the present type of hovers.

This style of heater warmed the brooder floor as well as the air, and when the lamp was turned up strong, often gave so much bottom heat as to cause leg weakness. The elevated floor was another objectionable feature, but the chief defect was the danger of overheating the lamp, especially in brooding chicks in cold weather when it was necessary to have a high flame. Brooders made by standard concerns now-a-days are practically fireproof, but many of the extremely cheap brooders offered for sale leave much to be desired in this respect, and if used at all should be located where they will not endanger valuable property. It is better to avoid all such brooders however, and buy only those that are known to be safe and reliable. Nowhere is it more true than in the purchase of brooder equipment, that "it is better to be safe than sorry."

Some outdoor brooders have built-in heating systems, such as the one shown in Fig. 117. Others consist of a comparatively simple case equipped with an independent hover as in Fig. 115. A well-built brooder should give good satisfaction when used under reasonably favorable conditions, and will last for many years if stored in a dry place when not in service. It is always better to buy first-class brooders and take care of them, than to purchase cheap, flimsy ones that may not give good service even when new, and whose limited usefulness at best is of only short duration.

If necessary to economize in first cost, a practical plan is to secure a hover and build the case at home, which can readily be done by any one handy with tools. As usually built, outdoor brooders are about 3x6 feet, which makes them large enough for 100 newly hatched chicks or 75 after they are two or three weeks old. It is not considered practical to build brooders of larger size than the dimensions just given, and it is extremely unwise to attempt to crowd into any brooder more chicks than it is designed to accommodate. In buying brooders, or hovers for homemade brooders, be sure to get those that have sufficient heating capacity to keep the chicks warm in severe weather.

An outdoor brooder should have at least three compartments, which give the chicks some opportunity to choose the temperature best suited to their requirements. These conditions are best secured by a hover compartment about three feet square, where the temperature under the hover can be kept in the neighborhood of 100 degrees at first, lowering it as the chicks grow older. Around or in front of the hover, depending upon its shape, there should be a space large enough to accommodate all the chicks without crowding. To this space they can escape if the hover becomes too warm and in it they are to be fed for the first few days. Connected with this should be an exercising compartment, also three feet square. This will be warmed somewhat from the heating system in the hover end, but can be opened up as desired to give the chicks air and gradually to harden them off before turning them outdoors.

If the brooder is to be used outdoors in stormy weather it is desirable to provide covered runs as shown in Fig. 115, where the chicks can get out to scratch and exercise without being exposed to wind, rain, or cold. This run may be any convenient size, but should seldom be smaller than 3x6 or 8 feet. If a covered run is not provided there must be some sort of an enclosure to keep the chicks within bounds at first, to prevent their straying away and getting lost, and under many conditions this enclosure is required to protect them from enemies of various kinds. Such enclosure may take the form of the one shown in Fig. 115, which is covered on top as well as sides, or may be like the one illustrated in Fig. 131.

Location for Outdoor Brooder

The brooder and its covered run or yard should have as dry a location as possible. There is no better place for them than a smooth, closely clipped lawn, if such is available. If the brooder is moved frequently to a new location the chicks will do no harm to the grass, and this will provide much of the green feed that is so essential a part of their ration. An additional advantage in brooding newly hatched chicks on the lawn is that they are within easy reach and can be kept under observation all the time, which is highly important during the first few weeks of their lives. When they are past the danger point and need no longer be confined to small runs, they may be moved to some other location where they can have more room. Fields covered with high grass or weeds should be avoided but a few clumps of weeds or bushes to which the chicks can have access for protection from the hot sun, also from hawks, crows, and other enemies, are desirable.

Protection for the brooder and the chicks often does not receive the attention that should be given to this important detail. Not only is it easier to operate the brooder when suitably sheltered, but the chicks will do better. Early in the season the brooder should be placed in the shelter of a building or other substantial windbreak and, if necessary, the sides of the run should be covered with burlap. Still cold will not harm the chicks seriously after they become hoverwise, but a run swept by a raw, cold wind will cause great discomfort and generally results in their staying indoors much of the time, to their great disadvantage.

It may be worth mentioning in this connection that outdoor brooders can be conveniently operated indoors early in the season, if there is a building or even an open shed in which they can be placed. In such a location a small pen or run can be provided for the chicks so that they can get out for exercise regardless of the weather, whereas, if the brooder is out in the open, the chicks may have to be confined to its narrow limits for days at a time. The added convenience and comfort to the attendant, who will be able to care for the brooder and the chicks without being exposed to storms, are in themselves a sufficient reason for keeping the brooder indoors at this season, if possible. In summer the brooder should be placed in the shade, as it is apt to become overheated if exposed to the direct rays of the sun.

FIG. 115—OUTDOOR BROODER AND COVERED RUN
Outdoor brooders are used by many, especially after settled weather has arrived. Covered runs are highly desirable for additional protection after the chicks are old enough to run outdoors. The brooder alone will not afford sufficient room for them, when confined on account of sudden cold snaps, rain, etc

Who Should Use Lamp-Heated Hovers and Brooders

While the better grades of brooders and hovers such as have just been described, have been brought to a high degree of efficiency, and leave scarcely anything to be desired in the way of practical, convenient, and reasonably automatic brooding devices, they all are open to the important objection that they are capable of brooding flocks of only moderate size. Where chicks are to be raised in large numbers it is highly desirable to brood them in as large flocks as are practicable, in order to reduce the labor cost. To meet this demand and to keep as low as possible the cost of equipment and houses, colony hovers, each with a brooding capacity of many hundreds of chicks, have been introduced and have in a short time attained a high degree of popularity. While these huge brooders have been an unqualified success and are now regarded as indispensable wherever chicks are extensively raised, it is not probable that they can or should entirely displace lamp-heated brooders. Each has a distinct place to fill in practical and economical brooding.

No one questions the fact that the person who is operating on a small scale will find lamp-heated brooders better adapted to his requirements. As his plant develops and his flocks grow larger there will come a time when, in the interest of economy and efficiency, he clearly should change over to colony hovers. Just when that point is reached will depend upon a number of considerations and is a matter for individual decision.

One of the most important advantages possessed by lamp-heated brooding devices is that chicks in the comparatively small flocks made necessary by this method of brooding will do much better, as a rule, than when they are herded together in great numbers. The death rate will be lower and the chicks will have better individual opportunities for growth and development. While remarkably good results often are reported in colony hover brooding, the general accuracy of the above comparison has never been seriously questioned. It follows that those who wish to grow valuable chicks with small loss, and with the best opportunities for individual growth and development, will continue to use lamp-heated hovers in spite of the admittedly greater cost of brooding them in this way.

FIG. 116—NONCROWDING PARTITION DOOR FOR BROODERS
With these noncrowding doors in the partition between hover and exercising compartments there will be no corners on either side for the chicks to crowd into.

Similarly those who may be raising comparatively large numbers of chicks but whose seperate broods are small, will find lamp-heated hovers well suited to their use. For illustration, the person who has incubators of 250-egg capacity or less, and who has only a single machine hatching at a time, will find that he can brood his chicks to much better advantage in lamp-heated hovers than with colony hovers. In making a choice of brooding equipment it is worth considering that the best lamp-heated hovers have been brought to a degree of mechanical perfection which makes it possible to operate them with the slightest of attention. A further advantage is that while fuel for colony hovers sometimes is difficult to secure, kerosene can be obtained in practically every section of the country.

Colony Hovers

Colony hovers, while of comparatively recent introduction, have been developed to a good degree of efficiency and are in high favor among those who have large numbers of chicks to brood and who wish to do this in the cheapest and easiest manner. With these hovers chicks may be brooding in flocks of many hundreds and without much more labor than would be required in caring for one small lamp-heated brooder. Single flocks of 1,000 chicks or more having been brooded successfully with colony hovers, though the present tendency is to discount extreme claims as to brooding capacity. Under ordinary conditions 500 chicks are considered enough even for the largest hovers, and many prefer not to exceed 300 or 350.

Various types of colony hovers have been developed and are offered for sale, the chief differences between them being due to the nature of the fuel employed. They all provide a warm brooding room, in any part of which the chicks will be fairly comfortable, and with a circle or zone near the stove or heater where a uniform brooding temperature is to be maintained by the action of a regulator controlling drafts or fuel supply. This brooding zone usually is at a little distance from the heater and its diameter is determined by the size and elevation of the canopy or dome. In some instances, as in the case of the heater shown in Fig. 119, no hover is used, but only a comparatively small heat deflector, the temperature about the heater being maintained at a point sufficiently above the brooding temperature so that the chicks will not collect here, but will gather in a circle outside the too-warm zone.

During the day the chicks scatter all over the room, exercising and scratching for food in the litter and readily finding their way back to the vicinity of the heater when in need of warmth, provided they have been properly trained. There is, however, the same necessity of teaching them to find their way to the source of heat as in the case of lamp-heated hovers—greater in fact, owing to the much more serious consequences that are apt to ensue if a flock of several hundred chicks should begin huddling in some corner instead of spreading out contentedly in an open ring in the comfortable temperature near the stove or heater.

The colony hover was developed, or at any rate attained its first popularity, on the Pacific Coast, where oil or distillate-burning heaters have been in general use for a number of years. These hovers are installed in suitable rooms with the oil supply on the outside, or at least at a distance from the burners. With suitable thermostatic control of fuel they will maintain a fairly uniform temperature in the brooding zone and throughout the room, and are easily regulated and controlled.

The number of chicks that can be brooded with a colony hover is determined as much by the size of the room in which it is operated as by the capacity of the

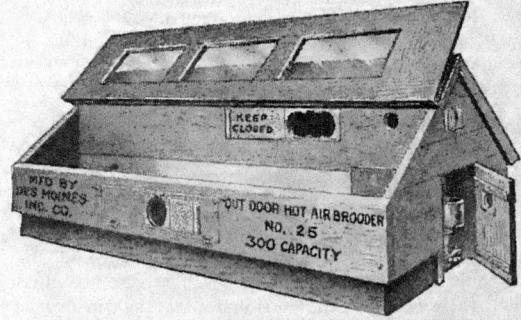

FIG. 117—HOT AIR OUTDOOR BROODER
This brooder has an enclosed lamp and a "built-in" heating system, and affords a comfortable home for outdoor chicks. Courtesy of Des Moines Incubator Co.

heater. By regulating fuel consumption and adjusting height of canopy or hover, the brooding temperature can be extended far enough beyond the heater to give a circle sufficiently large to accommodate many hundreds of chicks. Regardless of heating capacity however, there is a practical limit to the number that can be kept in a room of given size and it is just as objectionable to overcrowd in a brooding room as to do so under a lamp-heated hover. It is difficult to give a general rule governing colony hover capacity, since something depends upon the type of hover, and more perhaps upon the

THE SELECTION OF BROODING EQUIPMENT

FIG. 118—CHOOSE A PROTECTED LOCATION FOR OUTDOOR BROODERS
A southern expose with a windbreak of trees on the west and north is extra desirable for early season brooding.

weather and whether the chicks have an opportunity to get outdoors or not, also the care and attention that they receive. In general, it may be said that a house providing 100 square feet of floor space will afford sufficient room for a flock of 400 to 500 chicks for the first 10 to 15 days, after which they should have additional floor space for exercise, unless the weather is mild and they can spend most of the day outdoors.

In sections where hard coal is obtainable, colony hovers with stoves for burning this fuel are quite popular. Several such hovers installed in a long brooder house, are shown in Fig. 122. They are low in cost, the fuel is comparatively inexpensive, and they give excellent service. They are not so easy to operate as the oil or distillate-burning hovers, nor are they as desirable as the latter in the south where the extremes between night and day temperature are wide, and where it is difficult to check a coal fire sufficiently to keep the room temperature within the proper limits during the day, without having it go out. Efforts to operate coal-burning hovers with soft coal have been made with but limited success, as their fuel capacity is too small to carry a good fire through a cold night. If hard coal or coke is not readily obtainable it usually will be better to purchase kerosene or distillate-burning heaters instead. Another type of brooder suitable for large flocks, and one that has been in successful use for a number of years, is the Cornell gasoline brooder. This brooder was developed by the Poultry Department of Cornell University. Gasoline is far from being popular as fuel but it has some advantages, and if properly handled is safe.

As poultry keepers have begun to favor colony flocks of more conservative size, manufacturers have made an effort to effect a compromise between the small lamp-heated hovers and the requirements of colony brooding, retaining kerosene as fuel. The hover shown in Fig. 120 is one of this type. If not operated under too extreme conditions, they give good results.

How to Use Colony Hovers

Colony hovers can be used successfully at almost any season, though if operated in cold weather it is necessary to provide especially warm quarters. The average coal-burning hover does not have sufficient fuel capacity to heat a large house with single walls and generally cheap construction in severe winter weather, and in the case of oil or gasoline-heated hovers the fuel cost in such houses is practically prohibitive. Almost invariably it is true economy to build with double walls so as to retain heat and reduce fuel consumption.

Flocks of 300 to 500 chicks can be successfully brooded in a house 10x10 feet or 12x12 feet, provided the chicks can spend most of the day outdoors after they are a couple of weeks old. For use early in the season however, more floor space should be provided, doing so either by making the room larger, say 16x16 feet, or by providing a two-room house. There are several reasons why the latter is much better than having the floor space all in one large room. In the first place if the room is large enough to provide comfortably for the growing chicks it will be unnecessarily large for newly hatched broods, and since these must have a comfortable temperature more or less all over the room, the cost of heating will be much greater than is necessary. Another important objection to rooms of large size is the danger from floor drafts which are almost unavoidable in cold weather, and as a result of which epidemics of colds and roup are liable to break out, often causing great losses.

These difficulties are largely overcome by the use of a two-room house such as is illustrated and described in Chapter XII. The brooding room affords comfortable quarters for the chicks during the first two weeks, after which they are allowed access to an adjoining room of about the same size, which will be warmer than outdoors, but decidedly cooler than the brooding room. This arrangement affords an opportunity for the chicks to get hardened off before they are turned out, and provides ample floor space for them if they must be confined indoors on account of cold or stormy weather. The hover room is practically free from floor drafts, and it will cost only about half as much to heat it as would be the case if the entire space were in one room. The brooding room should be built with double walls and windows that can be made tight, but the exercising room need only have single walls, and the front should be arranged so that it can be thrown open when weather conditions permit, thus giving the chicks practically outdoor temperature without exposing them to

FIG. 119—OIL BURNING COLONY HOVER
No hover at all is used with this colony brooder, which is readily regulated so as to maintain a "zone" of correct brooding temperature at a reasonable distance from the heater. This is indicated by the position of the chicks in illustration. Heater burns kerosene or distillate and will successfully brood several hundred chicks at one time.

storms, rain, snow, or high winds, and without cooling down the brooding room.

Colony hovers usually are located in the center of the brooding room. They should be fired up and thoroughly tested so that the operator can be certain that he will be able to maintain a fairly uniform temperature before entrusting chicks to them. When the chicks are first placed under the hover they should be confined by a strip of galvanized wire cloth. This should be about 18 inches wide, and long enough to form a complete circle about the hover at a distance of at least three feet. This guard should be drawn up at first, so that the circle does not extend more than about a foot or so beyond the hover, but after the chicks become familiar with their surroundings and have learned where to go for warmth the circle can be enlarged.

When certain that the chicks can be trusted to return to the hover promptly when uncomfortable, the guard may be entirely removed, though it is a wise precaution

FIG. 120—OIL HEATED COLONY HOVER
This brooding device is provided with a hover under which the chicks gather for warmth. It does not heat the room to as high a temperature as the brooder shown in Fig. 119, and is, therefore, more economical in the use of fuel.

to continue to draw it up around the hover at night, so that the chicks cannot stray off into corners and huddle there as they sometimes do even after they seem to be thoroughly trained. It is important to give these large flocks careful attention, and the greatest pains must be taken never to let the fire go out in cold weather or to permit the temperature to drop too low at night, either of which is liable to start the crowding that is so greatly to be feared. As a further precaution it is wise to round out the corners of the brooding room using wire netting, pieces of prepared roofing, or anything else that will answer the purpose.

Hot Water Brooding Systems

Where large numbers of chicks are to be brooded in cold weather many persons prefer to use hot water pipe systems. These have the disadvantages of exceeding all others in first cost, and their operating season is comparatively short, as it seldom is desirable to brood chicks by this method in warm weather. Hot water brooding systems are fairly easy to operate however, when properly installed, and the advantage of having many hundreds of chicks in comparatively small flocks under one roof with one heater or furnace for all, is especially important in cold weather.

There are two general systems of pipe-heated brooders, each with its own advantages. The method most commonly used in New England is what is known as the open-pipe system where the pipes are entirely exposed or covered only with a cloth-covered frame which is laid over the pipes, this being done in the case of newly hatched chicks or when it is desirable to raise the temperature for any given pen. No hover cloths are provided and the temperature is kept fairly high throughout the room, the chicks getting up close to the pipes for added warmth at night and as needed during the day. A full description of such a brooder house is given in Chapter XII.

The covered-pipe system has various forms, from overhead pipes with a tight hover over the top, to pipes placed under the floor and confined in a box in order to heat air, which then is discharged under a round or square hover, adjustable in height and provided with hover cloths to confine the heat, the chicks being warmed by a hot-air circulating system very much as in lamp-heated hovers.

Both systems give good results when properly managed, the open system being the cheaper to install, probably a little more expensive to operate, and calling for pretty exact control of room temperature. It is not practical to install pipe-heated systems in small houses. Colony hovers or lamp hovers with auxiliary heat are more desirable as well as much cheaper.

Electrically Heated Brooders

Electrically heated brooders probably are the most convenient type of brooding equipment available. Such brooders are easy to operate and when of correct design and provided with reliable regulators require practically no attention. As usually made they may be attached to an ordinary lamp socket, and have a regulator which automatically turns the current on and off as necessary to maintain the desired temperature. No attention whatever is needed aside from adjusting the regulator for more or less heat as occasion requires. Reliable appliances of this sort will maintain an almost uniform temperature under ordinary conditions, and as the current is only on when the heat falls below the point for which the regulator is set, there is no waste of current. If favorable rates can be obtained it is possible to brood chicks in this convenient, labor-saving way as economically as with oil or gas. Since there are no lamps to fill or clean, no coal or ashes to handle, no danger from fire, and no lamp or stove to taint the air, it is possible to operate electric brooders where it would not be desirable to use any other kind. A brooder of this type is illustrated in Fig. 121.

Homemade Brooders

There is little demand for plans for homemade brooders nowadays and still less excuse for them. It is possible for any one who wishes to do so to build a brooder of the general type as the one shown in Fig. 107, using a similar heating method, but such brooders are so inferior to those now made by reliable manufacturers, and so unsafe as regards fire, that there is no good reason for giving them any consideration.

Most manufacturers furnish complete heating and brooding systems or independent hovers for installation in homemade brooder cases, for either indoor or outdoor use, and it is entirely practical to use them in this way.

Local tinsmiths cannot make them as cheaply nor as well as those regularly manufactured, and the use of a makeshift heating system is unwise. With no other purpose in view than to safeguard the interests of the chick grower, we most earnestly advise against wasting time or money on homemade brooding outfits, other than outdoor or indoor cases to be equipped with hovers or brooder heaters especially designed for such use. There is too much at stake both in the chicks that are brooded and in the danger to valuable property which results from the use of lamp-heated brooders of the usual homemade construction, to warrant any one in experimenting with such devices.

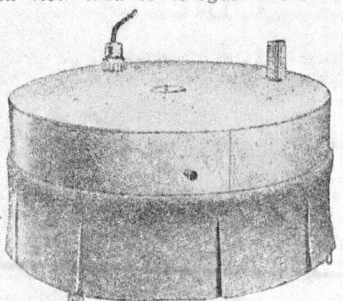

FIG. 121—HOVER HEATED BY ELECTRICITY
This hover has a heating plane in the top and is a most convenient brooding device where current can be obtained at a reasonable rate. It is equipped with a regulator which automatically cuts out the current when the temperature goes above the desired point.

No Economy in Skimping On Brooder Equipment

It is scarcely possible to overemphasize the importance of providing sufficient brooding capacity for the chicks that are to be raised. The average chick raiser almost invariably is short on brooders at the time when he needs them most, which is false economy in about its worst form. There is no disputing the fact that millions of chicks die from exposure every season—chicks that would have lived and returned to their owners a substantial profit, if only they had been properly brooded. The incubator often is unjustly blamed for hatching out weakly chicks that could not be raised when, as a matter of fact, they were sturdy and vigorous when hatched but were sacrificed to their owner's neglect to provide suitable brooders for them—none at all in some instances, and in others cheap, inferior makes with inadequate heating capacity, resulting in the chicks being exposed to low or irregular temperatures that they could not possibly endure.

In still other cases first-class brooders may be provided but not in sufficient numbers, so that the chicks are injuriously crowded, and perhaps are removed from the brooder to make room for younger lots weeks before they should be deprived of artificial heat. Overcrowding of brooders is a most common practice, and while a little slower in action, is about as serious in its final effect as having no brooders at all. The wise chick raiser will learn the actual capacity of his brooders and will then either limit his hatching to that number, or will provide the additional equipment needed in good time, even though to do so may necessitate spending more money for the purpose than is convenient. Skimping on brooders is in no sense economical or practical, though it is extraordinarily difficult to get beginners, and even many experienced growers, to realize how much they lose and how seriously they imperil their whole poultry enterprise, by such a pennywise policy.

How to Estimate Brooding Capacity Required

So far as the beginner is concerned, it is possible that a good deal of this deficiency in brooding equipment is due to the fact that he does not understand just what his requirements are going to be, nor what is a reasonable number of chicks to place in a brooder. Speaking generally, hover capacity may be figured on the basis of floor space following the rules for doing this which will be found on page 80. The capacity of the average round hover, measuring 20 to 24 inches in diameter, is in the neighborhood of 65 to 75 chicks at three weeks old. With these rules or estimates for general guidance, it should be a simple matter for the most inexperienced to determine the amount of hover space he will need for a given incubator capacity. Counting the average hatch at about two-thirds of the egg capacity of the machine, which is a reasonable basis on which to figure, a 100-egg incubator will require one good lamp-heated hover to take care of a hatch. For a 150 to 200-egg machine two such hovers will be needed, and for a 350 to 400-egg machine three hovers, or one colony hover will be required, the latter being large enough to take the entire hatch from two such incubators when necessary. These estimates apply to a single hatch in each case.

Chicks can seldom be weaned from artificial heat until they are over four weeks old, and in early spring will need to be brooded for six weeks or more. Hence, if the incubators are being run continuously there must be brooder capacity for two successive hatches, or double the number required for one hatch. This is where a great many chick growers make a most serious mistake, failing, as they do, to provide brooders for the second lot. This makes it necessary to put the first chicks into cold brooders when only about three weeks old—a step that is practically certain to result in heavy losses, es-

FIG. 122—COLONY HOVERS IN LONG POULTRY HOUSE
Illustration shows several coal-burning hovers installed in a long house. For this purpose a regular brooder house may be used or a laying house divided by means of suitable temporary partitions.

pecially in the early part of the season. Either provide the extra brooders or hovers needed, or delay the second hatch until the first lot of chicks can be removed to cold brooders without injury.

CHAPTER X

Care and Management of Brooder Chicks

When to Take the Chicks From the Incubator—How to Determine Capacity of Any Brooder—Teaching Chicks to
Use the Hover—How to Make and Use Cold Brooders—Importance of Litter and
What Kind to Use—Labor-Saving Methods.

IT IS assumed in this chapter that the chick grower has selected the brooding equipment best suited to his requirements, and that he has looked ahead and has purchased it well in advance of the time when it will be needed, so that there will be ample time in which to set it up and test it out before entrusting valuable chicks to its care. That is assuming a good deal too much in many instances, for unpreparedness is the average poultry keeper's besetting sin, and he frequently pays dearly for it. The beginner especially, and all who are trying out new equipment, should realize the importance of thorough testing in order to learn just what results can reasonably be expected, doing this in ample time so that any adjustments that may be needed can be made before the brooder or the hover, as the case may be, must be put into active service. The too common plan of placing chicks in a brooder whose limitations are not known, expecting to be able to meet conditions as they arise, is responsible for enormous losses each year —losses that might readily be prevented with a little forethought and timely preparation.

In testing out a new brooder or hover it is not enough to be sure that it is in good general working order, that the lamp burns steadily and evenly, and that it heats up readily. All this is important; but it is even more important, from a practical point of view, to learn what the brooder will NOT do. Every brooding device, of whatever kind, is capable of supplying just so much heat, and when the outside temperature drops below a certain limit it is impossible for it to maintain the proper brooding temperature. Just what that limit is will depend not only upon the capacity of the heating system, but also upon the conditions under which it is used. This information each operator must secure himself, and it can not be too plainly stated that until he has done this he is not ready to begin brooding chicks. The operator has only himself to blame for the trouble and losses that he is about certain to meet if this precaution is neglected.

The importance of learning the limitations of whatever brooding devices are used is all the greater because average expectations regarding them are entirely too high; that is, more is expected and demanded of them than is reasonable or possible. The conditions that the brooder must meet, especially early in the season, are hard enough at best, what with the cold, raw winds, sudden and extreme cold snaps, belated snow storms, and days of continuous rain that then are to be expected in most sections of the country. Winter fires may have to be resorted to in dwellings, but still it is expected that a little, one-inch lamp flame will furnish sufficient heat to maintain a temperature of approximately 100 degrees under a hover that has only a thin board wall for protection against storms and perhaps almost zero temperatures. The better class of brooding devices are marvelously efficient in the use of the comparatively small amount of heat available, but there is always a limit beyond which they cannot reasonably be expected to go in supplying warmth, especially in the case of broods of newly hatched chicks which require much higher temperatures under the hover than those that are several weeks old.

All brooder tests should be made with a thermometer in the room as well as under the hover, and a written record should be kept of the temperature in both locations. If this is done the brooder's natural limits will quickly be learned and there need be no uncertainty then as to just what may reasonably be expected in the future. With the flame turned as high as it is desirable to have it, if the hover heat can be kept up to 100 only when the room or outside temperature is at or above 50, then that must be accepted as the brooder's limit, and if it is to be operated at lower temperatures some means of conserving the heat must be provided. The worst thing that can be done is to risk chicks in the brooder when it is known that the temperature to which it is to be exposed will go well below its limit— "taking a chance" on their coming through alive. The operator can depend upon it that if his brooder, in a definite test, fails to maintain sufficient heat when the outside or room temperature drops below a certain point, whether that is 40, 30 or 20 degrees, it will always fall short thereafter at about that point.

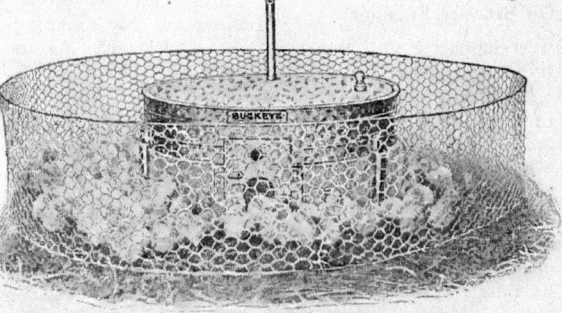

FIG. 123—PORTABLE HOVER WITH WIRE GUARD
Enclosed within a circular wire guard chicks cannot stray away from hover and get chilled. If one-half or three-fourth-inch mesh netting cannot be secured it will be safer to use galvanized wire cloth. Courtesy of Buckeye Incubator Company.

What to Do When the Brooder Does Not Heat Up

Most complaints in regard to the brooder's failing to heat up are due to unreasonable demands—to expecting it to maintain brooding temperatures under impossible conditions. There are, however, various measures that may be taken to help out in emergencies, and there are some things that must not be done. The heating system, whether it is oil, gas, or coal, can never be forced with safety. If the lamp or heater, working at a safe limit, will not furnish enough heat to meet necessary requirements, then there is only one thing to do, and that is to find some way to save more of the heat. NEVER take chances on a smoking or overheated lamp by turning the flame beyond what is known to be the safety point.

The simplest way to handle an outdoor brooder that

CARE AND MANAGEMENT OF BROODER CHICKS

is not furnishing sufficient heat is to get it indoors where it will be warmer and where it will be protected from wind. If that cannot be done it may be possible to put it in a more sheltered place such as setting it close to a building or other windbreak, banking up around it with leaves, straw, planer shavings, or anything that will stop the circulation of the air around it and conserve heat. Practically all ventilation in the brooder compartment can be cut off under such conditions, as there will still be a sufficient circulation of air to meet all necessary requirements. If there are two or more flocks of the same age to be protected, it may be practical to put them both together in one brooder so that their bodily heat may reinforce that from the lamp. If nothing else can be done, the brooder can at least be covered with blankets, rugs or pieces of carpet.

Where hovers are used it always is wise to have a few cloth-covered enclosures such as the one shown in Fig. 109 in order to be prepared for emergencies, and these enclosures also can be helped out under extreme conditions by banking up with planer shavings, etc., as shown in Fig. 128. In banking up or blanketing any sort

FIG. 124—MUSLIN COVERED HOVER ENCLOSURE
Where there is danger of floor drafts, a hover enclosure for newly hatched chicks like the above is better than open wire as shown in Fig. 123.

of brooder or hover there is danger of cutting off the supply of air needed by the lamp, or reducing the free circulation of air required to keep it cool, and pains should always be taken to see that this does not occur. Many smoked and overheated lamps result from this cause.

All such precautions as have been here suggested are merely makeshifts intended to meet sudden and unexpected emergencies, and must not be relied upon regularly. They add greatly to the labor of caring for the chicks and are only fairly satisfactory at best. If the brooder is going to require frequent helping out in this way it will be much more practical to set it aside for warmer weather and provide some other appliance that will supply enough heat to meet the requirements.

Under all ordinary conditions the thing to do where chicks are to be brooded early in the season, is to have a permanent brooder house, warmly built and equipped with some source of auxiliary heat if necessary. Regular hot-water heating systems are best and cheapest in large houses, but in small ones a coal-burning stove will give good satisfaction. This will keep the room fairly comfortable and make it comparatively easy for the hover or brooder lamp to keep up the brooding temperature, and will afford much more favorable conditions for the chicks when out of the hover.

When to Take the Chicks Off

If the incubator can be spared for the purpose and the chicks are not too much crowded, it is desirable to leave them in the nursery for about 24 hours after they are all out. If it is necessary to reset the machine at once they may be taken out as soon as they are all dry, but where this is done, careful attention must be given to prevent their chilling. When chicks must be taken from the machine at this time, the best plan is to put them in warmly

FIG. 125—METHOD OF MARKING CHICKS
A hole punched in the web of the chick's foot is a convenient way of permanently marking the chick. The hole will never grow over, and chicks so marked can always be identified. There are 15 different combinations possible, as shown in this illustration.

lined baskets or boxes and keep them covered up and in a warm place for a day or so. If it is not practicable to do this, especial pains must be taken to have a reliable brooder or hover ready for them, thoroughly warmed up and accurately regulated to incubator temperature. If possible, the brooder should be in a warm room where the chicks will not be exposed to cold the instant they get outside the hover.

Whenever they are moved, the chicks must be carefully protected against chilling. A warmly lined basket or a tray such as is shown in Fig. 80 should be provided. The top of the box should be covered with a cloth frame, and two light partitions, put together in the form of a cross, should be provided to divide the chicks into four lots and prevent crowding when the tray is filled, or to keep them together in one or two compartments if only a few are to be handled. Fasten the partitions together but leave them loose in the box so that they can readily be taken out for cleaning and disinfecting, which should be done for each brood. Do not try to move too many chicks at a time if the room is cold, but take out a few and then close the machine and dispose of these before removing any more.

Record Marking for Chicks

When the chicks are taken from the incubator is the time to mark them, if any sort of breeding or hatching record is to be kept. One way of doing this is by the use of leg bands as shown in Fig. 129. As there is more or less trouble with leg bands, however, owing to the necessity for changing them as the chicks grow, the system of marking them by means of a band in the wing is regarded as more satisfactory. A leg band is employed until the chicks are about a month old and then it is transferred to the wing as shown in Fig. 130.

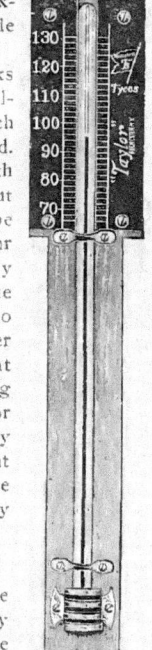

FIG. 126—BROODER THERMOMETER.

A simpler way where flock or hatching records only are to be kept and not individual numbers, is by the

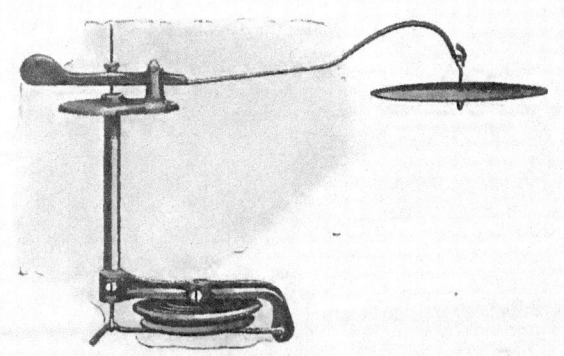

FIG. 127—A BROODER TEMPERATURE REGULATOR
While regulators are not as essential on brooders as on incubators, they will be found well worth the extra cost—particularly during the first few days when the hover temperature should be fairly uniform. The regulator illustrated above has a wafer thermostat. Courtesy of Prairie State Incubator Company.

familiar toe-punching method. This is illustrated in Fig. 125. A record is kept of the significance of each combination of punched webs and chicks so marked can readily be identified ever after, as the holes in the web will never grow over. A more systematic method of identifying by toe-marking is described by Prof. F. C. Hare, of Clemson College, S. C., as follows:

"In the system that I am using at Clemson College, the toe punches are always known by number, and not by inside or outside, left or right, or any location term. Four valuations are given to the webs between the six toes thus: The outside web of the left foot is 1; the inside web of the left foot is 2; the inside web of the right foot is 4; and the outside web of the right foot is 8. These marks must be memorized, but if you will say them over a few times that will readily be accomplished. Just remember that the series is 1, 2, 4, 8, with the 1 at the left or PROPER UNIT place.

"Now, let us see how we will punch that chick from pen three so that every time we catch him, or any of his brothers or sisters, we will know at once that the youngster is a progeny of pen three. The outside left web is 1, and inside left is 2. Three (3) is made by punching both 1 and 2 (both webs on the left foot). So that we have this rule: Always add the value of the punched webs and the result is the number of the chick. For example, 4 is one punch, the inside right; 5 is 4 plus 1, or inside right and outside left, and so on up to 15—8 and 4 and 2 and 1, or every web punched. When you catch any bird, examine his feet and add up the value of his punched webs. You've got his number at once. I like to associate the bird's number with the pen from which he was bred, as that saves all the annoyance and trouble of looking up his number in a note book.

"We have been using this method here, and it is so much more satisfactory than the ordinary way that I want others to profit by it. The students can read the number of a chick from his feet without error, and tell to which pen he belongs. They have never heard the terms "inside left" or "outside right," and are not bothered with a complicated system of identification that is impossible to keep in mind."

Teaching the Chicks to Use the Hover

Place the chicks under the hover and keep them there for at least several hours before feeding or watering. A wire guard such as is illustrated in Fig. 123 is indispensable at this time, setting it up just far enough from the hover so that the chicks can get outside the curtain, which should be pinned up here and there so that there will be no possible chance for them to lose their way. If the hover is square or oblong and open on only one or two sides, make suitable wire-covered frames instead, and set them up in front of the hover, moving them back as the chicks learn how to use the additional space. After they are once settled under the hover they should not be confined to it but should have an opportunity to run in and out, thus learning the source and location of heat and how to find their way to it. Keep them under constant observation at this time and push them back under the hover at frequent intervals not only to prevent any possibility of their getting chilled, but to make certain that they do not form the habit of huddling together for warmth outside the hover, which habit, once formed, will be a source of continual trouble during the entire brooding period.

Gradually give the chicks more liberty, moving the guard farther back from the hover, but never leaving them for long at a time until certain that they will voluntarily go in when cold or uncomfortable.

Different broods of chicks vary more or less in the promptness with which they become hoverwise. A single day may be sufficient in some cases, but usually it takes at least two or three days, and sometimes longer. Bear in mind that every increase in liberty, such as removing the guard, giving the chicks the run of the entire brooder or house pen, letting them out into yards, and increasing the size or shape of these, is a danger point. Chicks readily get confused and lost in unfamiliar surroundings, and every such change should be made gradually and the chicks kept under observation until certain that they

FIG. 128—INDOOR BROODER INSULATED WITH PLANER SHAVINGS
This illustration shows measures taken to save heat in cold-weather brooding. The indoor brooder case is placed a few inches from the house wall and the space between is packed with planer shavings. Courtesy of Wisconsin Experiment Station.

thoroughly know their way back. This trouble is especially liable to occur during the first week or two, when the operator is impatient to get rid of guards, etc., which are somewhat troublesome, but without which heavy losses may result. If the chicks have been properly trained they will be thoroughly familiar with their surroundings by the time they are two weeks old and thereafter they may be allowed to go and come at will.

Correct Brooder Temperature

The temperature to be maintained under the hover will vary with the style of brooder used, the kind and position of thermometer, the outside temperature, and the age and development of the chicks. For this reason an exact schedule of hover temperatures cannot be given, though it can be approximated. The conduct of the chicks themselves is a fairly accurate indication as to whether the heat is right, but is not to be entirely relied upon, as it is possible to accustom young chicks to a higher temperature than is good for them by continually keeping the brooder a little too warm.

Whatever the theoretically correct temperature may be at any given time, it is only correct in practice when the chicks themselves have put their O. K. upon it. If they are restless and dissatisfied the temperature must be raised sufficiently to make them comfortable, whatever the increase may be. However, any marked variation from normal requirements is good ground for suspecting that something else is wrong. Possibly the thermometer is inaccurate—that is a matter of frequent occurrence with the low-priced ones commonly used in brooders. Sometimes the chicks are weakly, due to inferior breeding stock or to injuries received during incubation; and sometimes there is a defect in the brooder itself that needs correction. Remember that a somewhat higher temperature than normal is always required in cold or windy weather.

Because of the various conditions that may modify temperature requirements and because the chicks themselves must be the court of last resort, many operators discard the thermometer entirely and depend solely on the chicks and the "feel" when the hand is thrust under the hover. This method may prove satisfactory for operators of experience but it would seem unwise to recommend it for general adoption, especially during the first few weeks of the chicks' lives when there are other things besides low temperatures that may cause discomfort and restlessness among them and when, without a thermometer, the inexperienced operator may be completely misled as to actual conditions under the hover.

Brooding Temperature for First Four Weeks

In general, it is wise to start with the temperature at 100 when the chicks are all under the hover, reducing it at the rate of about 5 degrees each week until the chicks are four weeks old, when the temperature should be about 80. These temperatures are to be taken with a thermometer so placed that the bulb will be about on a level with the chicks' backs and well inside the hover curtain but not necessarily in the warmest spot. The schedule here given represents a fair average of temperature requirements at all times during the first four weeks, but may safely be varied 5 degrees either way as weather conditions and the conduct of the chicks dictate.

Chicks when settled for the night should not be huddled together in a bunch under the hover—that means too little heat; neither should they collect outside the hover curtain—a sure indication that it is too warm. Instead, they should all be under the hover but spread out loosely with a few heads sticking out around the curtain. As the temperature drops during the night the chicks will gradually draw back toward the warm center. The caretaker must see to it that there is plenty of surplus heat when the temperature is liable to drop low during the night. If the hover has a regulator, as it should, this surplus heat will be allowed to escape until it is needed. If not, the chicks will have to get away from it by keeping close to the hover curtain in the evening. In warm weather when it sometimes is almost impossible to supply any heat at all during the day without having too much when the chicks gather under the hover, it is a good plan to raise part of the hover curtain. It is much better to do this than to let the lamp go out, in which case there will be no reserve heat at all in case of a sudden change.

FIG. 129—CHICK WITH LEG BAND

Numbered leg bands must be provided where each chick is to have a separate number. At the Kansas Experiment Station the newly hatched chicks are banded on the leg with pigeon bands. When they are three or four weeks old the bands are transferred to the wing. See Fig. 130.

After the chicks are large enough to run out more or less during the day, it still is well to keep up a good temperature under the hover so that any that get chilled can warm up quickly. In brooders that have square or oblong hovers and in which one side or end is noticeably warmer than the rest of the hover space, the temperature must always be high enough so that the chicks will keep away from the warm end. If it gets cold enough so that they crowd to the warm spot there is likely to be trouble.

From the time the chicks are hatched until they no longer need artificial heat, they must be protected against getting chilled. It is expensive and unnecessary to have a great excess of heat, but it is always better to err on the side of too much rather than too little. The chicks can get away from too much heat, but they have no recourse when there is too little. Great losses occur annually on account of brooders being operated at too low temperatures, either through carelessness or on account of inadequate heating systems. Many operators persist year after year in using brooders that are known to be unequal to the demands that will be placed upon them—that cannot supply the heat needed or cannot be relied on to keep it uniform over night, though they well know that a single chilling is certain to cause serious trouble and may result in the loss of the entire flock.

How Many Chicks to the Brooder

One of the most common sources of disease and loss among brooder chicks is overcrowding in the brooder or house pen, and it is important that the actual capacity of the brooder, hover, or pen be clearly understood. There are no definite standards for estimating brooder capacity, but as the average egg occupies approximately 3.5 square inches in the incubator it is clear that the chicks should each have at least 4 square inches of floor space under the hover. This means that to accommodate 100 newly hatched chicks the hover must be not less than 20 inches square, or about 23 inches in diameter if round. By the time the chicks are two or three weeks old they will be badly crowded if allowed no more space than this, and the number should be reduced to 65, or 75 at the most.

Since the claims of various manufacturers as to the capacity of their brooders are based on different standards, it will prevent confusion and disappointment if the following general rule is applied to all: Learn the number of square inches enclosed under the hover and divide this by 4 to get the capacity in newly hatched chicks; divide by 6 to learn the number of chicks that can be accommodated when 3 weeks old; and by 8 to get the capacity in chicks 5 weeks old. If there are any lamp boxes or heat drums occupying floor space under the hovers, this must be deducted before making the division. If the weather is quite warm so that it does not matter whether the chicks can all get under the hover or not, these limits may be somewhat exceeded. On the other hand, the regular estimated capacity should always be discounted in cold weather.

Inasmuch as there are few instances where it is practicable to divide or reapportion broods at the end of the third week when additional room is imperative if the brooders have been filled to capacity at first, the most practical plan is to base all estimates on the number of three-week-old chicks the brooder can accommodate, and limit the original flocks to about that number. Where the maximum capacity of the brooder is required at the start, the chicks usually are left in it indefinitely, with the result that they are badly overcrowded as they reach larger size.

Do not guess at the dimensions of the hover or in regard to the proper number of chicks to be brooded in it. Learn just what its capacity is, and never exceed it. If there are more chicks than there is brooder capacity for, and it is impossible to provide additional space in any other way, at least make some fireless brooders and put the surplus in these. It is useless to hatch out good chicks simply to kill them off in overcrowded brooders where they do not have sufficient liberty of movement, are apt to get overheated when the brooder is too warm, or where they cannot all get under the hover when it is cold. Even though no direct losses should result, there will be a general lack of thrift, and the chicks will be weakened and made increasingly liable to ailments which they probably would have entirely escaped if they had had a fair chance in the brooder.

The amount of houseroom that should be provided for chicks will depend to some extent upon the climate. Comparatively little room outside the hover will be sufficient for the first week, after which it should be increased as rapidly as is found to be safe. Where the chicks must be confined indoors most of the time it is usual to provide a pen about 4x10 feet for the use of a flock of 100 after they are about three weeks old—an average of about 2.6 chicks to each square foot of floor space. Naturally, if the chicks can be outdoors most of the time during the day less floor space will be needed.

Much less space than this usually is allowed to colony-hover chicks, a room 10x10 or 12x12 feet being considered sufficient for a flock of 300 to 500 chicks. The latter number however, will be badly crowded in even a 12x12-foot room, after the chicks are a few weeks old, unless the weather is so mild that they can be outdoors most of the time. A portable colony house 8x8 feet is recommended by the Poultry Department of Cornell University, for a flock of 250 newly hatched chicks, which allows one square foot to four chicks.

Providing Ventilation

Ventilation, so far as the hover space itself is concerned, generally is taken care of by the heating system which in most brooders is designed to furnish a supply of fresh, warmed air under the hover, making any especial attention to this point unnecessary except in warm weather when little heat is supplied and the movement of the air is slow and uncertain. If the hover is one of the indoor type the lamp fumes must either be piped out of the house or special ventilation provided to get rid of them. This is not necessary in a large room which can be freely ventilated, but in small or tightly closed houses, also where a number of hovers are being operated in one room, it will pay to provide a direct outlet for the fumes. After the chicks are far enough along so that they do not require artificial heat, ventilation becomes more important.

As a rule, it is desirable to leave the chicks under the hover for some time after heat is no longer required, opening up the curtain sufficiently to provide some circulation of air.

Just how long the chicks should have heat will depend on season and breed, also on the condition of particular broods. In quite warm weather the chicks may

FIG. 130—CHICK WITH WING BAND
Many persons who keep a pedigreed record of their chicks prefer to remove the leg band after the chick is a few weeks old and transfer it to the wing. A little slit is made in the web, using a sharp penknife, and the band is slipped through and bent into place. It remains here without further attention during the life of the chick. Photo from Kansas Experiment Station.

be able to supply sufficient bodily heat without using the lamp at all. Usually they need heat for three to four weeks in mild weather, and for as long as 7 or 8 weeks in the case of extra-early broods. The conduct of the chicks themselves should be the guide in deciding this. As long as they require heat in order to be comfortable it should be supplied, no matter how long that may be. Great harm will be done by cutting off the heat too soon. This practice is of common occurrence where not enough brooding equipment is provided, making it necessary to take the brooders for new flocks before the older chicks are sufficiently developed to get along without them. There is no economy whatever in doing this. It is always better to have a little more brooder equipment than is needed, rather than less. The man who has one or two hovers that he never has to unpack will raise more chicks and will raise them more successfully than the one who must continually push his chicks along into cold brooders before they are ready for them.

In the changeable weather of early spring it is wise to leave the hovers in position for some time after the lamp is permitted to go out, since a sudden cold snap may necessitate firing up again. However, as soon as it is reasonably certain that no more heat will be required, it is advisable to substitute cheap, homemade cold brooders or hovers. These will answer the purpose as well as the manufactured ones and will add many years of usefulness to the latter. Allowing chicks to continue using the regular hovers after they no longer need artificial heat results in rapid deterioration of equipment.

The Use of Cold Brooders

A cold brooder that may be made quite cheaply, and is easily substituted for heated hovers, is shown in Figs. 133 and 134. This cold hover originated at the Poultry Department of Wisconsin Experiment Station, and has been in successful use there for some years. An open, four-sided wooden frame on an elevated floor is provided for the circular lamp-heated hovers that are used as long as the chicks need artificial heat. Afterwards the "cold frame" is substituted for the hover, the method of doing this being thus described in Wisconsin Bulletin 261:

"On a mild night remove the hover from the brooder box and insert a 'cold frame.' A cold frame is made twenty-seven inches square with eight-inch plain boards on three sides, the fourth side being open, except for a slitted curtain of soft, warm cloth of the same color, if possible, as the curtain around the hover. The top of the cold frame is made of strips an inch thick and three inches wide, nailed together at the ends to form a frame which fits inside of the side pieces and rests on blocks nailed in each corner. This frame is covered with single-faced eiderdown or other warm cloth tacked loosely so that it sags in the center and rests on the chicks' backs when they go into the frame to sleep at night or warm up during the day. The open side is placed against the south side of the hover box through which the chicks enter. The chicks are accustomed to go through this opening in search of warmth and usually take to the new home without trouble. If they do not go in, put them in carefully. The corners of the frame must be well banked with litter (planer shavings) so that center of frame is the lowest, with a gradual rise to each corner,

"The cold frame boxes are about six inches smaller than the brooder box. This space is banked full with litter so that chicks cannot fly on top of the brooder box and get into this narrow space. This packing of litter helps to make the cold frame warmer. On cold nights if the chicks seem inclined to huddle together, cover the top with two or three burlap sacks for additional protection. As the chicks get older and no longer need the protection of the cold frame, they begin to stay outside or just inside near the opening. Do not disturb them and in a few more nights practically all will be inclined to stay outside. Then the cold frame can be removed, disinfected, and dried for the next lot. While it is in use the cloth top should be carefully sunned or dried each day and the litter should be frequently changed if best results are to be secured."

In warmer weather it is sufficient to replace the round heated hovers with wooden ones a few inches greater in diameter, enclosed in the usual way with slashed hover curtains and supported on legs so that the hover space will be about 8 inches high. It is a sim-

FIG. 131—OUTSIDE BROODER WITH ENCLOSED RUN
Outdoor brooders should be provided with some sort of enclosed run to which newly hatched chicks can be confined. If the covered run shown in Fig. 115 is considered too expensive, at least have one like this. It will pay for itself in a short time.

ple matter to take out the regular hovers and set these cheap, simple substitutes in their places, and if this is done in mild weather the chicks will not notice the change. Do not make the mistake of doing this right at the beginning of a cold spell however, nor should the preparation of these hovers be postponed until the need for them is pressing. The brooder season on the poultry farm is the busiest of all the year and there is never time enough for doing the things that need to be done then.

Chicks do not readily take to changes, and it will simplify this part of the work greatly if the lamp-heated and cold hovers do not differ greatly in appearance. By all means avoid moving the chicks to new quarters and changing the hover at the same time. The almost inevitable result is to have them crowd together in some corner, smothering and sweating and laying the foundation for sore eyes, colds, diarrhea, and other ailments.

Transferring chicks from brooders or brooder houses to colony houses is always a danger period. Even though they may be accustomed to cold brooders or none at all, when they are moved to strange quarters they are apt to crowd in some corner, and serious injury may occur. There should always be some means provided for rounding out the corners of the house such as by the use of boards, a strip of prepared roofing, a piece of netting, etc. These can be lightly tacked or hooked in place and removed when no longer needed.

Cleanliness and Disinfection

Cleanliness, as applied to brooders, means that they shall be dry and free from unpleasant odors, and that the litter shall be removed frequently enough to prevent an undue accumulation of droppings. This does not necessarily mean that there is to be no accumulation at all, but there must be no dampness or foul smell.

Whether the floor under the hover should be cleaned every day will depend on the number of chicks and the thickness of the litter, also on the kind of litter used. The ideal way perhaps, is to clean out under the hover once a day, but in practical poultry keeping much time and labor may be saved by using plenty of litter and cleaning less frequently. A deep bed of litter with a liberal percentage of dry, odorless droppings mixed in it may actually be more sanitary—may be "cleaner"—than a floor laboriously cleaned every day, but so sparingly littered that the brooder is always smelly and the chicks' feet continually soiled with fresh droppings. Whatever may be done elsewhere it will pay to use litter freely in and about brooders and hovers. Keeping chicks on practically bare floors cannot be excused on the ground of economy or any other. The floor of the house pen or brooder need only be cleaned infrequently if litter is freely used. For example, where deep litter feeding is adopted (see Chapter XI) it is not necessary to remove the litter for weeks at a time. However, if it gets noticeably damp from any cause it must be removed at once.

The need for disinfection depends somewhat on conditions. If there is any reason to suspect that there is disease in the flock, more frequent disinfection will be called for than would be the case where the chicks are all healthy. However, the brooder should at least be disinfected for each new brood. For this purpose formaldehyde or a good coal-tar disinfectant can be used, applying it with a spray pump or, in case of the hover floor, with a scrub broom or brush. Always have the brooder thoroughly dry before using for the next brood of chicks and if it is to be disinfected during occupancy, let the work be done on a warm, sunny day, and have the brooder thoroughly dry before turning the chicks back in. If they are too young to stay out for the time necessary to do this, transfer them to another brooder or put them in clean fireless brooders or the chick trays used in transferring them from the incubator.

These steps will be about all that will be required under ordinary conditions but it will be found a wise precaution to keep some disinfecting solution on hand at all times. Use it in washing the water founts and feeding vessels at frequent intervals, especially if milk or soft feeds are supplied.

Under the head of cleanliness comes the injunction to see to it that the litter is kept dry and reasonably free from droppings. Extremely dusty litter also is highly objectionable and it must be renewed frequently enough to prevent its becoming so. If feed, especially moist mash, is scratched into the litter it should promptly be removed and replaced with new. Also, when the water fount is left standing in one place, the litter frequently becomes water-soaked and in this condition is a menace to the health of the flock. Always remove litter that gets wet from any cause, and shift the location of the fount frequently, unless an elevated platform is provided for it and the feed hoppers, which is by far the better plan.

FIG. 132—GET THE CHICKS OUTDOORS AS SOON AS POSSIBLE
Chicks that can get down on the ground in direct sunlight will do much better than when shut indoors. Keep them confined close to the door until they can readily find their way back and forth.

The runs or yards also should receive regular attention. When outdoor coops or brooders are used they must be moved frequently to new ground, and if for any reason the covered runs or yards are allowed to stand in one place until the ground becomes bare it should be well covered with a coat of air-slacked lime. As a rule, the yards should not be permitted to get into this condition however, but should be moved frequently enough to avoid it. If bare yards must be used they should be kept clean either by scraping and sweeping them every week or so, or by spading. The latter method will aerate the soil and the chicks will derive additional advantage from having loose earth to scratch in. If the soil is sandy or the yard is filled in as described in Chapter XII, probably nothing will be necessary aside from renewing the surface material every year, but clay soils require extreme cleanliness to keep them sanitary and free from disease germs.

Litter for the Brooder

Short-cut alfalfa hay is by far the best material generally available for litter. If it cannot be secured or if the price is too high to make its use practical, there are other materials that can be employed. Mow chaff or "shatterings" are good if free from mold, but if from

CARE AND MANAGEMENT OF BROODER CHICKS

FIG. 133—A HEAT SAVING COLD BROODER
The brooder here illustrated serves as an enclosure for lamp-heated hovers until artificial heat is no longer required, after which the hover is removed and the brooder arranged to operate as a cold brooder. Courtesy of Wisconsin Experiment Station.

clover hay, examine them carefully for this. Dusty mow chaff is a frequent source of an epidemic disease affecting brooder chicks. Clover hay or shredded corn fodder or stover run through a feed cutter and reduced to short lengths will answer fairly well, also dried lawn clippings if free from mold. After chicks are two or three weeks old, coarse sawdust or planer shavings may be used, but are not recommended for newly hatched chicks. Coarse bran often is recommended for litter for young chicks, but shortcut alfalfa is much better and usually is cheaper.

In the absence of anything else, coarse, clean sand may be used. It will keep the droppings from sticking to the floor and will absorb moisture, but cannot be regarded as litter or even as a substitute for it. The practice of placing paper on the floor of brooders, especially under hovers, is objectionable unless well-covered with litter. A bare paper surface is too smooth, does not afford a foothold for the chicks, and may cause cripples.

Getting the Chicks Outdoors

The age at which chicks should be given access to outdoor yards depends upon the season and the method of brooding. Many chick growers insist on the chicks being out on the ground by the time they are a week old, letting them out for at least a few minutes daily even though it may be quite cold. Coddling the chicks will make them weakly and hard to raise, it is true, but it is doubtful whether there is any advantage in exposing them to severe cold at an extremely early age. The general practice is to keep chicks indoors until they are at least two or three weeks old in cold weather, provided there is plenty of room for them. With outdoor brooders, where the floor space is necessarily quite limited, the chicks must get out about as soon as they become hoverwise. In permanent brooder houses, also in colony houses of sufficient size, the chicks will suffer no injury if kept indoors for two or three weeks, if properly cared for. If on hard floors however, with little or no litter to scratch in, a number of difficulties will quickly develop, such as toe picking, leg weakness, etc., and in addition there will be a general lack of thrift which, while less noticeable, may cause even more serious loss in the long run.

No matter how comfortably the chicks may be housed and brooded, there seldom is any condition that will make it desirable to keep them indoors longer than three weeks, and to keep them in for even that time without injury necessitates ample floor space, plenty of litter, and careful feeding. In mild weather chicks may be out much sooner—usually within 10 days. Let them out for only a short time at first and in the warmest part of the day, increasing the length of the period as conditions and the conduct of the chicks suggest. If the yards or runs are covered with tall grass, weeds, or growing crops, do not let the chicks out until the dew has dried off.

In introducing the chicks to their outdoor run, they should be confined close to the brooder or house door at first. A convenient way of doing this is to use a strip of one-inch mesh netting with wire supports, or panels of netting, both of which are illustrated and described in Chapter XII. If the door of the brooder or house is above the ground level, take pains to see that the approach to it is made flush with the doorstep or sill, and is not too steep, so that the chicks will have no trouble in getting into the house.

After they have become thoroughly familiar with their small yard, its size can safely be increased to include whatever space is available. By the time the chicks are four weeks old they should be spending most of their time outdoors, and the more room they have thereafter the better it will be for them. When the chicks are fair-

FIG. 134—COLD BROODER READY FOR USE
This is the brooder shown in Fig. 133, made ready for use with the hover in place. This brooder is built to retain as much as possible of the bodily heat of the chicks, but the operator should not depend too much upon this. Leave the lamp-heated hovers in place as long as there is need for them. Courtesy of Wisconsin Experiment Station.

ly well feathered out, they may be given free range if available. Chicks can be successfully grown to adult size in quite limited space if they receive the needed extra care and attention, but when they can have free range, that is by all odds the cheapest and best way in which to raise them.

Teaching Chicks to Use Perches

There is no advantage in, and no necessity for having the chicks perch at too early an age. As long as they are satisfied under the cold hover or on the floor it is wise to let well enough alone, at least until they are eight to ten weeks old or thereabouts, after which no doubt, they will be better off on perches. There seldom is any trouble in getting Leghorn chicks and those of similar breeds to use perches, most of them doing so before it is really desirable, but chicks of the larger breeds often are extremely slow in learning. It is not difficult to teach them however, when they are old enough, if they are handled properly.

A week or two before the cold hover is to be taken away, a perching board should be put in place in the house near the hover. This board should not be over a foot above the floor and should be eight to ten inches wide. It should be placed back against the wall, moving the hover forward, if necessary, so that it will not be under the board. The chicks will take to the perching board and will enjoy using it in the daytime even though they may abandon it for the hover in the evening. As they grow familiar with it however, some will remain on it at night, the number gradually increasing until all or nearly all will voluntarily perch there. Until they do this the cold hover should be left in place. After the chicks have become accustomed to the board, a perch may be installed, placing it a little above the board and in front of it, so the chicks on the board will not be soiled by the droppings from those on the perch, but so that they will all be close together, the board serving as a sort of step to the perch. The chicks will not be long in passing over from the one to the other, and when they do so the board may be removed, and the perch put back and raised to a height of 18 inches to 2 feet. The essential point in this as in other advance steps that the chicks are required to take all along the line from the incubator to adult size, is to make no abrupt changes. Let them pass gradually from one thing to the next, giving them time to become accustomed to each successive step.

Care of Brooding Equipment When Not in Use

The better makes of brooders and hovers contain so good materials and are so well made that they are to be regarded as permanent assets. If they are properly cared for when not in use, they will last for many years. As a rule, it is not legitimate use but neglect, rust, and decay that cause these articles to wear out. Just as soon as they have served their purpose for the season, they should be removed from the houses where they have been in use, or brought in from outdoors in the case of brooders, and thoroughly cleaned, disinfected, and stored in a dry place where they will be safe from rats. Wooden surfaces on which the paint is getting dull, should be repainted, and if the brooder has been standing on the ground it should be turned up so that the bottom will dry out thoroughly, after which it also should have a good coat of paint. Metal surfaces that are liable to rust, should be oiled or painted, and hover curtains that are badly soiled should be washed and then put back in place. Lamp bowls should be emptied, cleaned, and dried. Any repairs that may be needed should also be attended to at this time, and loose articles of equipment such as thermometers, regulator parts, etc., should be collected and carefully stored in a convenient place. These attentions and repairs take only a little time, but they will more than double the effective life of the appliances.

The Growing Stock

After the chicks no longer need brooders, either heated or otherwise, their treatment will be determined mainly by the future use to be made of them. Surplus stock to be marketed as squab broilers will be ready for special fattening almost as soon as they leave the brooder, or very shortly thereafter. If to be sold as regular broilers or frys, they should have a few weeks on range and then be penned or put in fattening crates for special feeding. If intended for next season's breeding pens, they will receive the general care and management outlined in Chapter II. Pullets intended for winter layers should, as a rule, be separated from the cockerels, placed in colony houses, and given all the liberty possible. The various details of care and feeding beyond brooding age do not properly come within the scope of this book, but will be found quite fully treated in "The Chick Book"—see page 112.

FIG. 135—CHICKS BROODED IN COLONY HOUSE
As soon as settled weather arrives chicks can be brooded from the start in portable colony houses like the above. For suggestions in regard to making portable fence panels such as are shown herewith, see Chapter XII. Photo from United States Department of Agriculture.

CHAPTER XI

Feeding the Brooder Chicks

When to Begin Feeding Newly Hatched Chicks and the Special Feeds That Should Be Provided—Rations That Secure Rapid Growth—Practical Methods of Saving Labor—How to Economize in Feed Cost—The Advantages of Hopper Feeding, and Its Limitations—Formulas for Home-Mixed Rations— How to Feed After the Chicks Are Out on Range.

WHILE the embryo has drawn upon the yolk for food practically throughout the developing period, a large portion of it still is unabsorbed, and it forms approximately one-sixth of the entire weight of the chick when hatched. This left-over yolk is drawn into the abdomen just before hatching. It is connected with the intestine about midway between the gizzard and the anus, by means of a "stalk" through which it is rapidly assimilated. Only a trace of it should be left on the sixth day.

The chick's digestive organs are not fully developed at hatching time and the overzealous caretaker who promptly places food before them is inviting trouble of the most serious kind. Careful investigations have shown that the chick's stomach is not fully developed until the second day after hatching, while the pancreatic ferments are not normally developed until the seventh day. Because of this fact, when newly hatched chicks are fed too soon or too heavily, the food cannot be digested, but remains undigested in the crop, gizzard or intestines, where it ferments and causes one of the commonest forms of so-called "white diarrhea."

Too early feeding also interferes with the prompt absorption of the yolk which is believed to result in unfavorable changes in its composition that further complicate the situation and increase the difficulty of successfully raising the chicks. It is not necessary nor desirable that the yolk should be entirely absorbed before feeding begins, but it clearly should form the chick's sole means of subsistence for the first two days at least. After that, in gradually decreasing proportions, it serves to reinforce the food obtained from outside sources and appears to have some influence in regulating the chick's bowels at this critical time, starting them to function in the natural way.

Normally developed chicks usually demand some food by the end of the second day, and while they apparently are not seriously inconvenienced by going without for a day or two longer, the general practice is to begin feeding them lightly at this time. Chicks will live for many days without any supplied food. The United States Post Office Department accepts parcel post shipments of day-old chicks that can be delivered within seventy-two hours, or three days, and there are numerous reports of shipments that have been on the road for five days without any apparent injury.

When to Begin Feeding

In determining when the first feed should be given, the beginner sometimes is confused by irregular hatching which may extend over an entire day or longer, leaving him uncertain as to just when the two-day period begins or ends. In a general way, it may be said that the hatch is assumed to have begun when the chicks commence to come out freely—not when the first few make their appearance, which may be several hours in advance of the general movement.

While the two-day period is a convenient approximate guide in determining when to begin feeding, the conduct of the chicks should also be considered. If they do not appear particularly hungry after the two days are up it will be wise to delay feeding a little longer. If on the other hand they clearly are ready for food it is safe to supply it a little in advance of the regular time. However, when the chicks become dissatisfied and noisy on the second day the cause is apt to be thirst rather than hunger. If they have been dried down a little too much in the incubator, or are kept close under the hover, as usually is necessary for the first day or two while they are learning where to go for warmth, they will need water before food, and it is well to supply it regularly after the first day, using for the purpose small founts similar to the one illustrated in Fig. 138.

FIG. 136—FEED THE CHICKS OUTSIDE THE BROODER
As soon as the chicks can find their way back to the hover readily, all feeding and watering should be outside the brooder. Doing this saves work and litter.

Place these where the chicks can get at them readily, and provide enough of them so that the thirsty ones will have room to drink without crowding, and there will be no danger of their getting wet. If the chicks become very thirsty however, and must all drink from a single fount they are apt to pile up about it, dripping and splashing the water over each other until they are thoroughly soaked and chilled—thus laying the foundation for intestinal disorders and an epidemic of diarrhea.

In order to avoid this danger, also to make it easy for the chicks to find the water and learn to drink, it is practical to use ordinary pie pans for water dishes for the first two or three days, putting just a little water in each. In this way the chicks can get at the water readily, and there need be no crowding. If the water is lukewarm, as it should be, getting into it with their feet will do them no harm, and they will keep drier than when ordinary founts are used. Some prefer to fill the pans with coarse gravel so that the chicks can get at the water without standing in it. In either case the pans must be emptied and refilled often enough to keep the water clean. After the chicks have learned to drink, founts are entirely satisfactory and more convenient.

As a rule there will be no difficulty in teaching chicks to drink. The brightest ones will learn quickly when the opportunity is afforded, and the rest will promptly imi-

FIG. 137—FEEDING TRAY FOR SOFT FEED
This tray is made from a smooth board of suitable size, with strips of lath around the edge. These should extend about half an inch above the board. Soft feed should never be thrown upon the floor or into the litter.

tate them. There is no danger of their drinking more water than is good for them if it is regularly provided after the first day and they are never allowed to get extremely thirsty. The water vessels should be placed directly upon the brooder floor at first, close to the hover, but after the chicks have become hoverwise it is advisable to put them on boards or slightly raised platforms so that litter will not be scratched into them. Drinking vessels filled with litter and dirt are a constant menace to the health of the flock.

Founts manufactured for this special purpose are best and cheapest for ordinary use but, in an emergency, a homemade fount can readily be extemporized from a one-quart vegetable can and a small dish or pan (see Fig. 139.) Punch one or two holes in the can so that they will be a little below the top of the dish when in use; fill can with water, place dish over it and invert. If the hole is properly located the water will stand a little below the top of dish and will be renewed from the can as the chicks drink it. The dish should be only one to one and one-half inches larger in diameter than the can, for best results.

It is important for the chicks to have some grit from the start, and many experienced chick raisers place this before them a few hours in advance of the first feed. In order to be certain that they all get their share of this highly important part of the ration it should regularly be mixed with each soft feed until certain that the chicks will voluntarily help themselves to it from the hopper. Use a good grade of commercial chick grit if obtainable. In the absence of this, supply clean, sharp sand.

FIG. 138—DRINKING FOUNT
There is no better way of supplying drinking water for chicks than by the use of a two-piece fount similar to this one.

Importance of Careful Feeding

The exact character of the ration that is fed to chicks is of less importance than the way in which it is fed—but still highly important. Strong, vigorous chicks will do well on rations that are far from being correct, provided they are carefully fed; but they will only make their best growth and development when their rations are properly adapted to their needs. If some chick raisers realize a measure of success with distinctly inferior rations, that does not affect the fact that the more suitable the feed provided, the easier it is to raise the chicks, and the better they will develop. No ration however, can be made up that will relieve the feeder of the necessity for exercising care and judgment in supplying it. Many a watchful, earnest farmer's wife with painstaking skill, and with the added advantage of farm conditions generally, is able to raise a larger percentage of chicks on cornmeal dough (which is about the worst feed to give them) than other persons who use the best of "balanced rations," but who feed them carelessly.

It is not meant by the foregoing to imply that there is any one method of feeding, or any one ration, that is to be recommended above all others. On the contrary, the well-informed chick raiser has a rather wide range of choice in both respects, being able readily to adapt the ration to available supplies and to modify methods of feeding to suit personal convenience. The beginner however, should not presume too much upon this fact. Lacking in the exact knowledge required to make such adjustments successfully, and quite apt to underestimate the importance of seemingly minor details, he almost invariably finds that he is more successful when he adopts a definite ration and method of feeding, each of proved value and then adheres strictly to them. Other methods may seem simpler or less laborious; other rations may be cheaper or more easily provided; but

FIG. 139—A HOMEMADE DRINKING FOUNT
A one-quart can inverted over a saucer makes a good fount for emergency use, but the regular manufactured ones are more substantial, less easily upset, and the chicks are not so apt to get wet.

without personal knowledge and skill, changes are almost invariably unsatisfactory and often disastrous. It is for this reason that in the latter part of this chapter some definite methods of chick feeding are given in detail. Unless there is a good reason for doing otherwise, the beginner should adopt one of these and follow it exactly. It will be time enough to simplify or cheapen it, when there is a substantial foundation of experience upon which to base the changes.

Nursery Feeds

During the first few days the food should be quite limited in quantity and of an easily digested nature. Cooked feeds are considered extra desirable and many experienced feeders depend almost exclusively upon bread crumbs at this time, moistening these with milk if obtainable, otherwise with water. Some add to the bread crumbs a limited amount of hard-boiled egg, using for this purpose infertile eggs tested out of the incubator. These are boiled for half an hour and then crushed or run through a food chopper, shells and all, and mixed with bread crumbs in the proportion of about six parts of the latter to one of the former. In view of the fact that chicks frequently have difficulty in assimilating the original unabsorbed yolk, the advisability of adding hard-boiled eggs to the nursery food appears questionable.

After the chicks are a week old there will be no objection to using them, but for the first few days the need for animal feed can be much better supplied in the form of skim milk, either sweet or sour, or a very limited amount of finely cut fresh meat.

In place of bread crumbs many use commercial "chick starters," or prepared nursery foods, several of which are excellent for the purpose and much more convenient than bread crumbs. Johnnycake is another nursery food in common use. In Farmers' Bulletin 624, of the United States Department of Agriculture, directions for making johnnycake are given as follows: "To one dozen infertile eggs or one pound of sifted beef scrap add ten pounds of cornmeal and one tablespoonful of baking soda, and mix with enough milk to make a pasty mash." This mixture can be baked on a griddle or skillet, or in the oven, as convenient. Whatever feeds are used, no pains should be spared to insure their being thoroughly wholesome and untainted. Nothing that has heated or that is moldy or sour should be fed under any condition. It does not seem to matter whether the milk given to chicks is sweet or sour.

It is not possible to give exact directions in regard to the amount of feed to supply during the first few days, but the quantity should be limited. The feeder must learn to be governed by the condition and conduct of his chicks, following the general rule to "feed often, but keep them hungry." The usual plan is to let them have all the moist mash they will eat in three to five minutes, after which the surplus is promptly removed. Three feeds will be sufficient the first day, but thereafter it is advisable to feed four or five times, at regular intervals.

Great harm is done by leaving soft feed before the chicks so that, after eating what they need and running back under the hover to warm up, they can come out later and stuff themselves with what they do NOT need. If the chicks are slow about learning, it may be advisable to give them a little more time for the first feed or two, to be certain that all have had a chance, but do not be overanxious about this. Some chicks will be nearly a day younger than others and these will be better off if they do not eat at all. After the first two days however, the rule should be "every chick out at feeding time," whether they eat much or little.

Probably the best way to give soft feed is to provide a sufficient number of wooden trays, such as the one shown in Fig. 137. This consists simply of a smooth half-inch board (six inches in width by twelve inches in length is a practical and convenient size for a small flock) with a strip around the edge about the width of an ordinary plastering lath, to prevent the contents from being scratched out. Use nothing but smooth, surfaced lumber in making them, and provide enough so that all the chicks can get to the feed at the same time, without crowding. Keep these trays clean and free from taint by daily scalding or sunning.

For reasons already given the chicks' food, during the first few days of their lives, should be chosen with care, but thereafter their feeding offers no peculiar problems. Chicks should be regarded simply as fowls—quite small, it is true, but fowls just the same. So far as feeding is concerned, their appetites and needs differ from those of adult fowls only as modified by their smaller size. The same grains that are good for adult fowls are good for chicks, and they may be fed in about the same proportions. If some feeds are provided for the chicks that ordinarily are not given to adults, that usually is because they are too expensive to be fed to the latter, but

are required in so small quantities for chicks that the slight additional cost is unimportant compared with the desirability of giving them the best possible start.

Whatever the nursery feed may be, the general practice is to begin the use of a mixture of finely cracked grains, generally called chick feed, about the third to the sixth day of feeding, also adding a limited amount of some good mash mixture to the nursery feed. Gradually increase the proportions of both chick feed and mash so that by the beginning of the second week, or shortly thereafter, the nursery feed can be entirely omitted, and the chicks placed on the ration which they are to receive regularly for the next three or four weeks.

What to Feed Up to the Fourth Week

Just what this ration shall be will depend a good deal upon available supplies, and the personal preferences of the feeder. The simplest and easiest way is to use the ready-mixed commercial chick feeds and mashes that are for sale in practically all markets. These special

FIG. 140—CONVENIENT MASH FEEDERS FOR YOUNG CHICKS

These flat troughs with strips of wire cloth over the tops are just the thing for providing dry mash for chicks. The wire cloth should be cut to fit inside the trough. It rests on the mash and follows it down as the chicks consume it. So protected the mash is always readily accessible but the chicks cannot scratch it out. Courtesy of Missouri State Poultry Experiment Station.

feeds, if the buyer is careful to secure the best brands, are wholesome, nutritious, and well balanced, containing practically everything that the chicks need with the exception of green feed. Some chick feed mixtures contain grit and charcoal but, except when buying in quite small quantities, it is better to purchase these materials separately and feed them in hoppers rather than to scatter them in the litter. If the mash mixture does not contain meat scrap this should be added in proper proportion.

Ready-mixed mashes are available in which powdered milk is used in place of meat scrap and this material is believed by many to be especially good for chicks. Where skim milk or powdered milk is fed, only a limited amount of meat scrap, if any, need be supplied, though an occasionally feed of fresh meat or finely ground butcher scraps are always a desirable addition to the ration. As a rule, the poultryman can buy ready-mixed feeds cheaper than he can make up good mixtures at home, unless he is using large quantities. Careful tests at state experiment stations, and the general experience of practical chick raisers, indicate clearly that chicks will do better on a ration affording reasonable variety and consisting of about equal proportions of cracked grains and mashes.

FIG. 141—FEEDING COOP FOR YOUNG CHICKS
In order to protect the young chicks from being trampled by the larger ones at feeding time, an enclosure similar to the one shown above will be found very convenient. It will also protect the food from rain in wet weather, if the top is covered with prepared roofing.

Chicks Must Be Kept Busy

Almost any method of feeding that makes the chicks work for their ration most of the day is a good one. The problem of keeping them busy is quite simple if the chicks can run at large, as their natural activity will keep them on the move practically all the time. If in confinement however, either indoors or in small yards, it is scarcely possible to maintain them in good thrifty condition without the liberal use of litter on the floor of the brooder or pen. As has already been pointed out in Chapter X, the best litter for chicks is short-cut alfalfa hay. The chicks will eat some of the leaves and finer particles, and will be the better for doing so. The material is just fine enough and light enough to make good scratching, and if the hay is properly cured it will be reasonably free from dust. Short-cut alfalfa may seem rather expensive but, in the long run, it is the cheapest litter that can be used for the first three weeks, results considered.

Persons who have clean clover hay, free from mold, and can have it cut into short lengths at little cost, will find it desirable and less expensive than alfalfa. In the absence of either of these, clean oat or wheat straw, chopped as fine as possible will answer fairly well, but there is no other material generally available that is so desirable as alfalfa or clover. By the seventh day the chicks should be able to handle about two inches of litter and thereafter the amount should be increased as they grow, aiming always to have enough so that they will have to spend a good part of the day digging for the grain part of their ration.

Chicks need some form of animal matter by the end of the first week. Finely chopped hard-boiled eggs if available, may be added to the soft feed, and fresh meat cut in very small pieces is excellent. As a matter of convenience however, most chick raisers use a good grade of commercial meat scrap, sifting out the coarse particles until the chicks are large enough to eat it without waste as it comes from the bag. Start with not over five per cent in the mash, gradually increasing to fifteen per cent, beyond which it is not considered advisable to go until the chicks are out on range.

After the chicks are two or three weeks old it is practical to feed meat scrap alone in hoppers, provided the ration as a whole is satisfactory. If the chicks are dissatisfied with the rest of the ration however, there is danger that they will eat more meat scrap than is good for them, and overconsumption of this highly concentrated food will result promptly in digestive disorders.

Any danger of its being too freely consumed will be avoided when added to the mash, and it also will make the mash more appetizing, which usually is desirable.

Skim milk is especially good for chicks, and may be supplied with safety in any desired quantity. Use it for mixing all moist mashes, and supply it for drinking in water founts. Where it is freely used it is not necessary to provide any form of meat. It may be given either sweet or sour, though it is not generally believed to be desirable to give sweet and sour milk alternately. It is important to observe strict cleanliness in the vessels used in feeding milk, washing and scalding them thoroughly at frequent intervals.

The chicks need green feed, practically from the start, and should have it regularly at least once a day. It should be fed sparingly at first until the chicks become accustomed to it, after which they may be given all they will clean up. Use any succulent material available, such as cabbage or lettuce leaves, mangels, potatoes, etc. Feed the latter sparingly, however, as they are apt to cause diarrhea if too freely used. Tough, stringy green feed such as grass, overgrown oat sprouts, etc., cannot be safely fed unless chopped into quite small pieces. The more tender the material provided the better it will be for the chicks. If sprouted oats are provided, sprout them in a warm place so that they will grow quickly, and feed when the sprouts are not over two inches long, to insure their being tender. At this stage the chicks will eat both sprouts and roots, and also will find a good deal of healthful exercise in picking at the kernels. Be careful never to feed moldy sprouted oats, however.

The supply of grit must never be neglected. Probably a good limestone grit is most suitable for the purpose. It should be kept in hoppers where the chicks can help themselves to it at all times and, in addition, should also be mixed with the regular mash feeds as already suggested. Use fine chick grit at first, changing to a larger or intermediate size after the chicks are a few weeks old.

Young chicks like charcoal and will eat it greedily. As it appears to be quite helpful in preventing certain

FIG. 142—DEEP LITTER FEEDING
Several weeks' supply of cracked grains is buried in a thick coat of litter as illustrated above, and the chicks get plenty of exercise digging for it. There is little leg weakness among deep-litter fed chicks.

digestive disorders, it should always be supplied. Get granulated charcoal, with the fine dust sifted out, and feed it in hoppers.

Careful experiments, particularly those made at the N. Y. (Geneva) Experiment Station, indicate that it is desirable for the chick ration to have a larger proportion of mineral matter (ash) than is regularly provided

FEEDING THE BROODER CHICKS

by the ordinary feeds used. Meat scrap contains a sufficient amount of bone to meet most requirements, but the particles usually are entirely too large for small chicks. Until they are big enough to eat meat scrap as it comes from the bag, the best way of supplying this deficiency in the ration is to add about five per cent of bone meal to the mash mixture.

Home-Mixed Rations

While ready-mixed chick feeds and mashes are much more convenient for the average chick raiser than home mixtures, these may often be employed at a marked saving in cost, particularly on farms and in grain-growing sections generally, provided they are used in quantities sufficient to make it worth while to give proper attention to their preparation. Home mixtures are apt to be variable in quality or in composition, lacking in variety, and poorly milled. Grains cracked at local mills always contain a large proportion of particles either too coarse or too fine, representing a serious waste in either case unless screened out. Home-mixed mashes also are apt to be poorly balanced unless the feeder follows a definite formula.

If home mixing is practiced, see to it that the cracked grains are carefully screened to remove meal and particles too large to be fed safely. Provide reasonable, but not extreme variety, and follow a formula of proved value, which calls for grains and meals that are obtainable in the local market, if possible to do so. While some grains are generally regarded as more desirable than others, there are none that are indispensable, and the practical thing to do in any case is to use the cheapest and most available feeds, avoiding too great dependence on any one kind and making sure that the total ration is reasonably well balanced.

FIG. 143—CROSS SECTION OF MASH AND GRAIN HOPPER
This illustration gives all necessary dimensions for hopper illustrated in Fig. 146. Can be made in any desired length.

Since corn, wheat and oats are obtainable by most persons, a practical formula for the cracked grain or chick feed mixture is:

    100 pounds of cracked wheat.
    100 pounds of fine cracked corn.
    100 pounds of pinhead or steel-cut oats.

If the latter cannot be obtained, use fifty pounds of rolled oats instead. It is not advisable to use the latter freely however, as the particles are large and too easily found. With a mixture containing these three grains, it does not matter greatly whether anything else is included, though cracked kafir corn, milo, hulled barley, etc., may be used freely, if obtainable at reasonable cost. Such seeds as hemp, millet, etc., if used at all, should be added only in limited quantities.

A good mash to be fed either dry or moist in con-

FIG. 144—A SIMPLE SHADE FOR THE WATER FOUNT
The outdoor water fount should always be protected from the sun in hot weather. If natural shade is not available, put the fount in an open box of suitable size, with the open side turned toward the north or northeast.

nection with the above cracked-grain mixture is made after the following formula:

    100 pounds of cornmeal.
    100 pounds of coarse brown middlings.
    50 pounds of white middlings or low-grade flour.
    50 pounds of rolled oats or oat flour.
    15 to 30 lbs. of meat scrap (increase gradually to maximum).

After the chicks are two weeks old, substitute bran for brown middlings and increase the meat scrap gradually to forty pounds. The physical condition of the mash has a good deal to do with its palatability, and since the meals mentioned vary in degree of fineness, this formula should be considered as more or less tentative, changing the proportions a little, if necessary, in order to get a satisfactory mixture—that is, one that the chicks will eat readily and that will not be too sticky or gummy when moistened.

A Successful Feeding Method

The general principles of chick feeding both as to rations and methods, have been briefly covered in the foregoing treatment of the subject. There are many however, who require a specific method and more detailed instructions and for their benefit the following schedule has

FIG. 145—GROWING CHICKS ON RANGE
View on poultry plant at Wisconsin Experiment Station. Chicks with good houses, plenty of range, and plenty of shade in warm weather should grow without a check, and there should be few losses among them.

FIG. 146—MASH AND GRAIN HOPPER FOR GROWING CHICKS
When the chicks are a couple of months old and can have practically free range, they may be hopper fed on both mash and grain, if desired. The two-compartment hopper here illustrated, will hold several days' supply. It is provided with a rainproof top so that it can be placed outdoors.

been prepared. It is by no means the only way in which chicks can be successfully fed, but that it is a practical and successful one, the experience of countless chick raisers has abundantly proved.

First Day. Supply neither feed nor water. Allow the chicks to come out from under the hover, but give them only a limited amount of room and watch them carefully to see that at no time during the day do they become chilled, or even uncomfortable while out, and that the hover temperature is maintained at about 100 degrees at the level of the chicks' back and a short distance inside the hover curtain.

Second Day. The chicks are to have no feed during this period, but should be supplied with lukewarm drinking water. If they appear to be dissatisfied, sprinkle chick grit over a feeding tray and let them have all they want of this.

Third Day. Assuming that the hatch has begun during the night or in the morning, the first feed may be given on the morning of the third day—not too early however, if the house is cold. Give a light feed of bread crumbs moistened with milk, or water if milk is not available. Moisten the bread crumbs just enough to make them soft but not pasty. Sprinkle fine chick grit or sharp sand over the bread crumbs to make certain that the chicks will get the necessary amount of this highly important part of their ration. See that they all come out from under the hover for this first feed, but if there are any of the late-hatched ones that are not hungry or are still a little weak, let them go back under the hover at once or return them by hand. Give the others three to five minutes at the feeding trays, if they want that much time, but the instant their hunger is satisfied, put them back under the hover, unless they return voluntarily, and remove the feeding trays. Feed again at noon and early in the evening. Provide water in drinking founts and place these where the chicks can get at them whenever they come out from under the hover, but watch them closely and see that none get wet, and that they do not spend much time about the founts.

Fourth and Fifth Days. Feed moistened bread crumbs five times, or morning, noon, and evening, and middle of forenoon and afternoon. Give them about three minutes in which to satisfy their hunger and then remove the trays. Whatever feed is left on the trays should be scraped off and added to the ration given to the larger fowls. Mix a fresh batch for the chicks each time. Always sprinkle chick grit or sharp sand over the feed when putting it before the chicks, and continue to do this until they are ten days to two weeks old. Chicks apparently cannot be trusted to eat as much grit as they really need when it is supplied only in hoppers.

Sixth and Seventh Days. Give the chicks five feeds as on the preceding day, but limit the quantity and, after removing the surplus, sprinkle a little chick feed on the litter where the chicks can readily find it. Use only a small amount and provide an extra fine mixture for the purpose. The best way to secure this fine-cracked feed is to run some of the regular chick feed mixture through a hand mill or coffee grinder. A limited amount of a good mash mixture may also be mixed with the bread crumbs, gradually increasing the proportion of the mash and decreasing the bread crumbs until the latter can be entirely omitted early in the second week if it is desirable to do so. If bread crumbs are available at low cost however, they may continue to form a part of the mash mixture for an indefinite time. Sprinkle a little chick feed over the litter after each light feeding of moist feed as on the previous day.

Eighth Day. If the directions for preceding days have been properly carried out the chicks now will be ready for the alternate feeds of moist mash and chick feed which will form their regular ration for the next two or three weeks. Continue to feed the moist mash morning, noon, and evening, and feed the cracked grains lightly in the middle of the forenoon and afternoon. Some of this should be buried in the litter so that the chicks will have to dig for it. If they are healthy, vigorous chicks and only a limited amount of litter is used, they will soon learn to hunt for it, and will enjoy doing so.

FIG. 147—OUTDOOR FEEDING FRAME
This illustration shows a cheap enclosure for small chicks, where they may be fed without interference from the larger members of the flock. Photo from U. S. Department of Agriculture.

FEEDING THE BROODER CHICKS

At first it is necessary to use a good deal of care as to the amount of chick feed that is supplied and the depth of litter in which it is buried, but the latter may be increased rapidly, and by the end of the second week they should be able to negotiate several inches of fine, light material such as short-cut alfalfa. Thereafter, until they can be outdoors most of the time, they should be compelled to spend several hours daily searching in the litter for the cracked-grain portion of the ration. It is not advisable to try to make the chicks clean up every particle of the chick feed in the litter. There should always be a little that they can get by hunting for it, but do not supply it so liberally that they can find it without effort.

FIG. 148—QUICK GROWING BROILERS
The two chicks shown in above illustration were deep-litter fed, by the method described in this chapter. When 8 weeks old they reached a net weight of 4 lbs.

Second to Fourth Week. The method of feeding as outlined for the eighth day may be continued practically without change until the chicks are about four weeks old, when they will begin to tire of chick feed and will show a marked preference for larger grains. The mixture then should be changed to supply the regular scratch grains provided for adult fowls, or make up a special mixture to consist of equal parts by weight of coarse cracked corn, whole wheat and clipped oats. A double portion of corn may be used if price makes it an object, and if clipped oats are not available, whole oats may be fed after soaking them several hours or boiling for one hour.

Never feed dry whole oats to young chicks, as the sharp points are liable to cause serious trouble. Oats that have been boiled or soaked may be used with entire safety however, and if desirable they may form 50 per cent of the total grain ration after the chicks are several weeks old. The mash mixture also should be changed about the same time, using 100 pounds of corn meal, 50 pounds of bran, 50 pounds of white middlings or low-grade flour, 50 pounds of ground whole oats and 50 pounds of meat scrap. The number of daily feeds may now be reduced to three, and this modified ration may be continued without change until the chicks are practically full grown. Two of these feeds should be cracked grains in litter or scattered broadcast over the range, with one feed of moist mash, and a hopper of dry mash always available. Chicks fed by this method and with the ration here suggested should make rapid growth and escape many of the ailments and losses that result from less suitable rations or improper methods of feeding.

Simplified Feeding Methods

While the method that has just been described, and others of a similar nature, will produce results that cannot be equalled by "easy" methods, it must be conceded that they involve a good deal of labor and almost constant attendance, which many chick raisers are not able or willing to give. To meet such conditions there are various modifications that may be introduced, chiefly in the way of hopper feeding, that will materially reduce the time and labor required. If these changes are wisely made and if the caretaker does not pursue labor-saving methods and "efficiency" to the point where the well-being of his flock is sacrificed, reasonably good results may be secured.

It should be clearly understood that the exact number of feeds to be given daily is important only in so far as it assists in keeping the chicks busy. But the average chick raiser finds that in proportion as he reduces the number of feeds the difficulty of maintaining healthful activity increases. For this reason, it is not advisable for the beginner to attempt too much in the way of simplified feeding methods. It is much wiser for him to follow practices that are known to be safe and effective, rather than to endanger the thrift or the lives of his chicks merely to avoid a little labor.

In dry-mash feeding, the mash is placed in hoppers, or feeding troughs similar to the ones shown in Fig. 140, and the chicks are given access to it at all times. If care is taken in the preparation of the mash, making it sufficiently palatable so that the chicks will eat enough of it, and avoiding making it so appetizing that they will depend mainly upon it instead of scratching in the litter for grain, it is entirely practical to feed in this way. The chick feed, also, instead of being given in installments through the day can be supplied at one time, morning or evening as convenient, after the chicks are a couple of weeks old, provided sufficient litter is used.

Deep Litter Feeding Method

A method of feeding that has been adopted by many with good results, and which represents the practical minimum in labor required, is known as the deep litter method, which the chicks, during the first four to six

FIG. 149—A CORN FIELD IS EXTRA GOOD AS A RANGE FOR GROWING CHICKS IN HOT WEATHER

weeks, are fed exclusively on chick feed and meat scrap. The entire amount of chick feed required for this length of time is buried in the litter when the chicks are about one week old, and meat scrap is supplied in hoppers, allowing them to help themselves to it at will.

Assuming that the flock is to consist of 75 to 100 chicks, and will occupy an indoor pen measuring about 5x10 feet, the procedure is as follows: Spread on the floor of the pen a layer of about two inches of short-cut alfalfa and sprinkle over it ten to fifteen pounds of chick feed. Follow with alternate layers of litter and feed until the material is eight inches deep all over the floor and 50 pounds of chick feed has been buried. This amount should last the chicks about four weeks, and nothing else is fed except meat scrap as noted, also a liberal allowance of green feed daily. Since the chicks must scratch for practically every bit of feed they get, they will be found busily digging in the litter most of the time.

A modification of this plan, as adopted by many, consists in supplying a good dry-mash mixture in hoppers, adding to it the proper proportion of meat scrap. As this plan removes all danger of the chicks eating more meat scrap than is good for them, it probably is a safer method for the average feeder than the regular chick feed and meat scrap ration.

Whatever feeding method may be followed during the first month or six weeks, after the chicks are well grown and can be out on free range it is entirely practical to feed both mash and grain in hoppers, though the chicks undoubtedly will grow more rapidly if a little hand-feeding is practiced right along up to maturity. Many successful chick raisers make a practice of providing hoppers containing dry mash and cracked corn for growing stock on range, but continue to give mixed grains in the morning when the chicks are turned out, and a good moist mash in the evening. By doing this they undoubtedly secure more rapid growth and earlier maturity than can be expected where exclusive hopper feeding is practiced.

Cornell Rations and Methods for Chick Feeding

The approved method of chick feeding at Cornell University, as given in Bulletin 327, is as follows:

For the first five days feed the chicks five times a day with nursery feed (Mixture No. 1). This is to be moistened with sour skimmed milk, and shredded green food, fine grit, and charcoal are to be scattered over the food. In addition to this moist feed, a shallow tray containing cracked grains (Mixture No. 2) is kept before the chicks. To this grain mixture is to be added a small amount of dry mash (Mixture No. 3). After the first five days feed cracked grains (Mixture No. 2) in light litter twice a day. The nursery feed (Mixture No. 1) is discontinued after five days, and a mash (Mixture No. 3) is moistened with sour skimmed milk, and fed three times a day. This mash mixture also is kept before the chicks in shallow trays.

This feeding is continued to the end of the fourth week except that after the second week the moist mash is given only twice a day. From the fourth to the sixth week, or until the chicks are on range, one feed of moist mash is given daily, dry mash is always available in hoppers or trays, and cracked grains (Mixture No. 4) are fed in litter twice a day. From the sixth week to maturity, dry mash (Mixture No. 3) and grains (Mixture No. 5) are hopper fed, with one meal a day of moist mash if it is desirable to hasten development.

Cornell Chick-Feeding Mixtures

Mixture No. 1
8 lbs. rolled oats.
8 lbs. bread crumbs or cracker waste.
2 lbs. sifted beef scrap (best grade.)
1 lb. bone meal.

Mixture No. 2
3 lbs. wheat (cracked.)
2 lbs. cracked corn (fine.)
1 lb. bone meal.

Mixture No. 3
3 lbs. wheat bran.
3 lbs. corn meal.
3 lbs. wheat middlings.
3 lbs. beef scrap (best grade.)
1 lb. bone meal.

Mixture No. 4
3 lbs. wheat (whole)
2 lbs. cracked corn.
1 lb. hulled oats.

Mixture No. 5
3 lbs. wheat.
3 lbs. cracked corn.

FIG. 150—PROFITABLE RAPID GROWING CHICKS
When chicks have reached this size the "danger period" is past and with proper feeding and care they should grow rapidly to market size or maturity.

Iowa Station Method of Feeding Chicks
(Condensed from Iowa Experiment Station Circular No. 17.)

The chicks generally are taken to the brooder when 24 to 36 hours old. They may be given water with the chill removed, and limited amounts of bone, charcoal, and grit. After they are 48 to 60 hours old, they are given limited amounts of moist mash (Mixture C) and cracked grains, (Mixture A). No more is given than the chicks will clean up in 10 or 15 minutes, but they are fed moist mash five times a day for the first three or four days then reduced to four feeds, and at the end of the first week reduced to three feeds a day.

The first feeds of crack grains are fed in shallow litter. The amount of this feed as well as the depth of the litter increases as the chicks grow older. At the end of the first week the litter is two inches deep. A dish of bran or hopper of dry mash is kept before the chicks, also bone, grit, and charcoal. By the end of the second week the number of feeds of moist mash is reduced to two, and the depth of the litter increased to three or four inches. As the number of feeds of moist mash decrease the amount of cracked grain is increased.

During the third week the mash (Mixture D) is gradually substituted for the mixture C and is fed moist two times a day until the end of the four weeks. The litter is now five or six inches deep. From the fifth to the eighth week only one feed of moist mash is given daily and the same mash is kept before them in hoppers. Grain mixture B now is substituted for mixture A and is fed in the litter once a day.

Ration II

Grain Ration "A"
Fed First 8 Weeks
Cracked corn 2
Cracked wheat 1
Steel cut oat meal 1

Grain Ration "B"
Fed After the 8th Week
Coarsely cracked corn 2
Wheat 1
Oats 1

Ground Feed

Mash Ration "C"
Fed First Two Weeks
Stale bread 3
Oat meal 3
Eggs (tested from incubator) 4
Bran 1½
Corn meal 1½
Ground bone ½

Mash Ration "D"
Fed After the Second Week
Corn meal 3
Wheat middlings or high grade shorts 2
Wheat bran 1
Beef scrap 1
Ground oats 1
Ground bone ½
Salt 1-10

Ground feed made moist with sour milk and beef scrap or meat meal fed in hoppers. All numerals in above rations refer to proportions by weight.

Method of Feeding Chicks Recommended By U. S. Department of Agriculture

(Condensed from Farmers' Bulletin 624.)

Young chicks should be fed from three to five times daily. Undoubtedly chicks can be grown faster by feeding five times, than by feeding three times daily, but it should be born in mind that more harm can be done by overfeeding than by underfeeding, and at no time should they be fed more than enough merely to satisfy their appetites and to keep them exercising, except in the evening when they should be given all they will eat. The first feed given after the chicks are 36 to 48 hours old may consist of johnnycake, bread crumbs, or pinhead or rolled oats. Feed either of these as convenient, giving five feeds daily for the first week, then gradually substitute for one or two feeds of the nursery feed, finely cracked grains, consisting of equal parts by weight of cracked wheat, finely cracked corn and pinhead oatmeal or hulled oats, to which about five per cent of cracked peas or broken rice, and two per cent of charcoal, also millet or rape seed, may be added. The above ration can be fed until the chicks are ten days to two weeks old, when the nursery feed may be discontinued, supplying in place of it a good growing mash mixture composed of two pounds of bran, two pounds of middlings, one pound of corn meal, one pound of low-grade flour or red-dog, and ten per cent of sifted beef scrap. This may be placed in hoppers and left before them at all times. If fed wet use only enough milk or water to make the mash crumbly, but in no sense sloppy. As soon as the chicks will eat whole wheat, cracked corn and other grains, the small-size chick feed can be eliminated. Growing chicks on a good range may be hopper fed, providing in one hopper a mixture composed of two pounds by weight of cracked corn and one pound of wheat, or equal parts of cracked corn, wheat and oats. For the dry mash hopper the mixture previously described may be used.

Feeding Growing Stock

As the scope of this book only includes the management of chicks up to the end of the brooding period, their subsequent feeding and care has been described but briefly, and in the most general way. Those who are interested in detailed methods of feeding and care of growing stock, whether intended for market or for the laying pen, are referred to "The Chick Book" (see page 112) in which these subjects receive due attention.

What Not To Do

So long as the chick raiser keeps to a definite approved method of feeding, there will be no special danger of his getting into serious difficulties, but where changes are made in the ration or method, there are various mistakes that the beginner is apt to make. There also are certain errors in feeding into which every one is liable to fall at times, and in regard to which a special warning should be given. Among the most common of these are the following:

Sloppy Mashes. The moist mash fed to young chicks should be mixed with sufficient water or milk to make it crumbly, but never sloppy or pasty. In the latter condition it is positively unwholesome and in a short time will certainly cause serious digestive disorders.

Sour Mashes. Moist food should never be allowed to stand for any length of time after mixing, especially when intended for newly hatched chicks. A fresh batch should be mixed for each feed. Mashes that have begun to sour are thoroughly unwholesome. In this connection a warning should be given against providing too large quantities of cooked or baked foods, such as johnnycake, which often sours very quickly in warm weather.

Moldy Feeds. Nothing about which there is the slightest suspicion of mold, should be fed. This includes grains that have heated, corn meal that has caked, cracked corn with discolored hearts—anything in short that is "off" in condition.

Dirty Feed. A good many economical feeders gather up the surplus after the chicks have been fed and after they have trampled over it and mixed litter and droppings with it, and keep it for the next feeding. This is the poorest of economy. It may do no harm to give this material to larger chicks, or to adult fowls, but it should never under any conditions be fed to brooder chicks.

Indigestible Feeds. Certain seeds such as hemp and millet have very hard shells which little chicks are not able readily to grind, and if used at all should be supplied only in most limited proportions. Along with these may be included feeds carrying high proportions of hulls or crude fibre. A comparatively small percentage of fibre will seriously irritate the intestines even of adult fowls, and such material should never be forced upon chicks. For this reason, it is not desirable to load the mash down with excessive quantities of bran, oat hulls, corn hulls, or similar material.

Frozen Vegetables. Vegetables in a frozen condition or that have been frozen and subsequently thawed out, should never be fed to chicks, as they will quickly cause intestinal disorders. It is a good deal better to let them go without green feed rather than to use such material.

Feeding Whole Oats. As oats usually are obtainable at a lower price per pound than any other grain, many persons attempt to use them in feeding young chicks and nearly always with disastrous results. The sharp points of the hulls may cause direct injury while the excess of crude fibre will irritate the intestines. There is no objection to the use of whole oats if they are sprouted, boiled, or soaked for several hours before feeding. In this condition the chicks will be able to pick out the kernels and discard the hulls.

Sudden Changes in Rations. Sudden changes in the rations supplied to chicks frequently cause indigestion, even though the feeds supplied may be entirely wholesome. If for any reason it is desirable to make a radical change in the feeding, give the chicks an opportunity to become accustomed to the new ration gradually.

Lack of Variety. Where home mixtures are used, there often is a lack of variety which, while it may cause no serious trouble, usually results in slower growth and a noticeable lack of thrift. Numerous experiments have shown that a reasonable degree of variety is essential to best results, and it is worth while to go to some little trouble to provide it, even though it may somewhat increase the cost of the ration.

Ice Cold Water. Cold drinking water for young chicks is highly objectionable. It should never be more than moderately cool for small chicks, and if the water vessels must be kept in a cold place they should be refilled with warm water at frequent intervals.

Insufficient Number of Water Vessels. One of the commonest sources of trouble, particularly where large flocks are kept, is failure to provide a sufficient number of water vessels, so that the chicks when thirsty have to struggle and crowd around the only available drinking place, under such conditions often get soaked and chilled. Supply water vessels enough so that the chicks will never have any occasion for crowding to get to the water.

Feeding Whole Grains Too Soon. The use of fine-cracked grains should be continued for three to four weeks. Then whole wheat and hulled oats can safely be fed, but do not feed whole corn until the chicks are half grown. They will eat whole grains at earlier ages than here recommended, but it is not wise to supply them.

CHAPTER XII

Brooder Houses and How to Build Them

Essential Requirements in Brooder Houses—Where to Locate Such Houses and How to Build Them—Plans and Bills of Material for Desirable Portable and Permanent Houses for Lamp-Heated Hovers, Colony Hovers, Etc.—Yards, Fences and Fixtures.

WHETHER brooder houses should be of the permanent or portable type will depend on the brooding system used, the location of the plant, and the season of the year when chicks are to be raised. There can be no advantage in building portable houses for winter brooding and, for the most part, permanent houses are not desirable for warm weather brooding, except up to the age of three or four weeks. Where early chicks are to be raised however, it will pay to build a permanent house of suitable size. If lamp-heated hovers or brooders are to be used, the house should be provided with auxiliary heat in the form of a hot-water system, or even a large coal-burning stove, by means of which the room temperature can be made comfortable. This will be much better for the chicks, will prevent having to force the hover lamps, and will save fuel. A permanent house can be equipped with many conveniences such as oil tank, work table, feed bins, storage for extra parts or equipment, etc., which would not be possible in a portable house. If the soil is heavy and inclined to be wet and cold special provision can be made for drainage, in this way making the yards much more serviceable and less liable to become contaminated with disease germs.

Portable houses, as a rule, are more economically built than permanent houses, and as they may be moved to any part of the plant or farm where they may be desired, they are especially convenient where the plant is a large one, or on a farm where there are outlying fields over which the chicks can range and from which they can pick up a good part of their living after they are large enough to be safe from hawks and other enemies. If there is only limited range available so that the chicks must be raised practically on the same ground, year after year, it is probable that better results will be realized by building permanent houses, planning them so as to secure every practical convenience in carrying on the work.

Location of Brooder Houses

Chicks are especially liable to injury from being cooped or yarded on wet soil or in damp locations, and whether the house is permanent or portable this point must receive careful consideration. It also is important that the house should be so located that the chicks will not be exposed to severe winds when outdoors. For this reason, advantage should be taken of available natural or artificial protection such as groves, hedges, or buildings. If there is no natural protection it must be provided by erecting windbreaks, etc. In most sections a house shielded on the north and the west, will be much easier kept warm and the chicks can be out in the yard at an earlier age and in colder weather than would otherwise be permissible.

The size of the house must be governed by the brooding equipment to be used, but the tendency to build small and cheap should be avoided. Too cheap houses are not economical in the long run, and as they rarely are as convenient or as well equipped as first-class houses, they are harder to care for, take more time for the work, and require more fuel to keep the chicks warm. In portable houses there is a tendency on the part of many to build too small, making the house difficult to care for, increasing the inconvenience of tending the chicks, and preventing its utilization for other purposes. If to be used exclusively for brooding, a portable house built on the plan shown in Fig. 166 will be found to offer some especial advantages. Such a house encloses less air space than one with a high roof, and for that reason is warmer. Ventilation is secured without exposing the chicks to drafts, and the cost is comparatively low. Portable houses of this type usually are built 6x6, 6x8, or 8x8 feet in size—

FIG. 151—PORTABLE WIRE FENCE FOR CHICKS
For 2-foot netting make the iron rods 30 to 32 inches long and point them so that they can readily be pushed in by hand. Rods can be passed through the meshes to hold them in place but should be fastened securely to lower edge of netting so it will be held tight against the ground, preventing the chicks from getting out under it.

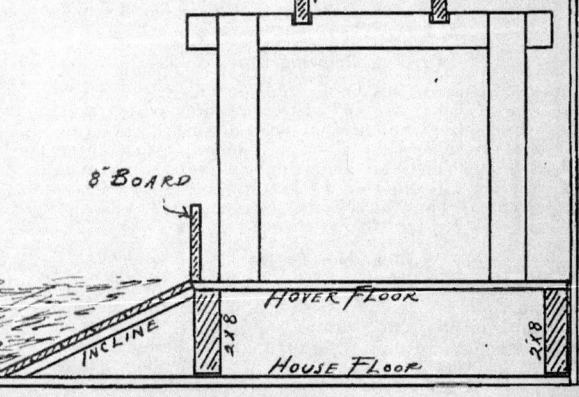

FIG. 152—BROODER HOUSE REARRANGED FOR LAYING PEN
Brooder houses with raised hover floors can readily be adapted for use as laying pens if partitions, hover platform, etc., are made movable. This illustration shows platform moved back against the house wall and provided with perches on trestles, for use of adult fowls. Board along the front edge of platform is to keep droppings out of the litter.

rarely larger—and for that reason seldom are employed for any other purpose, but stand idle when not used for brooding. A more practical house for general use is 8x10 or 8x12 feet, built with gable or shed roof, which will provide room for two or three hovers instead of one, thus reducing the labor of caring for the chicks, and giving a house large enough for a laying or breeding flock of 20 to 30 hens, a good-sized fattening flock, or the many other uses to which such houses can be put on the poultry plant more or less the year around. Whatever style of roof is adopted, the side walls should be high enough to provide plenty of headroom. It never is advisable to sacrifice this or any other practical convenience for a slight saving in cost. Piano-box brooder houses are quite popular with many, but are open to the objection just noted, that they usually are too small for any other use, and too low for comfort.

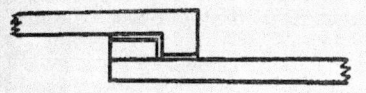

FIG. 153—LOCKING ENDS OF PORTABLE FENCE PANELS
This drawing shows manner in which ends of portable fence panels are locked. Also see Fig. 155.

Permanent compartment brooder houses usually

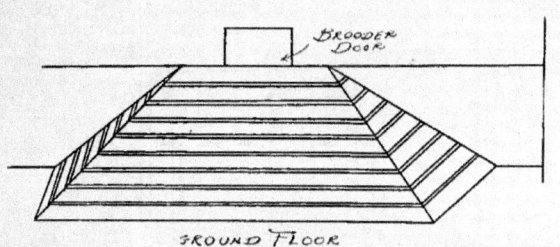

FIG. 154—CHICK INCLINE FOR BROODER OR HOUSE ENTRANCE
This three-sided incline, made of ordinary plastering lath, offers no opportunity for the chicks to get underneath or to huddle in corners. All sides slope to the brooder or house entrance.

should be designed so that they can be used for other purposes. The partitions may be made movable so that the house can be utilized by a winter-laying pen, or for fattening crates, surplus males, exhibition stock, or in any other way that may be desirable. If an elevated hover floor is provided it need not be nailed to the house floor, but can be loose so that it may be pushed back against the wall and the entire floor space utilized, simply setting trestles for perches on the platform, with an 8 or 10-inch board along the edge to keep the droppings out of the litter, as shown in Fig. 152.

Brooder House Construction

The brooder house should be warmly built and usually it should have double walls, though if not to be used in winter this may not be necessary. In order to reduce the enclosed air space and make the house easier to heat, the roof generally is sloped toward the south which makes it uncomfortably warm in the summer unless it is ceiled overhead and provided with gable ventilators.

The floor of the brooder house generally should be of concrete, if for no other reason than to make it rat-proof. Throughout the north the most serious enemy the chick raiser has to contend with is rats, and unless the house is made proof against them, they may be expected to take heavy toll from the brooder flocks. The house should have a solid foundation reaching well down into the ground and the floor should be 6 to 12 inches above the ground level so that it will always be dry. If a board floor is used it should be double-boarded, with building paper between to make it warmer, and with one-inch netting to exclude rats. If rats are allowed to harbor under the house they will get the chicks sooner or later, in spite of all precautions, for which reason houses with board floors should be high enough so that cats and dogs can get under.

Especial attention must be given to ventilation so that the chicks will not be exposed to drafts or direct air currents, but the windows should not be too high above the floor. As a rule, it will be found most satisfactory to hinge the windows at the bottom so that they will swing in at the top. The front eave should be wide enough to protect the windows when open. Whether the rest of the house is spouted or not, there should be a trough along the front so that there will be no danger of the chicks being caught in the drip from the eave as they gather in front of the yard doors during a storm.

In compartment brooder houses the passageway should be wide enough for convenience—at least three feet, and four is better, especially if there are lamps in it as shown in Fig. 164. Young chicks soon develop marked

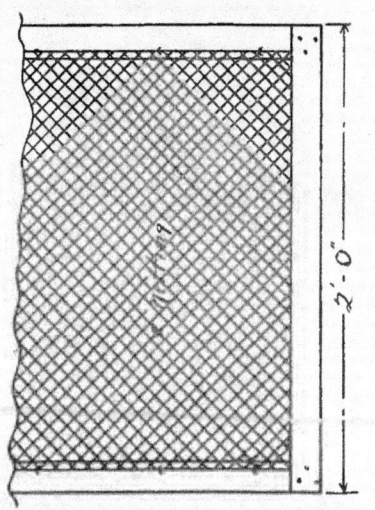

FIG. 155—END OF PORTABLE FENCE PANEL
Portable fence panels are indispensable on all poultry plants. Two and three feet are the most popular widths. Make them any convenient length, usually 10 to 16 feet, with one upright piece of furring in middle of panel to strengthen the rails. If ends are made as shown, they will lock, and when tied top and bottom with stout cord, will stand without posts. Use 1-inch mesh netting and 1x2-inch furring.

FIG. 156—CONCRETE INCLINE FOR PERMANENT BROODER HOUSES
Concrete inclines cannot be trampled down or washed away by the rain, and will last as long as the house itself.

FIG. 157—YARD FOR TWO PEN BROODER HOUSE
Where two broods are kept in one house, the yards may be conveniently arranged as shown. Use panels made as in Fig. 155, and provide a few short lengths for the ends. Reproduced from Bulletin 261, Wisconsin Experiment Station.

ability in flying over partitions and it is desirable to have these reasonably high. A width of four feet will answer in most cases. The base of the partitions should be of solid boards to a height of 18 to 24 inches, to prevent floor drafts, and the wire above should be 1-inch mesh. Pen doors should be strongly constructed and well braced or they will be a source of continual trouble. Double-acting spring hinges are desirable on such doors.

Auxiliary heat can be supplied in the form of a hot-water heater and a coil of pipe, or by means of an ordinary stove. Hot water gives a more uniform temperature and a comparatively simple outfit will answer the purpose, but if this is considered too expensive, a stove will answer, though it will be impossible to maintain as uniform heat during the night as with a hot-water system.

Yards for permanent houses should be built to meet adult requirements so that there will be no difficulty in putting the house to other uses when it is desirable to do so. Where the soil is heavy or not well drained it will pay to provide special drainage for the runs by filling in with sand and gravel where this material can be secured without too great expense. This can readily be done by setting 12-inch planks around the base of the outside fence and filling in to a depth of six inches with gravel, with a few inches of coarse sand on top. A yard filled in this way will be dry and much warmer than one on the ground level, and will be practically free from infec-

FIG. 158—ARTIFICIAL SHADE FOR CHICKS
Where there is no natural shade in the yards it must be provided in some such way as this. The air will circulate more freely underneath if the cover is supported well up off the ground.

tion with gapes which otherwise are liable to play havoc with young chicks raised on clay soil. Use durable posts and planks or better still, provide a concrete wall or lay up field stones in mortar. Do not provide a loose stone wall, as the sand will work out and also will push the wall out of place. In order to protect the chicks from hard winds, the yard should be surrounded by a tight board base two feet high, and in exposed locations there should be board bases for the partition fences also, using one-inch-mesh netting four feet wide above the boards.

Yards and Fences

Wherever chicks are grown there is need for more or less portable fencing. A plain strip of netting may be used, this being held upright by means of heavy wire rods pushed into the ground—see Fig. 151. A more durable and more generally desirable method is to provide fence panels such as are shown in Figs. 153 and 155. Almost innumerable uses will be found for such panels, if available, and as they can be cheaply made and will last many years when properly cared for, there is no economy in doing without them. For most purposes the panels should be of 1-inch netting 2 or 3 feet wide and ten to 16 feet long. The frames should consist of 1x2 or 1x3-inch furring of some kind of wood that does not split too

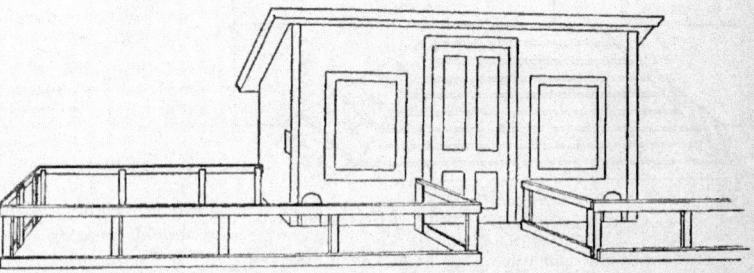

FIG. 159—ENLARGING YARDS FOR TWO PEN BROODER HOUSE
After the chicks have outgrown the first yards (see Fig. 157) these may be enlarged in the manner here indicated, without obstructing the entrance to the house door. Reproduced from Bulletin 261, Wisconsin Experiment Station.

easily. Make these frames about two inches wider than the netting so that the selvage will not lap over the edge. This will add a couple of inches to the height without cost, and the netting will last longer. Stretch the wire tightly and staple with plenty of double-pointed tacks. Netting staples are apt to split the frames and should not be used unless the wood is quite soft. Before putting on the wire, give the frames a double coat of paint.

The panel frames should be made by cutting the end pieces 2 feet 2 inches long for 2-foot netting or 3 feet 2 inches for 3-foot netting, laying these on top of the side pieces or rails and nailing with wire nails long enough to go through and clinch. Provide a middle crosspiece for long panels. Use box nails if obtainable in order to lessen the danger of splitting. When the panels are done they should all be exactly alike, but by turning them with the wire side out and in alternately the end pieces will engage each other as in Fig. 153 and if fastened together with a stout piece of cord or light wire, two or three panels will stand up without any other support, when properly connected by end panels. It costs comparatively little to make a supply of these panels, but in a term of years they will be found more economical than loose wire, which soon gets bent out of shape and is quickly destroyed, and in point of convenience there is no comparison between the two.

There are various methods of building inclines from

the house to the ground. With portable houses, inclines like the one shown in Fig. 154 are convenient, and being enclosed on the sides the chicks cannot gather under them. As this incline slopes to the door on all three sides, it prevents the losses that are apt to result from the chicks huddling in corners on either side of a straight runway. This incline is made of ordinary plastering lath nailed to four 2x2-inch pieces, the ends of which are cut to fit snugly against the brooder at the top and to rest securely on the ground or house floor at the bottom. This incline, properly made, requires no fastenings to hold it in place. For permanent houses earth may be banked up close to the door sill as in Fig. 132, or better still a concrete incline may be provided, as shown in Fig. 156, which cannot be scratched down or washed away by rain or the drip from the roof, and will last as long as the house.

Chicks are especially in need of protection from the sun in the summer. Even if the house is cool, which is not always the case, the chicks will be the better for outdoor shade, and if this is not provided naturally by trees, etc., the lack must be made up in some other way. Shade for yards may be supplied by clumps of corn, sunflowers, etc., or by quick-growing vines planted outside the yards and supported by the fences. For cheap, temporary shelters use some such device as is shown in Fig. 158, which will not only protect the chicks from the sun, but from rain if they happen to get caught out in a sudden shower, and will also afford a hiding place from hawks and crows. Such shelters may be made in any convenient size, and for large flocks are conveniently made with a gable roof high enough so that the enclosed space may readily be kept clean.

The preceding comments on house construction, yards, etc., will be found to apply quite generally to brooder houses of whatever type, and under practically all conditions where they are to be used. In the following pages some practical brooder houses are illustrated and described in detail. These will be found to conform closely to preceding statements as to what is desirable in such houses, and they are well adapted to the needs of chick raisers wherever located, or may be made so with slight changes. Persons desiring further information on this subject, are referred to "Poultry Houses and Fixtures" (see page 112) in which many additional plans for both permanent and portable brooder houses will be found. Plans for houses designed expressly for brooding ducklings are given in "Ducks and Geese" (see page 112).

Colony House for One Hover

The house illustrated in the plans in Fig. 160 is a good small house, and is designed for a single lamp-heated hover accommodating 50 to 100 chicks. If the cockerels are culled out as they reach market size the pullets can remain here until they are fully grown and are ready to go to the laying pens. The house is 6x6 feet with a window and muslin-covered opening on the south side and an opening for additional ventilation in the rear when needed. The siding should be of tongue-and-groove boards and it

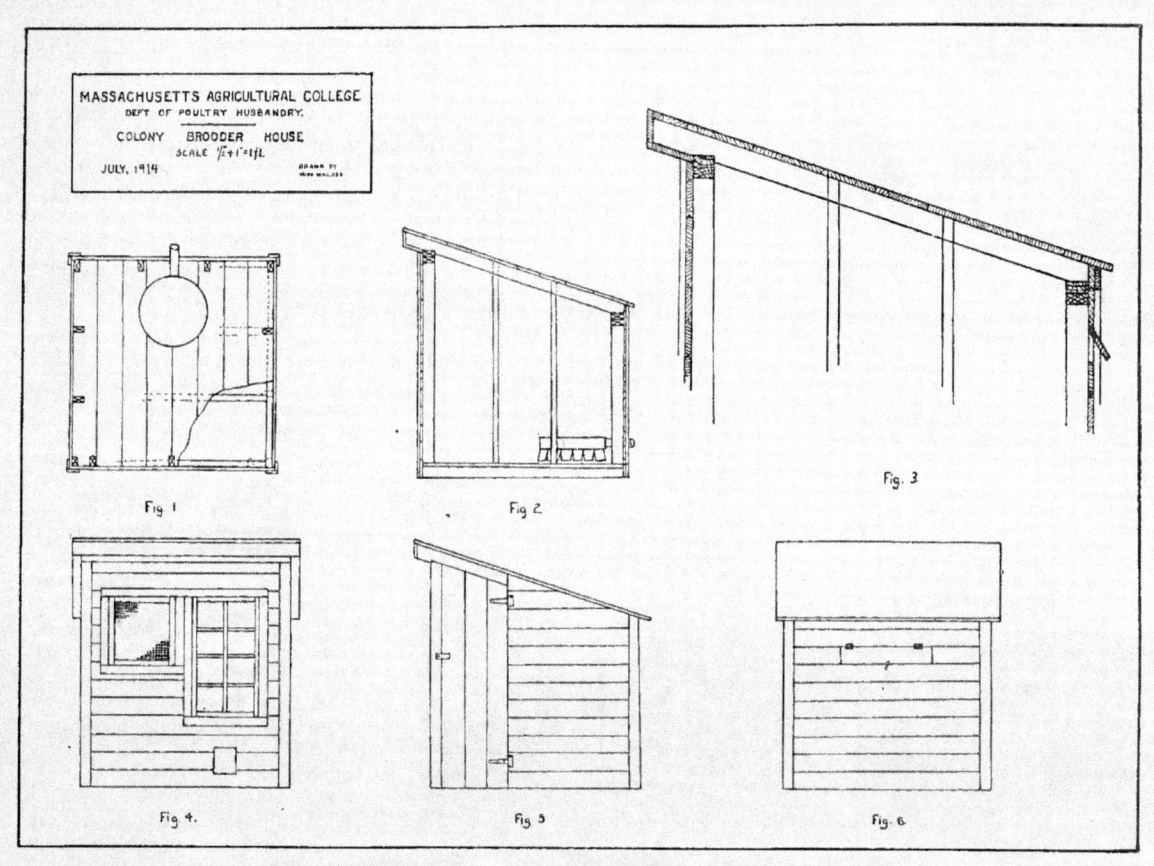

FIG. 160---PLAN FOR COLONY HOUSE FOR BROODER CHICKS
This plan, prepared by Massachusetts Agricultural College, gives complete details for a 6x6-foot portable house suitable for one lamp-heated brooder or hover. Will comfortably accommodate a flock of 75 to 100 chicks as long as they need brooding.

is roofed with a good grade of prepared roofing. This house is provided with a board floor, and no runners are indicated as the object with this house is to keep it close to the ground for convenience in teaching the chicks to run back and forth. This plan is safe however, only where there is no danger from rats. If the house must be blocked up to prevent rats harboring underneath, it will be better to provide runners which add greatly to the convenience of moving it.

House for Two Brooders

Having two or three hovers in one house reduces the amount of travel between the broods when small, and after the chicks no longer need artificial heat the hovers and partitions can be removed and all broods allowed to run together in one flock, which saves time and trouble all through the growing season. Such a house is shown in Fig. 162 which illustrates the kind in use at the Maine Experiment Station. It is described in Maine Bulletin 471 as follows:

"The houses are built on two 16-foot pieces of 4 by 6-inch timbers, which serve as runners. The ends of the timbers, which project beyond the house, are chamfered on the underside to facilitate moving. The houses are 12 feet long; some of them are 6 feet and others 7 feet wide; 7 feet is the better width. They are 6 feet high in front and 4 feet high at the back. The frame is of 2x3-inch lumber; the floor is double boarded, and the building is boarded and covered with a good quality of heavy roofing paper. Formerly shingles were used for the outside covering, but paper is preferred and is now used exclusively. This kind of covering for the wall is not so likely to be injured in moving as shingles. A door 2 feet wide is in the center of the front and a 6-light window, hinged at the top, is on each side of it. Two brooders are placed in each of these houses and 50 to 60 chicks are put with each brooder. A low partition separates the flocks while they are young. The houses are large enough so that a person can go in and do the work comfortably, and each one accommodates 100 chicks until the cockerels are large enough to be removed.

FIG. 162—A CONVENIENT TWO-PEN BROODER HOUSE
This house is 7x12 feet and accommodates two brooders of the kind shown in Fig. 108. After the hovers are no longer needed the yard partition (not shown in this illustration) is removed, and the two broods run together. Photo from Maine Experiment Station.

"An improvement has recently been made in these brooder houses by providing for better ventilation. When the weather is very hot there is no movement of air within one of these houses, even though the door and windows are open. The air within the house is practically stagnant and, on account of its relatively small volume, becomes intensely hot and stifling when the temperature outside gets high. The effect on the chicks under such circumstances is bad. They retreat to the houses to get shade, only to be injured if not killed by the hot, stifling air of the house. To remedy this difficulty a slot 2 feet long and 1 foot wide has been cut in the back of each house high up under the eaves. This slot is closed with a wooden slide running in grooves which are put on the outside of the house. The opening is covered on the inside with 2-inch mesh chicken wire. On very hot days the slide is pulled out completely so as to expose the whole opening of the slot. At night or during a period of wet, cold weather the size of the opening is regulated to suit the conditions. It enables one to keep a current of fresh air through the house in the warmest weather. The effect on the well-being of the chicks during a period of hot weather is most marked and satisfactory."

Yarding is something of a problem where two or three flocks are kept together, especially where it is desired to make certain that the two lots do not mix. They may be yarded as in Fig. 162, using a middle partition which is not shown here, or as in Figs. 158 and 159, the method employed at Wisconsin Station. Portable panels such as have previously been described are most convenient for making yards, short length panels being provided to make the yard narrow. If the short panels are 3 feet long the yards can be covered by using a regular 3-foot panel. Later on the yards may be enlarged as shown in Fig. 160, without obstructing the door.

At the Wisconsin Station a particularly good feature in use on colony houses for growing stock is a small door located about three feet above the floor, as shown in Fig. 165. This is left open at night so that the chicks can get out on the range at

FIG. 161—OPEN FRONT BROODER HOUSE
A cheap, simple house like this can be used to excellent advantage on many poultry farms. It is too open for portable hovers, but enclosed brooders, either indoor or outdoor, can be operated conveniently here early in the season when it would not be practical to have the chicks outdoors.

daybreak instead of having to await the convenience of the caretaker who may have too many duties to get round to all houses as early as is desirable. This door should not be used until the chicks are pretty well grown, nor should it be left open in stormy or cold weather. The illustration shows how the space below the door is protected by means of a piece of sheet iron, making it impossible for rats to climb up. A small platform is provided on the inside for the chicks to alight upon when they fly up, and they are never long in learning the use of the door.

Open Front Compartment Brooder House

For use with indoor brooders, fireless brooders, and for sheltering outdoor brooders early in the season, the brooder house shown in Fig. 161 will be found quite convenient and low in cost. It is not intended for use in extremely cold weather, but is designed simply to provide shelter for brooders and chicks when it is not convenient or desirable to have them out, and it contributes greatly to the comfort of the attendant in the uncertain, stormy weather that often is encountered early in the spring. It is not recommended for the use of lamp-heated hovers unless these are suitably enclosed, or the front of the pens provided with a cloth curtain.

The house is of the simplest and most economical construction. The size of the pens can be adapted to the particular type of brooder used, but should never be less than 6x6 feet, and 8x8 will be much better. For small flocks such as usually are placed in lamp-heated brooders, there is no advantage in making the house more than 10 feet deep. Good-sized doors are provided in the front of each pen, making them large enough so that brooders can be moved in or out without difficulty, and alternate partitions should be solid so that there will be no drafts sweeping through the house in windy weather. The open front is enclosed with small-mesh netting. Where sparrows are liable to be a nuisance, it will pay to use ½ or ¾-inch mesh netting, as they readily pass through 1-inch meshes.

No provision was made in the house here illustrated for protecting the front under any condition, but if located where rain or snow is apt to beat in, a hood extending forward three or four feet will assist greatly in keeping the floor dry. For convenience in caring for the chicks it is important to leave the front unobstructed by fences. If the chicks are not to be kept in the pens more than three weeks no yards at all need be provided, but as this house furnishes excellent summer quarters and probably will be in use most of the time, yards should be

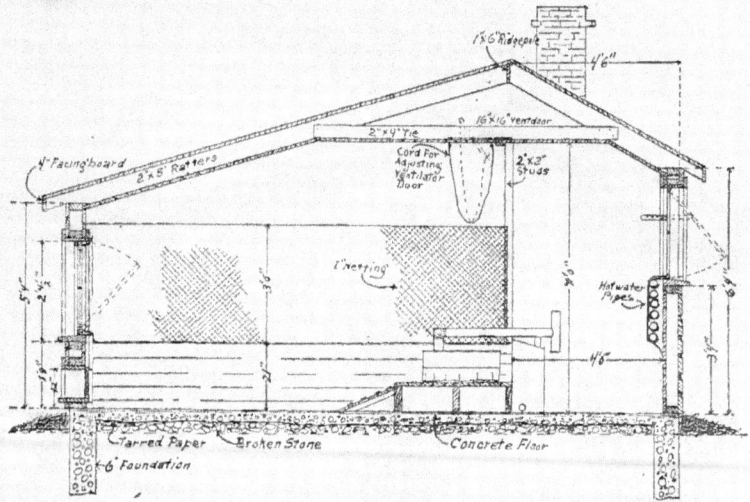

FIG. 163—CROSS SECTION OF PERMANENT BROODER HOUSE

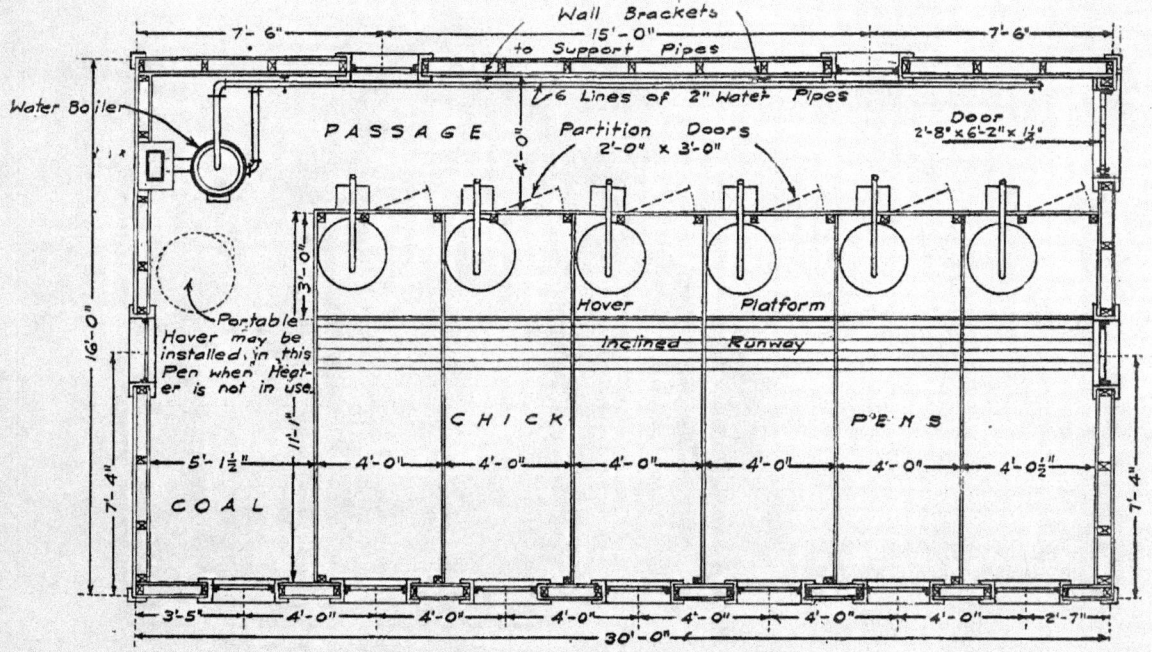

FIG. 164—FLOOR PLAN OF PERMANENT BROODER HOUSE

ARTIFICIAL INCUBATING AND BROODING

warm; 60 to 65 degrees is warm enough, as a rule. The individual hovers can be depended upon to provide the necessary additional heat without at any time having the lamps turned dangerously high.

As this house is intended for cold weather brooding it is ceiled with ⅝-inch ceiling boards. The additional cost of doing this will be amply repaid by the smaller amount of fuel required. Lath and plaster may be used if preferred, but, under ordinary conditions, ceiling is much better suited to poultry-house construction. Building paper should always be tacked to the studs before siding or ceiling is put in place. A layer of sheathing paper should also be nailed to the lower side of the ceiling joists or rafter ties before the ceiling is nailed on. Ventilation openings should be provided in the ceiling, as shown in Fig. 163. In small houses it is sufficient to have louvered ventilators in each gable, but in houses 50 feet or more in length it is necessary to provide roof ventilators also. The ground should be graded up to the front sill so that the chicks will have easy access to the yards. The siding should be carried up close to the roof boards, notching the top board carefully for the rafters. For cold climates, storm doors for all outside doors are advisable.

The cross section indicates adjustment of windows, etc., also construction of partitions. These are to be built up of flooring or any other tongue-and-groove lumber, to a height of 21 inches above the brooder house floor, with three-foot wire netting above. Note location of ceiling ventilator. This is hung flush with the lower face of the ceiling, making the opening wide enough so that the door will swing freely. It may be conveniently swung on a ¼-inch iron rod, stapling it tightly to the door and letting it turn in staples driven into the ceiling on each side. This rod should be stapled to the door just enough off center so that it will swing shut when

FIG. 165—ELEVATED CHICK DOOR
After the chicks are a couple of months old they should be let out of their houses at daybreak in good weather. This can be done without inconvenience by providing an elevated door for the colony house, which can be left open all the time. Rats and other enemies are prevented from gaining access by the strip of sheet iron or tin nailed over the siding below the door. Courtesy of Wisconsin Experiment Station.

built at the back. With the house facing south this will locate the yards on the north side where the chicks will be more comfortable in warm weather than in south yards.

A Permanent Brooder House

Floor plan and cross section for a permanent brooder house are shown in Figs. 164 and 163. As here shown the house is designed for lamp-heated hovers and is equipped with an auxiliary hot water heating system. If preferred, either coal or oil-burning colony hovers may be installed instead, no change in plans being required aside from omitting the hover floor and adapting the partitions to individual requirements. Equipped with lamp-heated hovers this house will accommodate six pens, each with a capacity of about 100 chicks. The number of pens may be reduced to five if preferred, and made five feet wide, which is a more convenient width for the caretaker. The heater is located at the farther end, where it is out of the way but easily cared for. A heater with a 12-inch grate should provide ample heat for a house of this size. Do not make the mistake of keeping the house too

FIG. 166—A-SHAPED PORTABLE BROODER HOUSE
Houses of this type are easier heated than those with higher roofs, since less space is enclosed. They are not so drafty in windy weather as houses with higher roofs and windows. Are especially well adapted to use with lamp-heated hovers or small-sized colony hovers. Photo from Iowa State College of Agriculture.

BROODER HOUSES AND HOW TO BUILD THEM

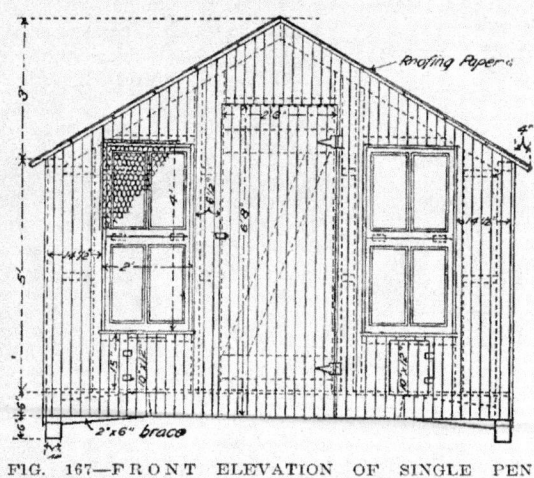

FIG. 167—FRONT ELEVATION OF SINGLE PEN COLONY HOVER HOUSE
From blue print furnished by Poultry Division of U. S. Department of Agriculture.

not fastened open. A couple of small blocks, nailed to the upper side of the ceiling at either end of the door, act as stops. The door may be held open by a weight, or by attaching the cord to stud or partition. These ventilators should be approximately under the highest point in the roof, providing two in this 30-foot house and spacing them 20 feet apart in long houses.

Where the brooding pens are five feet wide or more, it is desirable to have the pen doors hung on double-acting spring hinges, but this cannot be done with four-foot pens as in these narrow pens the door cannot swing in without striking the hover.

BILL OF MATERIALS FOR 16x30 FOOT BROODER HOUSE

Use	Size Inches	Length Feet	No. of Pieces	Remarks
Sills, side	2x4	16	4	
Sills, ends	2x4	16	2	
Joists for hover plat.	2x4	12	6	
Plates	2x4	16	4	
Studs, front	2x4	10	9	1 piece cuts 2
Studs, rear	2x4	12	8	1 piece cuts 2
Studs, ends and misc.	2x4	12	12	
Studs, partition	2x2	12	10	
Rafters	2x6	14	16	
Rafters	2x6	12	8	1 piece cuts 2
Ties for rafters	2x4	12	15	
Braces for rafters	1x6	8	15	
Sheathing for roof			660 ft. bd. meas.	Sfcd.
T & G siding			625 ft. bd. meas.	
Matched flooring for hover platform, partitions, etc.			260 ft. bd. meas.	
⅝-inch ceiling boards for walls and ceiling			1250 ft. bd. meas.	
⅞x6-inch boards for ridge pole, door and window frames			125 lin. feet.	Surfaced
Trim lumber, ventilators, etc.	⅞x4		430 lin. feet.	Surfaced
Door and window sills.	2x8		40 lin. feet.	Milled
Strips for inside window sills, and facing for front partition studs	⅞x1½		75 lin. feet.	Surfaced
Strips for window stops and chick runway	½x1		150 lin. feet.	Surfaced
Drip cap			30 lin. feet.	Surfaced

6 squares prepared roofing.
12 squares building paper.
266 sq. ft. 1-inch mesh netting for windows and partitions.
11 sashes, 1½-inch, 4-light, 10x12-inch glass.
1 4-panel door.
1 pr. 4-inch butt hinges.
1 rim lock.
6 pr. 3-inch butt hinges for partition doors.
11 pr. 2-inch butt hinges for windows.
18 2-inch screw hooks and eyes.
14 ft. of sash chain.
6 anchor bolts ½x12 in., with 2-in. washers for each end.
2 iron rods, ¼x20-inch, for swinging ventilator doors in ceiling.
1 6-inch chimney thimble.
350 bricks for chimney.

MATERIALS FOR CONCRETE FLOOR
50 bags of cement.
120 cu. ft. sand.
200 cu. ft. cinders or crushed stone.
160 cu. ft. cinders or stone for filling.

EQUIPMENT FOR AUXILIARY HEAT
Water boiler, 12-inch grate.
5 gal. expansion tank.
6 feet of 2-inch pipe.
100 feet of 1½-inch pipe.
Necessary manifolds, unions, elbows, etc.
4 wall brackets for supporting pipe.
2 joints of 6-inch stove pipe.
2 stove pipe elbows.

Portable Colony Brooder House

Brooding with colony hovers heated by means of oil or coal-burning stoves is a comparatively new method, but one that has become extremely popular wherever chicks are raised in large numbers, and that has practically revolutionized general brooding practice. As a rule, these hovers are placed in any buildings that happen to be available, and usually with good results, though specially designed houses are more convenient. Where a portable house for use with colony hover is desired, the plans shown in Figs. 167 and 168 will be found practical and economical. These plans were prepared by the Poultry Division of U. S. Department of Agriculture, and houses so constructed are in use on the Government Experiment Farm at Beltsville, near Washington, D. C.

The plans provide for a 10x10-foot house, on runners for convenient moving, and its general outlines are easily understood from the drawings. All dimensions are indicated. The floor is of tongue-and-groove flooring, laid on 2x6-inch joists set 2 feet apart. Rafters are 2 feet apart, and corners and runners are thoroughly braced.

BILL OF MATERIAL FOR PORTABLE COLONY BROODER HOUSE

125 sq. ft. T & G flooring ⅞x2½ in. x 10 ft.
325 sq. ft. T & G flooring ⅞x2½ in. x 12 ft.
6 pcs. 2x6 inch x 10 ft. for joists.
2 pcs. 4x6 inch x 12 ft. for runners.
6 pcs. 2x4 inch x 14 ft., for rafters.
16 pcs. 2x4 inch x 12 ft., for braces and studs.
150 sq. ft. sheathing ⅞x12 in. x 12 ft., surfaced 1 side.
1½ rolls roofing paper.
4 sashes, 2 ft. square.
2 sashes, 18x24 inches.
Nails, screws, hinges and paint.

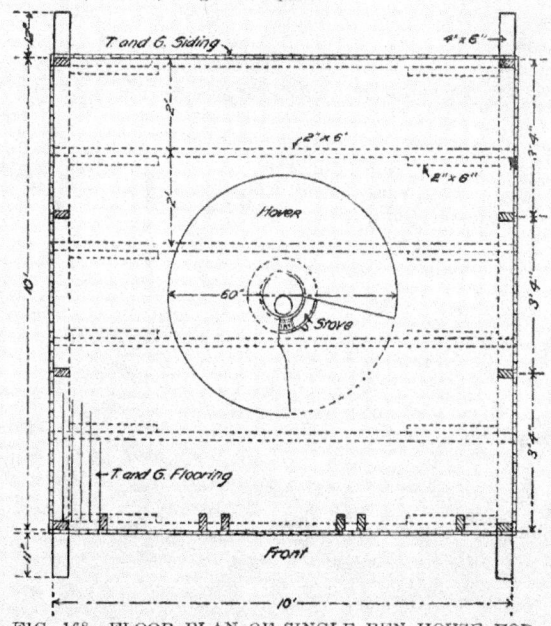

FIG. 168—FLOOR PLAN OF SINGLE PEN HOUSE FOR COLONY HOVER
From blue print furnished by Poultry Division of U. S. Department of Agriculture.

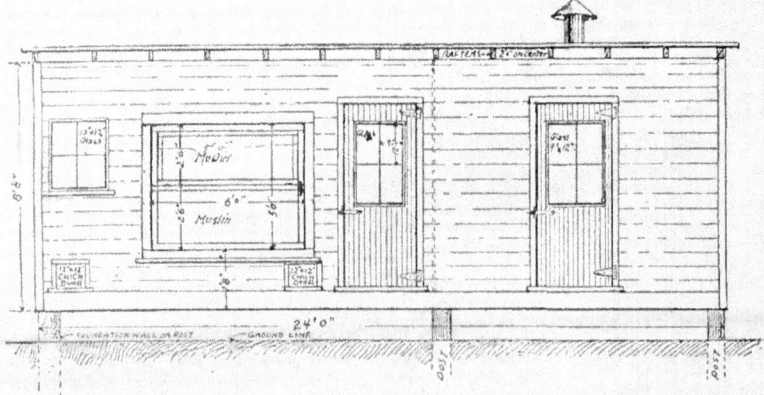

FIG. 169—FRONT ELEVATION OF TWO-COMPARTMENT HOUSE FOR COLONY HOVER

Permanent House for Colony Hover

Large brooder flocks necessarily require much greater floor space than is provided for flocks of 50 to 100, and larger houses or rooms, combined with the method of heating employed, frequently develop floor drafts to some extent. These must be reckoned with, especially in cold-weather brooding. One of the best ways of preventing this trouble is to build the house so that it can be divided into two parts of about equal dimensions, placing the hover in one section which is built quite warm but well lighted, the other section being used as an exercising compartment and generally built with a curtain front.

The house illustrated in Figs. 169 and 170 has been carefully designed to meet the special requirements of colony brooding and will be found suitable for the use of the great majority of those who are raising chicks by this time and labor-saving method. Fig. 170 shows floor plan of house, which is 10x24 feet, with a 10-foot hover section partitioned off at one end. When the chicks are first placed under the hover they are to be confined to this room. It is large enough for several hundred during the first week or two, but not so large as to invite floor drafts, and it can be comfortably heated with less fuel than would be required to maintain the correct temperature if the entire house were in one room.

The bill of material for this house provides for a double-boarded floor, the subfloor being of ordinary 10-inch sheathing, with a top floor of tongue-and-groove boards, and waterproofed sheathing paper between the two. Single board floors are almost certain to be drafty and cold. Under average conditions concrete floors are better for brooder houses than boards, because warmer, absolutely ratproof, and practically indestructible. Concrete floors must be well drained and insulated against dampness, and chicks must never be allowed to run on the bare surface, a common cause of leg weakness and rheumatism. Where there is no danger from rats an ideal plan is to provide a concrete floor in the brooding room and a plain dirt floor in the exercising compartment.

When the chicks are ten days to two weeks old, or when only a few days old in mild weather, they should be given access to the exercising compartment, which is provided with a muslin shutter for ventilation. In order to be able to graduate the ventilation, a double shutter is provided so that the upper part may be opened without disturbing the lower section, thus affording fresh air without exposing the chicks to direct drafts from the opening, as would be the case if the entire shutter were to be opened in severe or stormy weather. In mild weather or when the chicks are older and have become somewhat hardened, the entire shutter may be hooked up, thus giving the chicks practically outdoor conditions without exposure.

BILL OF MATERIALS FOR PERMANENT COLONY HOVER HOUSE

Use	Size Inches	Length Feet	No. of Pieces	Remarks
Sills, sides	2x8	12	4	
Sills, ends	2x8	10	2	
Sills, half width	2x4	12	4	Spike to inside face of side sill
Joists	2x6	10	11	
Plates	2x4	12	4	
Studs, front	2x4	8	10	
Studs, rear	2x4	10	6	1 piece cuts 2
Studs, ends	2x4	16	4	Cut to fit
Rafters	2x5	12	13	
Window sills	2x5	10	2	
Roof boards	1x10		325 ft. bd. meas.	Surf'd.
T & G siding	⅞x6		450 ft. bd. meas.	
Flooring	⅞x4		300 ft. bd. meas.	
Subfloor	⅞x10		265 ft. bd. meas.	
Ceiling	9-16x4		350 ft. bd. meas.	
Door & window frames	⅞x6		150 lin. ft.	Surf'd. 4 sides
Trim boards	⅞x4		60 lin. ft.	Surf'd. 4 sides
Frame for shutter	⅞x3½		25 lin. ft.	Surf'd. 4 sides
Frame for top shutter	⅞x2		20 lin. ft.	Surf'd. 4 sides
Strip under shutter	⅞x2½		6 lin. ft.	Surf'd. 4 sides
Strip under window	⅞x2¾		10 lin. ft.	Surf'd. 4 sides

3½ squares prepared roofing.
3 squares sheathing paper for floor
60 square feet wire netting for curtain front
4 4-light sashes, 10 in. x 12 in. glass
2 4-light sashes 9 in. x 12 in. glass (for doors)
3 pair 8-inch T-strap hinges
3 hasps
4 pair 2-inch butt hinges for windows
1 pair 2½-inch butt hinges for shutters
1 pair 3-inch butt hinges for shutters
4 2-inch screw hooks and eyes
Nails, tacks and paint

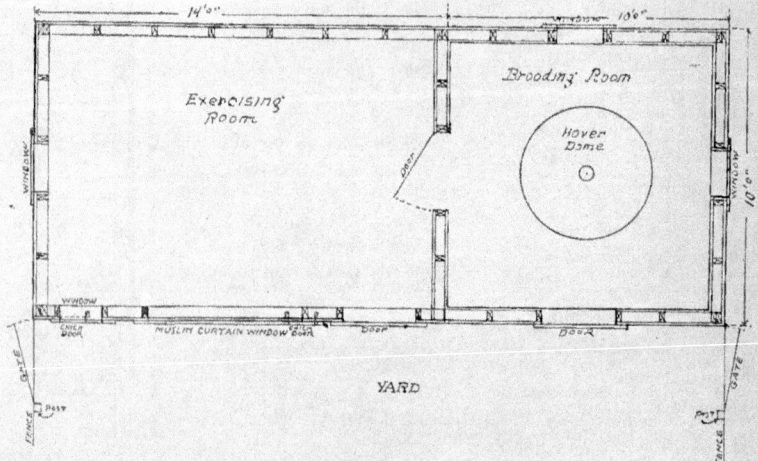

FIG. 170—FLOOR PLAN FOR TWO-COMPARTMENT COLONY HOVER HOUSE

CHAPTER XIII

Ailments and Diseases of Chicks

Importance of Being Able Promptly to Identify Ailments and Correct Conditions Before Serious Diseases Develop – How to Make Post-Mortem Examinations—Bacillary White Diarrhea and the Diseases With Which It Often Is Confused—How to Prevent and Cure All Common Ailments—Parasites and Enemies of Chicks.

CHICK troubles are of the poultry keeper's own making for the most part—the direct result of abuse or mismanagement. If there were no carelessness or neglect there would be comparatively little disease and few losses of chicks. The appearance of any considerable number of sick individuals in a brooder flock is positive proof that someone has not done his part. Nature is not a blunderer; chicks are hatched to live and grow, not to sicken and die.

Do not make the mistake of thinking of young chicks as weak. They are delicate organisms, it is true, but never weak unless mistreated. A watch is a delicate piece of machinery, but a good watch is not weak. If it is treated as a watch should be it will keep in good running order many years, doing more work and showing greater endurance, relatively, than most other pieces of machinery in common use. So a chick, if it is a good chick and treated properly, will live, keep healthy, and grow to adult size just in the way that nature intended. If it fails to do this, it is because someone abused or mistreated it or its parents. Chick troubles when they appear, can almost invariably be traced directly to low vigor in the breeding flock, weakened vitality due to improper methods with incubators or brooders, or to failure to supply well-selected and nourishing food.

It is to be expected, of course, that the beginner, with a new science to learn, a multitude of details to master, and a living to make, will find more or less difficulty in providing just the right conditions for his chicks at all times, and in avoiding mistakes. Sooner or later, he will have to reckon with various disorders in his flocks, and it is of the utmost importance that when disease does appear he shall be able to recognize it promptly in order to get the situation in hand at the earliest moment, before derangement becomes chronic—before simple ailments become incurable diseases.

To an extent that few realize, the difference between a nominal loss of 5 to 10 per cent and a loss of 50 per cent is determined by the promptness with which the caretaker recognizes the first appearance of trouble, and applies suitable correctives. One person sees that something has gone wrong—that his chicks are a little "dumpy," and he investigates the matter promptly, corrects the fault, and has no serious consequences to meet. Another, careless, thoughtless, or inexperienced, sees nothing wrong until the next day, which often is just one day too late. Twenty-four hours is a long time to a delicate young chick and twenty-four hours of neglect, discomfort, or disease may mean heavy losses that cannot be prevented by any subsequent care or treatment. One of the most important factors in the successful rearing of chicks, then, is the ability to recognize unfavorable conditions before they have a chance to produce serious results.

Chick's troubles usually are not diseases—not at first, anyway. They are simply ailments or slight derangements of the vital organs which, if noticed in time and their causes understood, can be corrected without serious loss. As a rule there is little to be gained in doctoring sick chicks. When the trouble has reached the stage where that becomes necessary there is little hope for them. Even if cured they will almost certainly be weakened and stunted, and about the worst thing that

FIG. 172—A HEALTHFUL LOCATION FOR THE GROWING CHICKS

can happen is to have such chicks recover, grow to maturity, and go into the breeding pen to pass on to the next generation, in increasing proportion, their weakness and liability to disease.

Methods of Sanitation

More attention should be given to sanitation in chick raising than is usually the case. Efforts to raise chicks with the smallest expenditure of time and money often result in providing makeshift coops and buildings, and in crowding the chicks into such inadequate quarters that injury inevitably results. While chicks apparently will do well under quite unfavorable conditions in warm, sunshiny weather, they lose ground rapidly whenever a cold, rainy spell occurs. There is no reason why this should happen if their brooders and coops are what they should be, and if these are kept clean. Overcrowding, foul hovers, poor ventilation, damp floors, and accumulated droppings reeking with ammonia fumes are not conditions under which any chicks can thrive, and it is only when they are raised during the most favorable season of the year that they are able to withstand such mistreatment.

Cleanliness ought not to be neglected at any time, and is especially important during the danger period—the first four weeks of the chicks' lives. It is not practical to lay down definite rules for cleaning coops and brooders, renewal of litter, disinfection, etc., since much depends upon the season, size of brooder, and number of chicks, but there are two rules that are of general application, and these are to renew the litter before it becomes damp and foul-smelling, and to apply some good disinfectant every time the coop or brooder is cleaned. When brood coops and outdoor brooders are used, with or without chick shelters, they should be moved to fresh ground every few days. Coops without floors should not be left standing in one spot until the ground becomes soaked with filth.

Some of the most serious diseases that affect young chicks are germ diseases, and the poultryman who is careless and slovenly in regard to the quarters in which the chicks are confined, is simply multiplying infection

FIG. 173—IT PAYS TO SPADE BARE RUNS
Spading the bare runs will sweeten the soil, help to keep them free from disease germs, and the chicks will greatly enjoy digging in the loose earth. If some oats or other grains are scattered broadcast over the ground before spading, so much the better. Courtesy of Wisconsin Experiment Station.

and cannot long escape the consequences of his indifference. Disinfectants should be used freely about all coops, brooders and runways where chicks are confined. Air-slaked lime is good for bare spots and general outdoor use, but is too caustic to be used where young chicks are liable to get into it with their feet. It should not be employed indoors, as the dust arising from it may cause serious inflammation of nostrils, throat or eyes.

Whitewash is an excellent disinfectant and may be used freely without any danger of ill effects. Most persons however, find the use of a good commercial disinfectant more convenient and more effective. Most of these are readily prepared for use at any time simply by adding water to the disinfectant in the proper proportion, and requiring no heating, straining or other preparation for use. They may be applied with a brush, whisk broom, sprinkling can, or spray pump, as convenient. Where liquid disinfectants are used, the brooders, coops, etc., should be dry before the chicks are turned back into them.

Constitutional Vigor

Constitutional vigor is the foundation of all successful chick raising, and it is useless to hope for success if this fundamental has been neglected. It is not necessary to repeat here what has already been said regarding this matter, but the beginner especially is urged to turn again to Chapter I on Selection of Breeding Stock, and review what will there be found on this vitally important subject. There is little that can be done to prevent losses due to lack of constitutional vigor, after the chicks are hatched, or to remedy the effects of mistakes in artificial incubation, though careful brooding and feeding will help.

First Symptoms of Disease

In many chick disorders the symptoms are similar, though not so much so but that the caretaker can detect shades of difference pointing toward specific causes. The successful chick raiser does not feel easy in regard to any brood so long as there is one mopy chick in it. It may be constitutional weakness or some other matter affecting a single individual (not all chicks will live under even the most favorable conditions) but if there is one weakly member of the flock there is reason to suspect that in another hour there may be two; and in a few hours there may be a dozen.

When chicks are noisy, when they huddle in corners or in the sunlight, when they stay under the hover for hours at a time, when they refuse to go out at mealtime and do not eat when they are out, there is every reason to fear serious trouble. Such conduct indicates weakness at least. It may not mean anything more serious than that, but study the chicks and review everything that has been done. Is the temperature of the brooder what it ought to be? Does the thermometer register correctly? Has the feeding been properly done? Have the foods been wholesome and pure? Has provision been made for plenty of healthful exercise?

Why Chicks Are Noisy

Chicks peep and are noisy because they are uncomfortable. Whether the cause of this discomfort is hunger or thirst or the first stage of disease the poultryman must determine for himself, and if he is a true poultryman he will not leave the chicks until he knows. Often this indication of uneasiness is the first warning of serious trouble, and if the caretaker is unable otherwise to reach a definite conclusion as to the cause he will find it worth while to take out a few of the weakest individuals and kill them and carefully examine their internal organs. Many an epidemic could have been arrested at the start by such a step. After a number have died it may be too late; by that time the whole flock may be seriously infected.

If with all conditions as nearly correct as the operator knows how to make them, the chicks do not promptly brighten up, it usually is wise to add a little pepper, ginger or mustard to their feed. One of these mild stimulants, especially during the latter part of the first week when the young chick is completing the absorption of the yolk and coming to depend entirely upon supplied foods, may prevent serious derangements. The use of digestive stimulants is better than resorting to drugs, but be careful! Use only enough to make the mash slightly warm to the taste and discontinue it as soon as it is no longer needed. Chicks that are regularly given highly seasoned food are apt to be injured, liver disorders being extremely common under such conditions.

AILMENTS AND DISEASES OF CHICKS

Milk Feeding for Young Chicks

In cases of weakness from any cause it will pay to provide a supply of milk for the chicks to drink if it can be secured at reasonable cost. It does not seem to matter much whether the milk is sweet or sour, but it is not considered desirable to give sweet milk at one time and sour at another. As it generally is difficult to keep milk sweet until the chicks have consumed it, usually the more practical plan is to supply it sour all the time.

Probably the most convenient and sanitary method of feeding milk is to use one of the commercial two-piece drinking founts, or a good homemade substitute may be made by using a saucer or similar dish with a one-quart can inverted in it, as illustrated in Fig. 139. Whatever is used, it should be thoroughly cleaned and scalded at frequent intervals. The milk feeder should be placed where the chicks cannot scratch litter into it. If the milk should become foul in any way, throw it away, clean the vessel thoroughly, and provide a fresh supply. Milk is a highly favorable medium for the development of disease germs of various kinds, therefore it must be kept free from contamination.

The Storrs (Connecticut) Experiment Station has carefully investigated the value of milk, both sweet and sour, in the diet of chicks, particularly those that are infected, or that are liable to become infected with bacillary white diarrhea. The results secured in an extensive series of such experiments are announced in the following conclusions, quoted from Bulletin 80 of that institution:

"The feeding of milk to young chicks has a most favorable influence on the growth and on the lessening of mortality of the chicks. It tends to prevent mortality from all causes, and if fed soon enough and for a sufficiently long period, greatly reduces the death-rate caused by bacillary white diarrhea.

"Sweet and sour milk are apparently of equal value in their relation to growth and mortality. Furthermore, different degrees of souring do not alter the results of milk feeding.

"The value of milk as a food for chicks does not depend upon any acids that may be present, nor upon any particular types of micro-organisms; but upon one or more of the natural constituents of the milk.

"When milk is supplied freely to chicks, it becomes all the more important that they have abundant exercise. This applies more particularly to early hatched chicks that are brooded wholly or for the most part indoors.

"The feeding of sweet or sour milk to young chicks has in no instance been found to be in any way injurious to the chicks employed in our numerous experiments. If the milk is clean, and not too old, none but the most favorable results should accompany its use as a food for chicks. There is no preference in the choice of sweet or of sour milk, except from the standpoint of convenience. The use of the one or the other should be determined by the circumstances. However, it seems very desirable that the same kind of milk be supplied throughout the milk feeding period. If the choice is that of sour milk, sour milk should be fed to the end."

General Treatment for Diarrhea in Chicks

The chick's digestive organs are peculiarly delicate during the first few weeks of its life and almost any unfavorable influence is liable to result in some affection of these organs. A chick that has been kept in an insufficiently ventilated nursery chamber in the incubator, that has been chilled either in the incubator or in the brooder, that has been fed too much, deprived of some needed element such as grit or green feed, given cold water to drink, permitted to get wet, crowded in the brooder, kept confined to the brooder too long, or exposed to any one of a number of possible resources of bacterial infection, will almost certainly have digestive disorders, generally accompanied with some form of diarrhea.

Since diarrheal discharges in chicks usually are "white," the tendency on the part of most persons is to jump to the conclusion that chicks so affected have that much-dreaded disease known as bacillary white diarrhea. As a matter of fact, however, cases of bacillary white diarrhea are few in number as compared with the other causes producing similar symptoms, and it is much safer

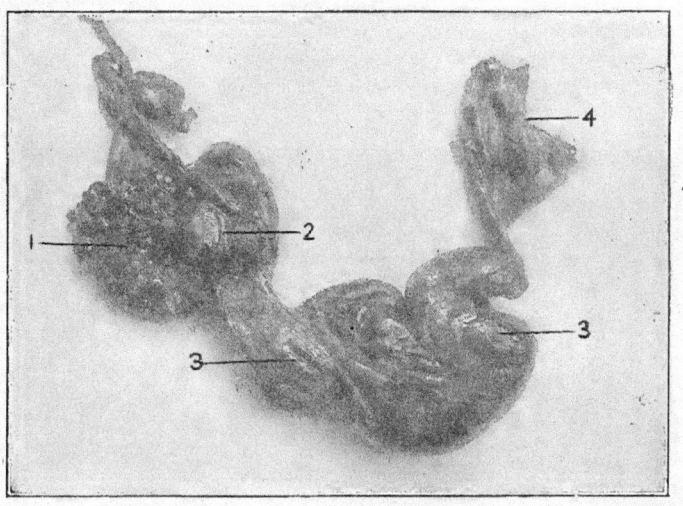

FIG. 174—INFECTED EGG ORGANS OF HEN
Illustration made from photograph of ovary and oviduct of hen badly infected with bacterium pullorum. 1. Ovary with many of the ova showing discoloration. 2. Large-size, infected ovum, showing decided-ed discoloration. As a rule will be found more or less cheesy in texture. 3. Oviduct showing indications of disease. 4. Cloaca. Photo from Storrs Experiment Station.

to assume that the trouble is NOT bacillary infection, until all the more probable causes have been eliminated by thorough diagnosis.

The careful observer finds that the character of diarrheal discharges accompanying different forms of ailments or diseases vary more or less. Generally speaking, a frothy condition of the contents of the bowels indicates intestinal catarrh resulting from chilling in or out of the brooder, exposure to floor drafts, rain, chilling winds, etc., though they sometimes indicate inflammation of the bowels, such as may accompany any form of acute indigestion. The presence of reddish mucus in the droppings also indicates inflammation. Watery droppings, when associated with extreme thirst, indicate aspergillosis—a disease acquired by inhaling mold spores from moldy grain, clover, etc., or picking them up with food. White, pasty droppings may indicate bacillary white diarrhea, but are much more apt to be the result of catarrhal or digestive disorders.

It hardly needs to be said that for the cure of diarrhea and the prevention of its spread throughout the flock, the cause must be discovered and removed. Often where this is done and a few simple measures taken to relieve the suffering resulting from diarrhea, the chicks may be restored to good health without any other treatment. In the earliest stages of the trouble it may be sufficient to use something that will act as a tonic and stimulant to the digestive organs, such as cayenne pepper, ground ginger, or mustard, used sparingly. An excellent soothing food for chicks suffering from bowel trouble in any form is boiled rice, which should be cooked thoroughly and boiled as dry as possible, taking up all surplus moisture at feeding time by stirring in sufficient brown wheat middlings, or wheat bran with all coarse particles sifted out. Let the chicks have all the boiled milk they will drink.

In order to avoid spread of infection, it is always desirable to use a disinfectant in the drinking water. For this purpose potassium permanganate generally is recommended. It loses its virtue quickly in exposed solutions, but if the supply of water is renewed several times a day, as should always be done when there are sick chicks in the flock, it will prove effective, and it is quite cheap, besides being simple and easy to use. The best way to provide it is to make a stock solution by dissolving in a large bottle or jar of water, all the crystals that the water will take up, and each time the chicks are watered pour enough of the solution into the water to give it a reddish color.

FIG. 175—CHICKS INFECTED WITH BACILLARY DIARRHEA
These chicks are of the same lot as those shown in Fig. 175, but have bacillary white diarrhea. They probably inherit the infection from the hens that laid the eggs from which they were hatched.

Charcoal is an excellent corrective in intestinal disorders and should be kept before the chicks all the time, placing it in any convenient, waste-preventing hopper. They will eat it more readily if supplied in granulated form with the fine dust screened out. It is taken for granted that the chicks will always have a supply of grit crushed to suitable size. Clean, coarse sand will answer at first, but a good grade of commercial grit is better.

In all digestive troubles with chicks a liberal supply of green food is important. This should be tender and succulent however, and if the chicks are not accustomed to having all they want of it, only a limited quantity should be fed at first, increasing the amount as the chicks get used to it and can be trusted not to overeat.

For the treatment of chicks affected with diarrhea in any form there are good commercial remedies on the market that are thoroughly reliable and effective, and they are much more convenient for use than home remedies. One of these should be secured and kept on hand ready for use at the first appearance of trouble. If none is immediately available in case of emergency, try bichloride of mercury. Get this in tablets of 1-1000 of a grain and dissolve twelve in each quart of drinking water.

Proper Dosage for Chicks

In administering medicines of any sort, chicks 1 to 5 weeks old should have one-sixth to one-eighth of the dose given to an adult fowl; chicks 5 to 10 weeks old, one-fourth to one-fifth the adult dose; chicks 10 to 15 weeks old, one-third the adult dose; chicks 15 to 26 weeks old, one-half the adult dose. However, where remedies are added to the drinking water, practically the same proportions should be used for both adult fowls and chicks, since the latter will drink proportionately less and so will get no more than the proper dose.

In giving Epsom salts, apply the following rule: For chicks 1 to 5 weeks old, give 1 level teaspoonful to 8 chicks; 5 to 10 weeks old, 1 level teaspoonful to 5 chicks; 10 to 15 weeks old, 1 level teaspoonful to 3 chicks; 15 to 26 weeks old, 1 level teaspoonful to 2 chicks. Salts may be given most conveniently when dissolved in water and mixed with a little wet mash, and the best time to give the treatment is in the morning before the chicks have had access to any other food.

Importance of Post-Mortem Examinations

There are few external symptoms that can be relied upon in distinguishing between different chick diseases, and careful examination of the internal organs of dead chicks is the only reliable means of doing this in many instances. The poultryman therefore, must overcome his dislike for this work and by repeated examinations thoroughly familiarize himself with the appearance of the organs of both normal and diseased chicks or he will never be able to identify diseases with certainty. It will prove a good investment for the beginner to sacrifice a few healthy chicks in order to learn exactly how their internal organs appear when in normal condition.

A good way to make the examination is as follows: Procure a shingle or board of white pine or other soft wood, into which tacks or pushpins can be easily pushed. Place the chick on the board, breast uppermost, and stretch out the wings and legs, tacking them in this position. Slit the skin covering breast and abdomen and peel it back sufficiently to expose the breast and the muscular wall of the abdomen. With shears or a knife make an incision below each side of the breast bone and remove the entire breast. This exposes the internal organs without disturbing them.

Liver Disorders

After removing the breast bone the liver will be in plain sight and should be carefully examined. The healthy liver has a uniform, dark chocolate color and is firm in texture. If it is abnormally dark in color, or pale with bright red edges or spots, or if the gall bladder is enlarged, sometimes discoloring the parts of the liver lying next to it, suspect congestion or inflammation. A pale liver with streaks and patches of red is a symptom in bacillary white diarrhea but is observed frequently when no trace of bacillary infection can be detected.

Congested livers frequently are due to a lack of green feed. Serious epidemics of diarrhea have been checked by correcting the ration in this respect. When the gall bladder is distended and the adjacent parts are discolored, the ration probably is lacking in animal matter. Congestion of the liver may be caused by feeding overstimulating foods or too much mash, or by the excessive use of cayenne pepper and ginger. Congestion of the liver may or may not be accompanied by diarrhea. It often causes heavy losses and there is no doubt that many epidemics of so-called "white diarrhea" arise from this simple, easily prevented cause. If suitable foods are used and proper methods of feeding are adopted as outlined in Chapter XI, it should be comparatively easy to prevent losses from this source.

Aspergillosis and Congestion of Lungs

After removing the liver, carefully examine the lungs. These should be light pink in color. If diseased they may be covered or filled with white cheesy nodules the size of a pinhead or smaller, or the lungs may be discolored and dark. If nodules are present the trouble is aspergillosis, sometimes called brooder pneumonia. Aspergillosis is caused by the growth of mold in the lung tissue—just the same kind of mold that comes on bread when it is kept too long in a can or box; the mold that is found in closets, cellars and damp, dark places generally. This mold usually forms in small, round nodules, white or yellow in color, cheesy in texture, and easily recognized wherever they exist. In another form of aspergillosis, small yellowish nodules are found all over the walls of the air sacs and various abdominal membranes, instead of being limited to the lung tissue. The kidneys are often a mass of these nodules. This disease sometimes occurs without noticeable development of nodules, when it closely resembles inflammation or congestion of the lungs.

The most common cause of infection is the use of moldy hay or straw for brooder litter. The general use of "shatterings" or chaff from the stable or haymow is responsible for a great deal of this trouble. Dusty shatterings often are quite full of mold spores and the chicks breathing this dust are rapidly infected. The disease may also be caused by moldy food. While it has never been completely proved, it is probable that infection may take place through the egg shells which, when damp, furnish conditions peculiarly favorable to the development of mold. Since the shells are quite porous it is possible for infection to penetrate the shell in this way. To prevent such infection eggs kept for hatching should be stored where mold will not form, and as an additional precaution they should be dipped in alcohol before being placed in the incubator. Since mold forms readily on eggs where they come in contact with each other, those that are kept for hatching should not touch, especially where there is any dampness.

While epidemics of aspergillosis are almost invariably reported as "white diarrhea," this disease seldom if ever produces characteristic "white" discharges. As a rule, they are quite watery, probably due to the fact that chicks affected with this disorder are feverish and drink excessive quantities of water. There is no known cure for aspergillosis. If its presence is promptly discovered much may be done to prevent serious losses by at once removing the source of infection. Use nothing but mold-free litter and feed, disinfect the brooder every time a new lot of chicks is placed in it, and be sure that it is absolutely free from mold. If these simple precautions are taken the disease will seldom be a source of serious loss.

When the lungs, instead of being full of nodules, are discolored and dark, and appear to be filled with frothy mucus when cut open, the trouble is congestion or inflammation. This disease sometimes is called brooder pneumonia, and frequently occurs in epidemic form. It is caused by improper brooding, impure air, also by allowing the chicks to become wet, chilled, or overheated. Many heavy losses from this cause are reported by persons brooding chicks in fireless brooders, especially in cold or changeable spring weather. Inflammation of the lungs is practically incurable but readily prevented. Use a brooder that provides an abundance of heat with a forced circulation of pure, warm air, prevent chilling or overheating, and losses from this source will be few in number.

Sour Crop and Gastritis

The crop, gizzard, and intestines should next be examined. Chicks often suffer from sour crop and gastritis or inflammation of the stomach. These ailments frequently occur together and both result from improper feeding or the use of unsuitable foods. The chief symptom is an accumulation of gas and liquid in the crop, causing distension and sometimes vomiting and gasping for breath, the latter symptom occasionally being mis-

FIG. 176—HEALTHY NONINFECTED CHICKS
These ten-day old White Leghorn chicks are free from infection with bacillary white diarrhea, and present a strong contrast with infected chicks of the same age on opposite page.

taken for gapes. These ailments may be almost wholly prevented by using due care in feeding, and by keeping the chicks liberally supplied with charcoal. When the symptoms are first noted give Epsom salts and change the ration. It is a good plan also to give bicarbonate of soda (common baking soda) in the drinking water, making the solution as strong as the chicks will drink it readily.

Coccidiosis

The intestines of healthy chicks are pinkish white. In some forms of bacillary infection they probably will be a dirty or blackish white. Their contents should be of a creamy consistency and light in color unless charcoal is fed. If hard, frothy or badly discolored, suspect indigestion, due to the feed or the method of feeding.

Near the lower end of the intestines are the ceca or blind guts. Carefully examine these. They should be about the size and color of the intestines, with walls of about the same thickness. The contents should be somewhat firmer. If solid and lumpy it is an indication of inflammation which probably originated in the intestines. If the ceca are enlarged, the walls thick, and the contents cheesy or resembling mucus, the trouble probably is coccidiosis, a bacterial disease. Chicks affected with this disorder usually die between the second and fifth week.

The symptoms are dullness and weakness accompanied by a white, pasty discharge. The presence of the disease is readily detected by examining the ceca, which will show symptoms as above described. There is little use in attempting to treat chicks that have coccidiosis, and preventive measures must be depended upon for protection.

Careful disinfection of the incubator, dipping the eggs in alcohol before placing them in the machines, disinfecting the brooder, and keeping the chicks on clean ground, all are advised where serious infection exists. This organism is widely disseminated however, being found in practically all members of the bird family and in other animals as well, and it is doubtful whether it causes serious trouble where strong, vigorous breeding stock is used and where the chicks' general health has not been weakened or injured by mismanagement.

FIG. 177—PAIR OF GAPE WORMS
A—Male.
B—Female.

Bacillary White Diarrhea

Bacillary white diarrhea is one of the most difficult chick diseases to combat successfully, though fortunately it is by no means as common as it generally is believed to be. Of the reported cases of white diarrhea, apparently only a comparatively small percentage is correctly identified. The general failure properly to diagnose the various affections that are confused with bacillary white diarrhea is unfortunate, as it leaves the real cause undetected and thus permits the spread of the disease and increases the losses. In all cases where the chicks have diarrhea, the first ones to die should be carefully examined, applying the tests already described, and if it is impossible to locate the trouble elsewhere, then (and not until then) bacillary infection may be considered probable.

In chicks that have died from this disease the intestines are pale, showing a dirty white color and usually are empty, but may contain a small amount of gray or brown matter. Unabsorbed yolk generally is present and has a stale odor but is not necessarily putrid. In bad cases of infection the first deaths may occur before the chicks are taken from the incubator. Affected chicks are chilly, listless, and with little or no appetite and are "short backed."

The heaviest death rate is from the fifth to the twentieth day, but infection is believed to occur within the first few days after hatching if it does not exist when the chick is hatched. If infection does not occur before the chick is a week old it is likely to escape altogether. Infection has been clearly traced to the hens that lay the eggs from which the affected chicks are hatched, and it has been found possible practically to eliminate the disease from certain flocks by testing the hens and removing all infected ones from the breeding pens. However, many chicks that are not infected when hatched become so through picking at the droppings from diseased chicks and for this reason it often is recommended that glass doors in incubators be covered at the time the chicks are coming out, to make the interior dark and discourage any tendency to pick at the droppings.

In all cases where there is reason to believe that the chicks are suffering from bacillary white diarrhea, arrangements should be made with the state experiment station to have some of the affected individuals examined. It is not desirable to forward dead chicks without previous arrangement, however, as the person who is to make the examination may wish to give some special directions regarding their shipment so that they may arrive in good condition.

There is no cure for bacillary white diarrhea so far as is now known. The only thing that can be done is to try to hatch chicks free from infection and then start them under the most favorable conditions, so that they will be strong enough to throw off infection if it occurs. Feeding milk—all the chicks will drink, is especially desirable, and the incubator and brooder should be thoroughly disinfected for each hatch or brood. Fine absorbent litter that will take up all moist discharges so that the chicks cannot pick at them so readily, is recommended.

Catarrhal Disorders

Chicks exposed to unfavorable conditions in or out of the brooders, such as chilling, overheating, impure air, etc., are more liable to develop catarrh of the bowels than the various forms of nasal catarrh. Under some conditions however, they may develop nasal discharges and "sore eyes"—forms of catarrhal inflammation. Keep the brooders clean and dry and at the proper temperature, and do not expose the chicks unduly to cold winds or rain. Whenever either symptom appears give potassium permanganate in the drinking water as previously directed.

Gapes

Gapes is due to the presence of gapeworms in the windpipe of the chick. The characteristic gasping for breath is caused in part by the presence of gapeworms and in part by mucus secreted as a result of irritation of the lining of the windpipe, to which the worms attach themselves. The adult worms are small, seldom over three-fourths of an inch long, and are found in pairs in the windpipe. This disease is comparatively unknown on sandy soils, but is so common on clay or limestone land that it is scarcely possible to escape it unless special precautions are taken. Earthworms are known to be instrumental in the

FIG. 178—CHICK WITH GAPES
Treatment of chicks affected with gapes is difficult and only practially successful, at best. The most practical plan is to prevent infection.

spread of infection, though they do not, of course, give gapes to chicks unless the worms are from infected soil.

In the case of gapes as in most other diseases, prevention is better and easier than cure and when there is sufficient room to do so, a good plan is to raise all chicks on land that has not been occupied by poultry for at least a year, and thus is free from infection. If it is possible to provide two nursery plots on which the chicks may be raised on alternate years, there will be practically no trouble from this cause. The following extracts from Circular 30 of West Virginia Experiment Station, by Horace Atwood and Dr. C. A. Lueder, give a summary of the results of some recent investigations on this subject at that institution, and are of unusual interest:

"During her lifetime no eggs are laid by the female, but these eggs develop in the ovary and accumulate in her body by the thousands. When the worm becomes fully mature and dies and is expelled from the windpipe the eggs which have accumulated in large numbers may be scattered about in various ways and thus perpetuate the disease.

"At room temperature, gape eggs freshly removed from a mature female and kept moist, hatched in fourteen days, and about the same length of time was required for the worms to mature after becoming attached to the upper part of the windpipe. Eggs buried in the ground between two watch glasses, in a cool, shady location, retained their vitality and hatched the following spring, but this period seems to be about the limit of their endurance, as they were found dead and disintegrated the second spring.

"It is probable that under natural conditions, such as prevail in spring and early summer, the eggs will hatch in from two to four weeks, depending on the temperature. The young gape worms when placed on a vertical surface covered with moisture always tend to travel upward. In this way they ascend grass blades, and the chickens, picking off the dew drops and tender blades, take the young worms into their mouths. From the mouth the worms make their way to the sinuses of the head, and their movement causes an irritation which brings about a discharge and makes the chicken sneeze. After being taken into the mouth of the chicken the worms are soon paired and attached to the upper portion of the windpipe.

"In 1900 the West Virginia Agricultural Experiment Station purchased a farm for general experimental work, on which gapes were present. The practice was adopted of burning all chickens that died of disease and of keeping the young chickens shut up until after the dew had dried off in the morning. This practice, without further procedure of any sort, thoroughly eradicated the disease from the premises in two or three years. Since that time chickens have been raised on this farm by thousands and not a single case of gapes has been present there for the past twelve or fifteen years.

"While studying recently hatched gape worms, the junior author observed that they were extremely susceptible to a very dilute solution of creolin or carbolic acid. A solution of three drops of creolin in a pint of water killed the newly hatched worms in from 30 to 60 seconds, and it was found that creolin added to the drinking water was an effective remedy, this medicated water flushing the surfaces to which the worms had just become attached and so killing them. Creolin should be added to the drinking water furnished the chickens, at the rate of three drops to each pint of water."

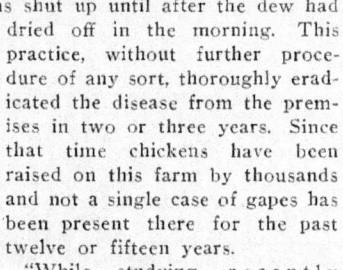

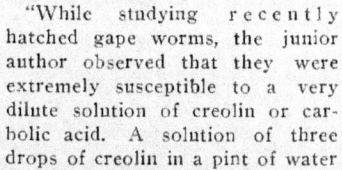

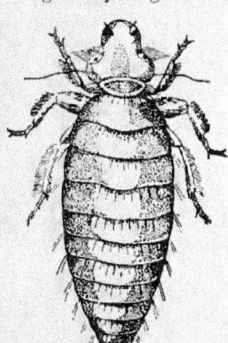

FIG. 179—COMMON HEN LOUSE

Leg Weakness

Leg weakness frequently occurs among chicks that are from one to four months of age. There are various causes for the trouble, such as lack of vigor in the breeding stock, bottom heat in brooders, overheating and crowding in brooders, poor ventilation, special feeding for rapid growth, lack of bone-forming material in the feed, etc. Constant confinement on board or concrete floors frequently causes leg weakness. Common symptoms are unsteadiness of gait, lack of activity due to inability to stand up, lameness, lying with legs stretched out behind or at side, etc.

The common practice of confining chicks indoors for long periods before they are allowed to run out, with little litter on the brooder or house floor and indifference to providing exercise, is the cause of three-fourths of all cases of leg weakness. Medical treatment is useless. Correct the conditions that cause the trouble and the chicks will soon recover. The weakest, however, should be removed and be given a separate brooder where they will not be trampled and abused by the healthy members of the flock.

Limberneck and Vertigo

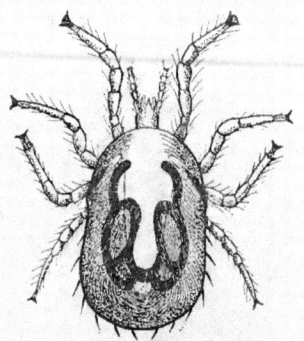

FIG. 180—RED OR "SPIDER" MITE

Young chicks frequently suffer from limberneck, caused by eating decayed animal matter, or the maggots that grow in such material. Do not confuse the symptoms of limberneck with those of vertigo. In vertigo (congestion of the brain), the chick's neck is drawn back over the shoulder or twisted to one side and the neck may be turned so that the chick looks directly upward. Affected birds will stagger, run backward, and make other peculiar motions, or may lie on one side. Congestion is caused by digestive disorders, sometimes by worms, and occasionally by injury. In well-developed cases of limberneck, the muscles of the neck are relaxed allowing the chick's head to droop until it often touches the ground, though in early stages the symptoms may resemble those associated with congestion. In either disease give the chicks a dose of Epsom salts and see to it that the cause is promptly removed.

Overgrown Wings

Young chicks, particularly Leghorns, frequently are found trailing their wings which appear to be out of all proportion to the size of the chick. This trouble occurs, occasionally, as a result of too high brooder temperature, but, as a rule, it indicates a lack of strength which may result from a number of causes. In many instances the wings really are not overgrown but are normal in length and only appear overlarge because of the relaxed position. When chicks are so affected it is a good plan to clip the wings, and relieve them of the extra weight. Then restore the chick's health by proper feeding and brooding, and there will be no further trouble.

Lack of Feathers

In many flocks there are found partially grown chicks that have failed to feather out properly, sometimes having no feathers at all except a few on the wings. This condition may be due to a lack of constitutional vigor or improper feeding, but more frequently to crowding in the brooder at night. Generally it is found that if these chicks are removed from the regular flock, warmly brooded in small numbers and well fed, they will promptly feather out and make fair growth. Such chicks however, should be sold as soon as they reach market size and should never be retained in the flock either as layers or breeders.

Stunted Growth

This condition generally is the result of weak constitutions, insufficient heat in brooders, or crowding and poor ventilation in brooders or coops. The general tendency to discontinue supplying artificial heat before the chicks are properly feathered out is responsible for much lack of thrift. With hen-brooded chicks it usually is the result of overcrowding. Coops that appear to be amply large when the broods are first placed in them, become badly crowded as the chicks increase in size. Confining growing chicks at night to hot, stuffy quarters in which they scarcely have standing room—a condition altogether too common in late summer and early fall, can have no other effect than to stunt their growth and impair their health.

Toe Picking and Cannibalism

Young chicks, especially Leghorns, are quite liable to form the habit of picking at each other when kept in close confinement, the toes being the usual point of attack. This sometimes goes so far as to result in the loss of a number of the weaker chicks that are literally torn to pieces by the stronger members of the brood. As a rule this vicious practice is the result of idleness, though a lack of suitable animal food sometimes appears to be partially responsible for it.

There is little danger of chicks forming bad habits if they are kept busy all day long, and for this reason there are few instances of toe picking reported by those who give especial attention to providing exercise. Where there is a special tendency to this trouble it often is a help to supply a little fresh meat, hanging it a few inches above the floor so that the chicks will have to work to get it, thus not only satisfying their craving, but at the same time inducing more exercise. It is stated that dipping the injured toes in pine tar will afford protection, provided this is done at once, before the chicks have become too familiar with the taste of blood.

Lice and Mites

Lice and mites cause heavy losses among chicks, especially when hen-hatched and brooded. Frequently their presence is not suspected and the chicks are believed to be dying from various diseases, when as a matter of fact, they are infested with lice and their coops and brooders are overrun with mites. Chicks that are hatched in incubators and raised in brooders will rarely have lice, unless they are kept in infested houses or where the parasites may be acquired from adult fowls. Chicks that are hatched under hens almost invariably are affected with head lice when taken from the nest, and should receive prompt treatment. Lice are readily killed by grease in any form, and a simple method of eradicating them is to grease the chicks' heads with a little unsalted lard, vaseline, olive oil, or something of a similar nature. If the chicks are badly infested it will be necessary to apply a little grease under the wings and below the vent as well as on the head. There are several preparations on the market which serve a similar purpose, and as they are more convenient and often much more effective, the use of home remedies is only to be recommended in case of emergency.

Red mites feed upon the chicks at night but remain hidden about the perches, brooders or elsewhere during the day. They rarely are found upon either chicks or fowls in the daytime, unless the sleeping quarters are completely overrun with them. Artificially raised chicks that are kept in clean brooders or colony houses, should never be infested with these pests, but if the mites are present on the premises, as they usually are to some extent in all houses occupied by adult fowls, there is always danger that they will be carried to the quarters occupied by the chicks. For this reason, coops, brooders, and colony houses should be sprayed with a good disinfecting solution and this, if frequently and thoroughly done, will prevent all trouble of this sort.

Enemies of Chicks

Chicks have a number of natural enemies, and to raise them without serious loss from this cause often is a matter of great difficulty. The provision of proper equipment for brooding chicks however, would prevent a large proportion of such depredations. On thousands of farms, enough chicks are lost each year from the depredations of minks, foxes, hawks, etc., to pay for all the permanent equipment that would be needed to protect them.

Cats. Cats can be trained to let chicks alone, and with proper attention there will be few losses from this source. In many cases they learn to take chicks by eating dead ones that have been left lying around instead of being picked up promptly as should always be done. Then they get to taking mopy ones that are not yet dead, and from this it is only a step to catching them as they run at large. As a rule, cats that have once learned to take chicks cannot be broken of the habit and should be shot at sight. Where losses occur from this source, covered runs are especially serviceable. Chicks can be kept in them for the first three or four weeks of their lives and will do well if the shelters are moved to fresh ground frequently. Portable fence panels also are used in making small enclosures within which the chicks are confined until they are large enough to take care of themselves.

Rats. Rats are extremely cunning, and where they are numerous it is almost impossible to protect chicks from them except by providing thoroughly ratproof coops and houses. Coops should have floors of inch boards, and all openings should be covered with one-inch wire netting. They should be raised off the ground and be moved frequently enough to prevent rats harboring under them. Chicks should not be brooded near buildings or rubbish piles where rats may hide, no tall grass or weeds should be permitted to grow near the coops or brooders, and if colony houses are used they should always be blocked up off the ground so that rats will not burrow under them. Permanent poultry houses with board floors should always be raised at least a foot off the ground for the same reason. When all grain and poultry feeds are kept in ratproof houses or bins, it is not a difficult matter to keep rats from becoming established on the premises. When they appear, a relentless war should be waged against them.

Minks, Skunks, Foxes, and Wolves. In some sections these animals cause heavy losses. Minks are especially dangerous as one mink may kill several dozens of chickens in a night. If the coops and houses are properly constructed, all openings covered with one-inch mesh netting and the doors regularly closed at night, there will be few losses. Where the chickens are liable to be attacked during the day, there often is no practical way to protect them when small, except by providing large yards enclosed with wire netting and keeping them confined thereto.

Hawks and Crows. These enemies are especially hard to combat, and when they get started on a flock will take many chicks. Crows are afraid of firearms, and shooting a few sometimes affords complete protection, especially if the dead birds are hung on poles located near the brooders. The plan of keeping brood hens confined to small coops or covered runs, which proves so satisfactory under ordinary conditions, is frequently impracticable where crows and hawks are numerous, as the chicks are thus deprived of the hen's protection. When these enemies are numerous it is advisable to confine the broods to a plot of suitable size, within which both hens and chicks may be given full liberty. This will enable the hens to warn the chicks of approaching danger and give battle when they are attacked.

INDEX

Air Cell, Development of the............ 42
Albumen, Analysis of 24
Albumen, Formation of 24
Allantois, The 29
Amnion, The 29
Animal Heat, Failure to Readjust for..... 51
Aspergillosis 107
Blastoderm, The 29
Bacillary White Diarrhea 108
Breed, Choice of 9
Breeding Board 18
   Flocks, Size of 16
   Fowls, Care of 13
   Fowls, Rations for 17
   Pen, Exercise for 18
   Pens, Mating the 16
   Stock, Care of Young 14
Bred-to-Lay Stock 10
Brooder, Cleanliness in 82
   Does Not Heat, What to Do When.... 76
   Electric 74
   Equipment, Skimping On 75
   How Many Chicks to the 80
   Litter for the 82
   Location for Outdoor 71
   Providing Ventilation in 80
   Related Fowls 10
   Temperature, Correct 79
   Use of Cold 81
Brooder House, A-Shaped Portable........100
   Construction of 95
   Location of 94
   Permanent Colony 102
   Portable Colony 101
Brooders, Fireless 65
   Homemade 74
   Indoor and Outdoor 70
Brooding Capacity Required,
   How to Estimate 75
   Equipment, Care of 84
   System, Hot Water 74
Catarrhal Disorders 108
Chalazae, The 23
Chicks All Out, Getting the 53
   Must Be Kept Busy 88
   Outdoors, Getting the 83
   Record Marking 77
   Selling Six-Week-Old 58
   When to Take Off 77
Chorion, The 29
Coccidiosis 107
Colony Hover, Permanent House for.....102
Colony Hover, Portable House for......101
Colony Hovers 72
Colony Hovers, How to Use 73
Congestion of Lungs 107
Constitutional Vigor 9
Cooling an Aid to Ventilation.......... 44
Custom Hatching 58
Day-Old Chick Industry, History of..... 54
Day-Old Chicks,
   Incubators Used in Hatching....... 55
   Prices Realized for 57
   Shipping Boxes for 57
   What to Do With Surplus 58
   Who Should Buy 55
   Who Should Produce 56
Diarrhea in Chicks 105
Disease, First Symptoms of 104
Door, Elevated Chick 100
Dosage for Chicks, Proper 106
Egg, Composition of Hen's 24
   Formation of the 22
   Structure of the 24
Eggs After Shipment, Resting 33
   Appearance of Fertile and Infertile..... 28
   Cooling 31, 44
   Defective and How Caused 26
   Failure to Test 51
   for Hatching, Undesirable 49

Eggs Held for Hatching 32
   How Long to Hold 33
   How Often Do Hens Turn 31
   Loss of Weight During Incubation..... 31
   Moisture in 31
   Position in Which to Keep 33
   Shape of 25
   Size of 26
   Size to Use 33
   Testing 41, 51
   Turning 40, 52
   Variation in Composition of......... 25
   Washing 33
   When Fertilized 28
Embryo, Development of Chick 29
Embryo, Position of 29
Enemies of Chicks 110
Epsom Salts for Chicks 106
Evaporation, Control of 43
Evaporation, Percentage of 43
Feathers, Lack of 109
Feed Hoppers 91
Feed, Unwholesome 93
Feeding Chicks,
   Cornell Rations and Methods for... 92
   Importance of Careful 86
   Growing Stock 93
   Iowa Station Method of 92
   Method, A Successful 89
   Method, Deep Litter 91
   Method Recommended by U. S. D. A... 93
   Methods, Simplified 91
   Milk for 105
   Trays 87
   What Not to Do in 93
   When to Begin 85
Feeding Coop 88
Feeds, Nursery 86
Females for Breeding, Selection of..... 12
Fertility and Hatchability 11
Fertility, Reasons for Low 20
Flock Matings 17
Floor Space per Fowl 15
Gapes 108
Germinal Disc, Location of 28
Growing Stock, The 84
Growth, Stunted 110
Hatch, Bringing Out the 45
   Cleaning Up the 46
   Starting the 37
Hatching Records 20, 46, 47
Hen, Bodily Temperature of 28, 39
House, A Permanent Brooder 100
   for Breeding Pen, Small Portable... 15
   for Colony Hover, Permanent........102
   for One Hover, Colony............... 97
   for Single Breeding Pen 15
   for Two Brooders 98
   Open Front Compartment Brooder..... 99
   Permanent Breeding 15
Hover, Cloth-Covered Enclosure for....68, 77
   Installed in Colony House 70
   Teaching Chicks to Use the 78
Hovers and Brooders,
   Who Should Use Lamp-Heated...... 71
Hovers, Colony 72
   Lamp-Heated 67
   Portable Lamp-Heated 68
Hygrometer 50
Inbreeding 10
Inclines for Brooders and Houses....... 97
Incubation, Loss of Weight During..... 31
Incubator, Changes in Equipment of..... 50
   Buying Too Late 48
   Cleaning the 53
   Correct Temperature for 38
   Details of Operation 46
   Location of 35, 48
   Operating Without Instructions...... 49
   Overcrowding in the 53

Incubator, Regulator 36
   Setting Up the 36, 48
   The Cost of a Good 35
   What Size to Get 35
Incubator House, A Small Aboveground.. 62
   at Oregon Experiment Station........ 63
   at Pennsylvania Experiment Station.... 63
   Concrete 64
   Details of Construction of 60
   Floors 64
   for Lamp-Heated Incubators 60
   for Mammoth Incubators 64
   Location for 59
Incubators, Electric 34
   Hot Air 34
   Hot Water 34
   Mammoth 34
Lamp Burners, Using Defective 52
Lamp, Care of the 37
   Flame, Ideal 49
   Flame Too High 49
   Flame Too Low 50
   Neglecting the 51
   Trimming the 52
Layers, Selecting the 12
Leg Weakness 109
Lice and Mites 110
Limberneck and Vertigo 109
Liver Disorders 106
Males, Selecting the Breeding 11
Marking Chicks, Methods of............. 77
Milk Feeding for Chicks 105
Moisture and Ventilation 42
Nursery, Overcrowding in 45
Ovary of Hen 22
Oviduct of Hen 22
Pedigree Hatching 45
Perches, Teaching Chicks to Use........ 84
Post-Mortem Examinations 106
Rations for Breeding Fowls 17
   Home-mixed 89
   Sudden Changes in 93
Records, Hatching 20, 46, 47
   in Use At Purdue University........ 46
   In Use at Ohio State University.... 47
Regulator of Incubator 36
Roosting Closet for Breeders........... 13
Sanitation, Methods of 103
Shade for Chicks 97
Sour Crop and Gastritis 107
Temperature, Correct Incubator 38
   Too High 51
   Correct Incubator 38
   Failure to Average the 51
Temperature of Eggs 39
   with Contact Thermometer 39
   with Inovo Thermometer 39
   with Suspended Thermometer 39
Temperature of Sitting Hens 30, 39
Tester, How to Use the 41
Tester, Magic Egg 52
Testers, Different Styles of 42
Thermometer Not in Correct Position.... 50
Thermometers, Incubator 38
Thermometers, Using Untested 50
Toe Picking and Cannibalism 110
Trap-Nesting 20
Trays, Shifting the 52
Turning Eggs 52
Ventilation and Moisture 42
Vertigo, Limberneck and 109
Water Founts 86
Water Vessels 93
White Diarrhea, Bacillary 108
Wings, Overgrown 109
Yards and Fences 96
Yolk, Analysis of 24
Yolk Sac, The 29

CPSIA information can be obtained
at www.ICGtesting.com
Printed in the USA
LVOW04s0012200617
538633LV00014B/430/P